UNRAVELLING
THE BOOK OF BOOKS

UNRAVELLING
THE BOOK OF BOOKS

BEING THE STORY OF HOW
THE PUZZLES OF THE BIBLE WERE SOLVED
AND ITS DOCUMENTS UNRAVELLED

BY

ERNEST R. TRATTNER

NEW YORK
CHARLES SCRIBNER'S SONS
1929

TO

MARCO H. HELLMAN

"As in water face answereth face—
so the heart of man to man."

CONTENTS

Part II

THE STORY OF BIBLES WITHIN THE BIBLE, OR HOW THE FOUR MOST IMPORTANT DOCUMENTS OF THE OLD TESTAMENT WERE INDEPENDENTLY WRITTEN AND THEN COMBINED INTO ONE VOLUME CALLED THE PENTATEUCH (THE FIVE BOOKS OF MOSES)

Part III

THE BIBLE KEEPS ON GROWING—AND THEN SUDDENLY STOPS

CONTENTS

THE NEW TESTAMENT
Part IV

THE "NEW" NEW TESTAMENT
Part V

ILLUSTRATIONS

FOREWORD

"Who wrote the Bible?"

That is one of the most natural questions for any thinking person to ask. For many centuries it was answered by both the synagogue and the church in a very simple and naïve way, not altogether free from superstitious awe. People willingly believed that the Scriptures were a supernatural product dictated by God from His throne in Heaven to certain of his chosen saints here on Earth who merely acted as His penmen. Without attempting anything more in line with historical accuracy it was sufficient to tell the inquirer that "Men spake from God, being moved by the Holy Ghost, and the result was the book which we call the Bible."

Under the influence of this crude idea the story of the making of the Scriptures was told from the "outside"—that is to say, from the standpoint of tradition, ecclesiastical teaching, and dogma which imposed themselves on the believer with the majesty of an unquestioned authority. During the mediæval ages no one thought of going directly to the Bible itself in order to learn the "inside" facts. Just because it was regarded as a sacred book—a stupendous supernatural forthputting of God himself—it became a sealed book. People did not so much know things *in* the Bible as they knew things *about* the Bible.

Not until the rise of modern scientific thought— particularly within the last two hundred years—was the true story of the origin of the Scriptures discovered.

It came about in this way. Thinking men could no longer bind themselves to mere Tradition which violated the most obvious facts of history and common sense. They stopped believing the earth to be flat when navigators found out that it was round. In like manner the great biblical scholars stopped believing in the divine origin of Scriptures when they discovered incontrovertible evidence which proved that both the Old and the New Testament were written like any other book under definite conditions of time, place, and race. Far from God being its sole author the Bible represents the remains of a vast literature extending over many hundreds of years. Not one author but scores of writers living in widely separated ages share the responsibility of its present appearance. . . .

The libraries of the world are full of books which tell the story of the Bible. They usually rehash the ancient and time-honored traditions which unfortunately rise no higher than the average Sunday-school lesson. That the time is now ripe for an altogether different treatment of this vast subject explains this particular effort as a concise account of the intelligent investigation of the Old and New Testaments.

It took stupendous daring coupled with unparalleled resourcefulness on the part of a handful of brilliant scholars to push their way into the inside of the Bible and present to the world an interior view. How all this was accomplished is a romantic tale full of high adventure. As a result of this indefatigable labor the Bible has been subjected to a greater and more careful analysis than any other book in the possession of the human race.

Beginning at first in a very feeble way, the process

of sifting the Scriptures soon developed into a real science of investigation so that its demonstrations became as important and revolutionary as the Copernican researches in astronomy or the Darwinian proofs in biology. It is not so well known to the general public that this science of biblical investigation has existed for more than two centuries during which it has developed definite methods and rules. Because of such a widespread unfamiliarity, the opening chapters of this volume deal with the discoveries of those great scholars who first achieved epoch-making results.

The science of Biblical Criticism—for that is what the investigation of the Scriptures came to be called—first got under way when men began to solve the puzzles of the Old Testament. It was only after the documents of the Hebrew Bible had been successfully unravelled that scholarly attention turned to the New Testament. This explains the rather lengthy treatment which is here given to the Pentateuch (the so-called Five Books of Moses). Modern Biblical Criticism actually began on the Pentateuchal problem and its foundation rests upon five main results which are here defined in five separate chapters constituting Book I of the present volume.

With these five main results clearly fixed, the next step is to reconstruct the literature of the Bible in terms of its original documents. This technic will be better understood when the reader is told at the very outset that the various books that make up the Old and New Testaments are compilatory productions. For example, the Book of Genesis was not written by one man: it represents the compacting together of widely different sources which were originally independent. Such dovetailing and interweaving of divergent types of writing was a common oriental practice. (It must always be remembered that the Bible is essentially an oriental book written by a people who lived on the shores of the Mediterranean.)

There has gone into the preparation of this volume the kindly interest of a host of friends to whom the author is greatly indebted. He wishes to thank his life-long companion and schoolmate, Lewis Browne, the distinguished author of *This Believing World*, for many hours of inspiration and counsel.

He is also deeply indebted:

To Prof. Carl S. Knopf of the University of Southern California for a careful reading of the entire manuscript and for many helpful suggestions.

To Prof. William Frederic Badè for a critical reading of the Old Testament section under the pressure of preparing a third archæological expedition to Palestine.

To Prof. C. C. McCown of the Pacific School of Religion for his keen interest in those chapters dealing with the New Testament.

To Lloyd Douglas, author of that delightful book, *Those Disturbing Miracles,* for his friendship and advice.

To Max Rosenblum of Cleveland, Ohio, for encouragement and faith.

ERNEST R. TRATTNER.

LOS ANGELES,
Jan. 15, 1929.

THE OLD TESTAMENT

PART I

THE STORY OF THE RISE OF SCIENTIFIC BIBLICAL THOUGHT—OR, HOW MEN CAME TO LOOK AT THE BIBLE INTELLIGENTLY

It is an immense relief to get the puzzles of the Bible rationally solved.

CHAPTER I

SPINOZA, THE PHILOSOPHER, FEARLESSLY UNDER–
TAKES THE FIRST MODERN SCIENTIFIC INVES–
TIGATION OF THE HEBREW SCRIPTURES

ALTHOUGH he was only twenty-three years old the elders of the Jewish Community of Amsterdam cursed him in the synagogue:

"Let him be accursed by day, and accursed by night; let him be accursed in his lying down, and accursed in his rising up; accursed in going out and accursed in coming in. May the Lord never pardon or acknowledge him; may the wrath and displeasure of the Lord burn henceforth against this man"—

And then they excommunicated him—

But he only smiled.

Monuments are now built in his memory, for he was not only one of the world's greatest philosophers but he was the father of modern Biblical Science.

In 1670 he wrote a book which he published anonymously, being very careful to take the added precaution of printing on its title-page a false place of origin. It created an immediate impression and was so widely read that thirty-seven edicts had to be issued against it—such was the spirit of the age in which it appeared.

"I set down nothing here which I have not long and seriously meditated," he writes in his epoch-making book which he called the *Theologico-Political Tract,* "and although from my youth I was imbued with the common opinions concerning the Scriptures, I have been compelled in my manhood to abandon these, and

5

to espouse these views which I promulgate in this place."

Who is this man of swarthy complexion who dares to combine a questioning attitude toward the Bible with the clear vision of the scientist and the devotion of the true seeker after the truth? Does he demand the right to think differently? Then he must be the foe of orthodoxy.

"Somebody ought to kill him!"

. . . But he managed to escape with only his clothing cut through by a dagger-thrust. . . .

2

Had he not escaped the madman's knife the world would have lost one of its most original and fearless thinkers. For here was a scholar of relentless honesty who asked deep and serious questions and answered them impressively. What he had to say was marked by an incorruptible conscientiousness and by that restraint and moderation in statement which befits the philosopher. Using his sight to eke out a living as a lens-polisher, he reserved his insight for Philosophy. And such was the high character of his personal life, that, although wretchedly poor, he refused a gift of two thousand florins and declined an offer of a handsome pension from King Louis XIV, the Grand Monarch of France. He carried a name that was half Hebraic and half Spanish; he lived in Holland and wrote his books in Latin; although born a Jew he died among Christians!

Baruch Spinoza—he afterward changed his first name to Benedict—initiated the preliminary stages of one of the greatest movements in human thought—

the scientific study of the Bible. Not only were his researches in the Scriptures, particularly the Old Testament, the most exhaustive of any up to his age, but he superseded all previous spasmodic efforts by laying down incontrovertible principles. His mind was brilliantly adroit and mathematical, which is revealed by the logical methods he used and the amazing results he achieved. Much of what modern scholars now agree is fundamental in Biblical Science was anticipated by him; and notwithstanding the fact that he had many predecessors, he was astonishingly original. . . .

To the enlightened mind of the twentieth century it seems incredible that there was a time when practically no one thought of the writings of Scripture as being the result of a slow historical growth. The idea of development so intimately wrapped up in what the modern man calls "History" is nowadays familiar even to school children. But in Spinoza's age men had been so long accustomed to look upon the Bible primarily as a supernatural communication that the true story of its origin was completely obscured. Some even went so far as to regard many of its chapters as having been actually written by the corporeal finger of God. It therefore took a free and clear mind to bring into recognition the fact that the writings of the Bible, coming through human channels, had an "earthly" history under definite conditions of time, place, and race. . . .

How did Spinoza proceed to a scientific study of the Bible? "I resolved forthwith to examine the Scriptures anew, in a spirit of entire freedom and without prejudice, to affirm nothing as to their meaning and affirm nothing in the shape of doctrine, which I did not feel plainly set down in their pages."

3

Spinoza's chief source of information and inspiration was drawn from the brilliant commentary of Ibn Ezra, a Jewish philosopher of the twelfth century who had led a life of romantic vicissitude. It is interesting to note that seven hundred years after his death this famous Spanish scholar became the inspiration of Robert Browning's master-poem "Rabbi Ben Ezra." He was the only predecessor to whom Spinoza acknowledged a debt, and rightly so, because he was the first to hint at the existence of contradictory passages in the Bible. But the bigotry of the age prevented Ibn Ezra from giving an open presentation of his discoveries. He had to venture discreetly and content himself with veiling his cautiously worded commentary in a cloud of obscure phrases. And here they remained "veiled" for five hundred years until unmasked by the austere fearlessness of Spinoza. "Ibn Ezra did not openly declare his opinion but put it in a kind of cipher which I do not hesitate to explain."

Shortly before Spinoza penned these audacious words, Thomas Hobbes, a free-thinking Englishman, had already declared that the first five Books of the Old Testament (The Pentateuch*) were documents written not so much *by* Moses as *about* Moses. In his book called the *Leviathan*, Hobbes noted many passages in the Pentateuch which were inconsistent with Mosaic authorship. It is a mooted question whether Spinoza was familiar with Hobbes, but it is significant that he too concluded that Moses could not have writ-

*Pentateuch is a Greek word meaning the Fivefold Work. It comes from *penta,* five, and *teuchos,* volume. The Fivefold Work embraces Genesis, Exodus, Leviticus, Numbers, and Deuteronomy.

ten the five volumes commonly ascribed to him. The idea that Moses was the author of the Pentateuch proved, upon close examination, to be simply a tradition having no basis in historic fact. The tradition itself was derived from old Jewish sources which held that every great leader wrote down by divine command the ideas and sometimes the actual words of God together with such events of the day as were deemed significant. Being thoroughly convinced that there was sufficient evidence within the Pentateuch itself to prove a plurality of authors who wrote at a date long after Moses, Spinoza proceeded to shrewdly reproduce the following instances from the Bible to prove his conclusions.

4

In the third chapter of Deuteronomy, verse eleven, mention is made of the iron bedstead of Og, King of Bashan. It was a gigantic relic $16\frac{1}{2}$ feet long by $7\frac{1}{3}$ feet wide. The passage here in Deuteronomy relates that it was preserved as an antique curiosity in the city of Rabbath, which belonged to the Ammonites. Now, on the face of it, this statement seems to be a perfectly innocent historical reference. Upon investigation, however, it proved to Spinoza to be a very important anachronism, for Moses never saw or heard of Rabbath! The idea of the Mosaic authorship of this particular passage in Deuteronomy was entirely upset by a note which appears in the twelfth chapter of the Second Book of Samuel, emphatically declaring that Rabbath was first conquered by the Hebrews under David. And David, of course, lived several centuries after Moses. Spinoza therefore rightly argued that if Moses was the

author of Deuteronomy he could not possibly have
written about a bedstead kept in the local museum of
a city which did not come into possession of the Hebrew tribes until the reign of David.

The incident of the iron bedstead is only one of a
large number of tell-tale anachronisms scattered
throughout the Pentateuch. Spinoza detected other passages which clearly indicate a plurality of authors.
There is, for example, the account of Moses' death, and
what happened after he was buried. Certainly Moses
could not have written his own funeral obsequies. Yet
in the Book of Deuteronomy there is a full report of
the burial of the great lawgiver. Did he then dictate
what was going to happen? Of course, the tradition of
both church and synagogue declared that Moses was
miraculously inspired to write it beforehand. But Spinoza could not agree with this tradition, and for a very
good reason: because he saw that the claim of tradition
was immediately cut off by the sentence with which
the account ends, which is: "No man knoweth of his
sepulchre unto this day." Unto what day? Would
Moses writing beforehand of his burial say that "no
man knoweth of his sepulchre *unto this day*"? Some
one living long after Moses, wrote the account of the
lawgiver's death and by "this day" he meant his own
later time.

Now look at Genesis. If that book is the work of a
single author how account for two entirely dissimilar
records of the origin of the name of the city of Beersheba? The first explanation given in the 21st chapter
says that it was named by Abraham and tells why he
called the place Beersheba. A little later on in the same
book a second explanation is given, in the 26th chap-

ter, with an entirely different story! And strange to say, this second account knows nothing about Abraham; it says that Isaac did the naming!

Spinoza clearly saw that if Genesis was the composition of Moses such a strange discrepancy would have been impossible. How could an author of fair intelligence, much less an infallibly inspired man, possessing good common sense and a reasonably firm memory, contradict himself that way? To charge Moses with such an error would be to rank his mentality with that of a child. Unless anachronisms and contradictions are proofs of unity of authorship, Moses could not have been the single writer of Genesis.

Another case in point, cited by Spinoza, deals with the inhabitants of Palestine whom the early Hebrew invaders constantly battled. They were known as Canaanites. According to the Bible it took many hundreds of years for the Hebrew newcomers to finally gain possession of the country from these people. Not until the reign of King Solomon, several centuries after Moses, were the Canaanites completely subdued. Yet, notwithstanding this historical fact, the sixth verse of the 12th chapter of Genesis contains these tell-tale words: "And the Canaanite was then in the land." Commenting upon this strange feature Ibn Ezra said: "There is in this a mystery, and let him that comprehendeth be silent." From this obscure hint of Ibn Ezra, Spinoza argues that the famous Spanish rabbi was convinced that Moses did not write Genesis. For does not this passage clearly imply that the Canaanites had disappeared from Palestine? The allusion is only intelligible when the Canaanites had ceased to be a distinctive portion of the population. Suppose we were to pick up a history in which the statement appears that "the Spaniards were then in possession of California." Would not these words be sufficient evidence for the reader to date the document as having been written after Spanish possession of California had passed away? With thousands of Canaanites about him in actual possession of Palestine Moses could not have written "and the Canaanite was then in the land." This is not the language of a contemporary: it is clearly retrospective. Some person living in Palestine many years after the disappearance of the Canaanites is responsible for this passage—not Moses.

In the thirty-sixth chapter of Genesis there is a similar case of retrospective or post-Mosaic writing where this note occurs in the thirty-first verse: "And these are the kings that reigned in Edom before there reigned any king over the children of Israel." Some author looking backward wrote of the kings of Edom and mentioned the fact that they ruled their people long before there were kings over Israel. Inasmuch as Saul lived many centuries after Moses, and was the very first king of the Hebrews, it can be plainly seen that Spinoza was correct in his contention that such a note could not have been written by one who died before kings in Israel were born! Certainly the character of this language had been determined by later political events.

In the Book of Numbers, third verse of the twelfth chapter, this statement is found: "Now the man Moses was very meek, above all the men who were upon the face of the earth." One cannot fancy Moses writing of himself like that, particularly when he was known for his modesty. Modest men do not use such language when speaking of themselves. And to urge, as some pious souls have done, that Moses said such things because he was so directed by divine inspiration would necessarily make egotism a supernatural product. The fact that Moses does not speak of himself in the first person led Spinoza to observe that some other writer speaks of him in the third—a writer who lived a long time after.

Neither was it possible for Spinoza to believe that Moses wrote the passage in chapter thirty-four of the book of Deuteronomy wherein these words occur: "There arose not a prophet since in Israel like unto Moses." It is difficult to believe that the modest Lawgiver would favorably compare himself with men living centuries later. The language is clearly that of a writer describing a retrospective condition, for Moses himself could not have written that no prophet had arisen "since" himself when he was yet alive—particularly when no prophet had yet been his successor. The writer is necessarily one who looked back to Moses through a long series of later prophets.

In Genesis, and elsewhere, places and localities are called by names which did not come into use until a later period. "We must note," says Spinoza, "that some places are not styled by the names they bore during Moses' lifetime, but by others which they obtained subsequently." For example, there is the story of Abraham's pursuit of his enemies. According to the fourteenth verse of the fourteenth chapter of Genesis Abraham led forth his trained men and pursued the enemy as far as Dan. Moses could not possibly have designated the terminus of the pursuit as "Dan," for this name was bestowed on that locality long after his death. Originally, the name of the place was Laish, and the story of how and when the name was changed to Dan is recorded in the twenty-ninth verse of the eighteenth chapter of the book of Judges, clearly indicating that this happened not only after the death of Moses but long after the death of Joshua. . . .

5

One of the main objects of Spinoza's *Tract* was to show the contradictory nature of many statements which appear in the Bible. With these statements once established his next object was to offer humanity a newer and more intelligent understanding of the Scriptures. He therefore patiently assembled a vast array of anachronisms, repetitions, discrepant accounts, mathematical impossibilities, and on the basis of this impressive evidence he unhesitatingly declared that the Pentateuch could not have been written by a single man and that Moses was far from being the sole author of the Five Books which tradition had piously ascribed to him. Every evidence taken directly from the writings themselves indicated to Spinoza a plurality of authors.

With the plurality of authorship once established the difficulties of the Bible solved themselves! The very fact that many writers, instead of one, had a hand in the compilation of the Scriptures is in itself a perfectly natural reason for the existence of differing accounts of the same story. Upon the old traditional idea that the Pentateuch was the infallible work of but one man, theologians had built up fantastic explanations in order to harmonize the stubborn inconsistencies of biblical literature. With Spinoza, however, a new process of thought begins—a complete departure from the old grotesque methods with their frantic but futile efforts to rationalize biblical discrepancies. By openly abandoning ecclesiastical notions as unsound, Spinoza became the Father of Biblical Science, for he presented the world this clear thought: that the Pentateuch must be understood as a natural book written by many men instead of a supernatural book written by only one man. Instead of being a Divine book containing a human message, the Bible became, in the hands of Spinoza, a Human book containing a divine message.

This was, of course, quite a startling conclusion which the humble philosopher himself anticipated would rock the orthodoxies of both church and synagogue. He therefore wrote these lines: "Those who look upon the Bible as a message sent down by God from Heaven, to men, will doubtless cry out that I have committed a sin against the Holy Ghost."

And so they did!

6

Yet the same keen mind which overthrew the crude superstitions about the Bible gave to the churches which condemned and villified him one of their most valuable formulas: "Scripture contains the Word of God." Ever since the seventeenth century, when accepted interpretations and blind faith began to crumble in the dust, this Spinozan formula has been constantly invoked. By it the churches have succeeded in saving thousands of the best minds in Europe and America to the cause of organized religion; for it meant a great difference to thinking men and women to tell them that Scripture *contains* the Word of God instead of dogmatically declaring Scripture *is* the Word of God. For this, the church and synagogue are indebted to the insight of an humble lens-polisher whom they at first hated—eventually, however, they saw "through the glasses which Baruch Spinoza ground."

The net result of Spinoza's labors was to underpin biblical study with fundamental principles of good common sense without doing violence to the great spiritual truth embodied in the pages of Scripture. Investigation proved to Spinoza that whereas the physical package containing the pearls of wisdom had come down through the centuries faulty, mutilated, and tampered with, nevertheless, "from the Bible itself we learn, without the smallest difficulty or ambiguity, that its cardinal precept is: To love God above all things and one's neighbor as one's self."

For these thoughts of majestic good sense Spinoza was regarded as a heretic and branded as an atheist. Of course, the whole world now knows that he was one of the most saintly men that ever lived, devoting himself to the pursuit of Truth which he called "The Love of God." To know something of the simple grandeur and excellence of his life is a spiritual bath, cleansing and stimulating. But at the bottom it is the old story: he whom one age stones another age enthrones—and herein lies the supreme irony of history.

Once having removed the benumbing and entirely mistaken fancies about the Bible Spinoza saw that a higher and more intelligent conception of God would now be allowed to take possession of the mind. His use, therefore, of scientific investigation was not an end in itself but a means to an end: to construct a firmer historical background for the spiritual element in the foreground. And now after almost three hundred years this Spinozan point of view has become the accepted attitude of the thinking world. By fearlessly sweeping away the scaffolding of worn-out tradition the humble philosopher of Amsterdam made it possible for those who came after him to see the Temple of Truth. . . .

In his great eulogy on Spinoza, Ernest Renan spoke these prophetic words: "The Truths which Science reveals always surpass the dreams which it destroys."

THE FIRST RESULT

The internal evidence within the Pentateuch itself indicates that Moses could not have been the exclusive author of the Five-Books commonly ascribed to him.

CHAPTER II

THE STORY OF RICHARD SIMON, A CATHOLIC PRIEST WHO WAS A HEBREW SCHOLAR

THE next step in the investigation of the Scriptures was made possible, curiously enough, by an opponent of Spinoza. He is the man whom the French regard as the first scientific biblical scholar of their native land—Father Richard Simon, priest of the Congregation of the Oratory.

Simon entered the Roman Catholic priesthood in 1670. It is a memorable date, for during the same year he wrote a pamphlet in defense of a group of Jews who had been foully charged with the murder of a Christian child in order to use its blood for ritual purposes. Such a barbaric accusation coming from his own fellow churchmen against an innocent and unoffending people aroused the hot temper of the young priest. He shot out a fearless and uncompromising exposure that seriously offended his ecclesiastical superiors, thereby damaging his own reputation. Like Savonarola of Florence, this man was singularly outspoken, exhibiting from the very beginning of his career a boldness of thought and action that forced him into a commanding figure playing upon the fringe of heresy.

It is much to the credit of the Catholic Church that she has had many priests who have been Hebrew scholars of ability—perhaps none more deeply steeped in the literature and lore of the Jews than Richard Simon. This monk was as much at home with a Jewish rabbi as with a Catholic bishop—"which thing was made a reproach unto him." As dogmatically-minded men dislike advanced thought more than anything else in the world it was only natural for Simon to constantly find himself knee-deep in the turbulent torrents of misunderstanding. From the members of his own church he frequently met with bestial unkindness: they not only personally disliked him but they burnt his books. Yet he continued to write with dauntless and unwearied zeal for what he thought might prove beneficial to mankind. . . .

2

Simon agreed with Spinoza that Moses could not have been the author of the Pentateuch; and in his *Critical History of the Old Testament*—the book which has made Simon's name famous to posterity—he gives substantially the same reasons as those advanced by the Hebrew-Dutch philosopher.

It was in 1678, eight years after Spinoza's *Theologico-Political Tract,* that Simon published his now famous critical *Histoire.* Almost immediately upon its appearance the book met with violent opposition and treacherous assault. Of the 1300 copies first issued only six escaped fire; and in all probability Simon's scholarship would have gone down in utter oblivion had not the liberal Elzevir Press of Amsterdam (so well known to book-collectors) come to the rescue. By printing three pirated editions it saved the *Histoire* and assured it a wide popularity. But in order to escape suspicion, these "Elzevirs" had to be published under fake titles which served their purpose by successfully misleading both the police and church authorities. . . .

It is no easy task to read Simon's *Histoire*, although the huge document is conveniently divided into three books, the first being entitled: "Concerning the Hebrew Text of the Bible from Moses to our Time." In this ponderous volume Simon showed that he possessed a genuine faculty for scientific investigation when he declared that "it is impossible to understand thoroughly the Holy Scriptures unless we first know the different states of the text of these Books according to the different times and places, and be instructed of the several changes that have happened to it."

Here is a clear and unmistakable understanding that the Hebrew Scriptures have shared the fate of all human productions in their transmission from hand to hand. Originally, the books of the Old Testament were written on skins which were usually cut into strips and sewed together so as to make a continuous belt. (The word "vellum" recalls the fact that a veal calf furnished the very choicest material for parchment making.) Each end of the belt had to be fastened upon a stick and the parchment was then rolled together so that it looked very much like our music-rolls for player pianos. Now, in the multiplication of a great variety of these "roll" copies many intentional changes, accidental errors, and divergences of readings crept into the text. It is not generally known that the Ten Commandments are reported twice within the Pentateuch: once in the twentieth chapter of Exodus, and once in the fifth chapter of Deuteronomy. A simple comparison of the text as given in Deuteronomy with that found in Exodus indicates how easily such variations made their way into the Hebrew Bible.

What then is the correct wording of the Scriptures?

ANCIENT HEBREW BOOK-ROLLS.

"Originally, the books of the Old Testament were written on skins . . . the parchment was then rolled together so that it looked very much like our music-roll for player pianos."

In order to properly answer this question, Simon declared that it was necessary to study the various ancient versions of the Bible and institute a close comparison between them. Only in this way, he urged, could scholarship arrive at the purest text. But this proposed manner of handling the Scriptures was contrary to the spirit of the age which fanatically regarded the Bible as too holy to be tampered with—an infallible revelation, infallibly received, recorded, preserved, transmitted, copied, and translated. Ecclesiastical teaching throughout Europe maintained that the Bible was written by men so perfectly inspired that they could neither spell a word wrong nor make a slip of the pen, for God must—so it was claimed—have protected His book from every error even in its transmission.

In the face of such blind belief it took an unflinching fearlessness to run counter to accepted notions; and it is largely because of his resoluteness that Simon's emphatic declaration gave a new impulse to research. Hundreds of investigators, demanding examination, now turned to the study of the "wording" of the Bible with minute and massive learning. Manuscripts were brought out of their musty hidings and carefully compared. When variations in the text appeared the task inevitably suggested itself of determining by comparison, and other evidence, which of the several readings might be the original one. Through this process amazing results were achieved, so that eventually the labors of these investigating scholars grew into a huge body of information commanding its own specialized workers and its own technic. This organized knowledge rapidly became known as "Textual Criticism," which, of course, is the technical name of the very Science that

this learned priest declared must mark the honest beginning of all biblical investigation. . . .

3

Just as the philosopher Spinoza had his predecessors
so too had Father Simon, particularly in this field of
the "text" study of the Bible. Important discoveries
in this department had been established long before the
French Oratorian began his investigations. For example, in 1650 Louis Cappel, an oriental scholar and
professor of Hebrew at the French School at Samur,
published a monumental work entitled *Critica Sacra*
in face of the opposition of the three Universities of
Geneva, Leyden, and Sedan. Cappel's book brought
forward a multitude of instances to show that the text
of both the Old and New Testament had become in
many places inaccurate, and that many different readings of the text of the Bible were already in existence.
Although Cappel was a Protestant, Simon did not hesitate to say of his book that it was "to be preferred to all
others who have treated the same subject."

What Simon owed to Cappel, Cappel in turn owed
to Elijah Levita, the foremost Jewish humanist of the
fifteenth century, who curiously enough introduced several famous Christians to a knowledge of the Hebrew
language. One day Levita made a very bold scientific
discovery regarding the Hebrew text of the Bible which
infuriated his fellow Jews. Taking the original words
of the Old Testament, Levita broke them up—that is,
he separated the vowels from the consonants, and con-
clusively proved that the Hebrew vowels (now known
as the Massoretic punctuation) were utterly unknown
to Moses! In fact, he showed that these tiny points and

accents found in the Hebrew Bible represented a late invention, having been added to the consonants many hundreds of years after the death of the pioneer law-giver.

To one unacquainted with the language of the Old Testament Levita's discovery might pass without the full recognition due it. Originally, Hebrew was written without vowels, a word being represented only by consonants. This, of course, was a very primitive and incomplete mode of writing which gave rise to many errors. The difficulties of reading accurately a script written in this manner can be judged if one will take a passage of ordinary English, eliminate the vowels, and then try to read it by the consonants. Take, for example, the first verse of Genesis: "In the beginning God created the Heavens and the Earth." When this same verse is written without vowels it appears: *"n th bgnng Gd crtd th hvns nd th rth."* Of course, this looks rather crude to the eye, but it must always be remembered that vowels are not necessary to any living language; they merely facilitate rapid reading at sight. Like several other Semitic tongues, ancient Hebrew was written without vowels for many centuries.

Eventually, however, a time came when the reading of the old Bible texts without vowels developed a very embarrassing situation which could only be relieved by creating a common system of vocalization. The need for such a system was long felt by the Jewish people in order to properly pronounce the sacred writings. After groping about for several hundred years a method of vowel "points" was finally evolved by a band of Jewish scholars who called themselves Massoretes (followers of tradition). This innovation took place during the seventh and eighth century A. D. partly in Babylonia and partly in Palestine.*

Levita's discovery proved a bombshell to tradition and orthodoxy, for it meant that the Hebrew text of the Bible in common use among the Jews was of relatively late origin and that the vowels had not been placed into the sacred writings by Moses as people firmly believed. It was a bold heresy for which, as Levita soon learnt, he had to pay a stiff price. For his able scholarship his own people rewarded him with insult and hostility; and like Spinoza, though born a Jew, he was forced to spend most of his life among Christians.

Of course, it is not difficult to understand why a wave of antagonism crashed over Levita's head. He lived in an age when both Jews and Christians regarded the Bible as a supernatural product and, moreover, were willing to persecute others in order to prove it! For many centuries various rabbinical writers and philosophers had succeeded in weaving around the sacred writings a web of legend and tradition designed to increase the veneration with which the ancient Scriptures were regarded. They surrounded the Bible with that glamor and halo of attraction which in the oriental mind belongs to the marvellous and supernatural. Consequently, it was commonly believed by both Jew and Christian that not only were the sacred writings themselves divine but also the very structure and wording of the sentences contained in them. And still more! —every letter of each word even to the tiny points by which the vowels were indicated!

---

*It is very interesting to note in this connection that the Bible of the Mohammedans, called the Koran, was also originally written (in Arabic) without vowels. Many years later the text was vocalized.

All sorts of fantastic notions were seriously entertained by the pious. According to one account, the mystery of the vowel-points was revealed by God to Adam in the Garden of Eden, according to another the Almighty presented them to Moses on Mt. Sinai. Still others believed that Ezra the scribe and his companions, under a special divine guidance, added them to the text, thereby finally settling the authorized method of reading it. Widely as these traditions might vary they all met on the same ground of belief: that every jot and tittle of the Law, every vowel-point and accent, had been accurately fixed by the will of the Most High. In nothing were the theologians quite so dogmatic or quite so loud as in their declaration that the Bible conveyed the word of God with absolute accuracy and without the slightest error. They even went so far as to deny the existence of a human element in the Hebrew Scriptures and, of course, Textual Criticism— that science which Simon championed—whose function it is to correct the errors of scribes and copyists, was denounced as an attack on the integrity of religion.

Cappel's adoption of Levita's conclusions relative to the late date of the vowel-points shattered the pet theological doctrine of a miraculously perfect text and thereby fanned the flames of a controversy which has lasted with curious persistency even to modern times. In the history of the Freedom of Thought this controversy is known as the question of Literal or Verbal Inspiration. Then as now, no more complete and crushing repudiation of the doctrine of divine dictation can be found than in Cappel's own words: "Wherefore, let this remain agreed upon and settled, that the codices underwent in the copying those varied and manifold mishaps which are common to all other books, arising from the ignorance, carelessness, and inattention of the copyists, and at times from the boldness and rashness of amenders; from which not even our present Hebrew Codex is exempt, nor could be, save by some stupendous and incredible miracle. . . ."

4

Originally, Simon did not aim to chart out new adventures in biblical study. His object was to gather together, recast, and discuss the investigations and researches of others and present them in an orderly and understandable form. However, he did achieve fresh discoveries which helped scholars to a clearer understanding of how the Bible was written. By a careful study of Hebrew, Simon was able to prove that the Bible is not a specimen of God's literary style, but the production of many authors widely divergent from each other in their use of words, favorite idioms, phraseology, and figures of speech. These many variations and marked peculiarities guided him in his efforts to unravel the original sources. Like a geologist intent upon tracing the earth's past by an examination of the various kinds of stratification Simon opened his Bible—and this is what he found:

On reading the early chapters of Genesis, he noticed that the Creation Story contained a diversity of widely different types of writing. He was quickly attracted to sudden and delicate changes in the text as if different men were speaking. "Sometimes," declared Simon, "we find a very curt style and sometimes a very copious one, although the variety of the matter does not require it." Pursuing this difference in style to the very boundaries of the story he recognized two independent and variant accounts which lie side by side, and that each account when unravelled according to its own literary style is a complete story in itself.

Now, when these accounts are properly separated and put into parallel columns it can be easily seen how they differ from each other not only in style but also on matters of fact. In the first account, for example, man's creation comes as the last act of God, whereas in the second account man is created first of all living things. Woman is created from man's rib according to the second narrative, but in the first "male and female" are created together. Plant life in the first story springs into existence at the direct command of God; in the second it results from a mist which rose from the earth and watered the whole face of the ground.

These duplicate statements of fact which sorely troubled both church and synagogue and forced thinking people to believe that the Bible contradicted itself proved, upon close examination, to be the natural results of two divergent accounts that had been dovetailed together. When properly separated the so-called inconsistencies vanished into thin air! So it was just at this point that Simon put forth his chief argument that Moses could not have been the author of these accounts. It arose from the impossibility of thinking that one and the same man would have used two different styles to write two complete stories of the same thing in the same book and place the one immediately after the other.

The following parallel versions of the Creation Epic will give a bird's-eye view of the complete severance of the opening chapters of Genesis into its two originally independent sources. For reasons, which will be explained later, the original Hebrew names for the Deity are here retained. In our English Bible the Hebrew word Elohim is translated "God";—where "Yahweh" occurs it is translated "Lord."*

First Account

Ch. I *1*. In the beginning Elohim (God) created the heavens and the earth. *2*. And the earth was waste and void, and darkness was upon the face of the deep; and the Spirit of Elohim was brooding over the face of the waters. *3*. Then Elohim said, Let there be light, and there was light. *4*. And Elohim saw that the light was good. Elohim caused the light to separate from the darkness. *5*. And Elohim called the light Day, and the darkness he called Night. And there was evening and there was morning, a first day. *6*. Then Elohim said, Let there be a firmament in the midst of the waters, and let it divide the waters from the waters. *7*. Thus Elohim made a firmament, and caused the waters which were under the firmament to separate from the waters which were above the firmament, and it was so. *8*. And Elohim called the firmament Heaven. And there was evening and there was morning, a second day. *9*. Then Elohim said, Let the waters under the heavens be gathered together into one place, that dry land may appear. And it was so. *10*. And Elohim also called the dry land Earth, and the gathering together of the waters he called Sea. And Elohim saw that it was good. *11*. Moreover Elohim said, Let the earth put forth vegetation: herbs which yield seed, and fruit-trees which bear fruit on the earth after their kind, wherein is

Second Account

Ch. II *4.b* In the day that Yahweh Elohim (Lord God) made earth and heaven. *5*. And no plant of the field was yet on the earth, and no herb of the field had yet sprung up, for Yahweh Elohim had not caused it to rain upon the earth, and there was no man to till the ground; *6*. But a mist used to rise from the earth and water the whole face of the ground. *7*. Then Yahweh Elohim formed man of the dust of the ground and breathed into his nostrils the breath of life. Thus man became a living being. *8*. And Yahweh Elohim planted a garden in Eden far in the East, and placed there the man whom he had formed; *9*. And out of the ground Yahweh Elohim made to grow every tree that is pleasant to the sight and good for food; the tree of life also in the midst of the garden and the tree of knowledge of good and evil. *10*. Now a river went forth from Eden which watered the garden; and thence it divided into four branches. *11*. The name of the first is Pishon. That is the one which encircles the whole land of Havilah, where there is gold; *12*. And the gold of that land is good; there is bedellium and onyx stone. *13*. And the name of the second river is Gihon. This is the one that encircles the whole land of Cush. *14*. And the name of the third river is Hiddekel. It is the one which flows east of Assyria. And the fourth river

*"Yahweh" is sometimes transliterated in various Bibles as "Jehovah." No modern scholar now uses this inaccuracy. The name Jehovah, which rests on the erroneous use of Hebrew vowels, was defended by Galatinus, father confessor of Pope Leo X, 1518.

their seed. And it was so. *12*. Thus the earth brought forth vegetation, herbs which yield seed after their kind and trees which bear fruit after their kind, wherein is their seed. And Elohim saw that it was good. *13*. And there was evening and there was morning, the third day. *14*. Then Elohim said, Let there be lights in the firmament of heaven to distinguish between day and night. Let them also be for signs, and for seasons, and for days and years; *15*. And let them be lights in the firmament of heaven to shed light upon the earth. And it was so. *16*. Thus Elohim made the two great lights: the greater to rule the day and the lesser light to rule the night; also the stars. *17*. And Elohim set them in the firmament of heaven to shed light upon the earth. *18*. And to rule over the day and over the night, and to distinguish between light and darkness. And Elohim saw that it was good. *19*. And there was evening and there was morning, a fourth day. *20*. Then Elohim said, Let the waters swarm with swarms of living creatures, and let birds fly over the earth in the open firmament of heaven. *21*. Thus Elohim created the great seamonsters, and all living, moving creatures with which the waters swarm, after their kind, and every winged bird after its kind. And Elohim saw that it was good. *22*. And Elohim blessed them, saying, Be fruitful, and become numerous, and fill the water in the sea, let the birds become numerous on the earth. *23*. And there was evening and there was morning, a fifth day. *24*. Then Elohim said, Let the earth bring forth living creatures after their kind: cattle and creeping things and beasts of the earth after their kind, And it was so. *25*. Thus Elohim made the beasts of the earth after their kind, and the animals after their kind, and everything that creeps upon the ground after its kind. And Elohim saw that it was good. *26*. Moreover, Elohim said,

is Perath. *15*. And Yahweh Elohim took the man, and put him in the garden of Eden to till it and to guard it. *16*. And Yahweh Elohim commanded the man, saying, Of every tree of the garden thou mayest eat freely. *17*. Except of the tree of the knowledge of good and evil; from it thou shalt not eat, for in the day that thou eatest of it thou shalt surely die. *18*. Then said Yahweh Elohim, it is not good for man to be alone; I will make a help suited to him. *19*. And out of the ground Yahweh Elohim formed all the beasts of the field and all the birds of the heavens, and brought them to the man to see what he would call them; and whatever the man called each living creature that was its name. *20*. Thus the man gave names to all cattle, and to the birds of the heavens, and all the beasts of the field; but for the man himself there was found no help suited to him. *21*. Then Yahweh Elohim caused a deep sleep to fall upon the man, so that he slept; and he took one of his ribs, and closed up its place with flesh. *22*. But the rib, which he had taken from the man, Yahweh Elohim fashioned into a woman and brought her to the man. *23*. Then said the man, This is now bone of my bones, and flesh of my flesh; she shall be called Woman, because she was taken out of Man.

Let us make man in our image, after our likeness, that they may have dominion over the fish of the sea, and over the birds of the heavens. And over the cattle, and over all the beasts of the earth, and over all the creeping things that creep upon the earth. *27.* Thus Elohim created man in his own image, in the image of Elohim created he him; male and female created he them. *28.* Elohim also blessed them, and said to them, Be fruitful, and become numerous, and fill the earth, and subdue it; and have dominion over the fishes of the sea, and over the birds of the heavens, and over every living thing that creeps upon the earth. *29.* Elohim also said, Behold, I give to you every herb yielding seed, which is upon the face of all the earth, and every tree, in which is fruit yielding seed; it shall be food for you. *30.* And to every beast of the earth, and to every bird of the heavens, and to everything that creeps on the earth, wherein there is life, I give every green herb for good. And it was so. *31.* And when Elohim saw everything that he had made, behold, it was very good. And there was evening and there was morning, a sixth day.

Ch. II *1.* Thus the heavens and the earth were finished, and all their host. *2.* When on the seventh day Elohim had finished his work which he had done, he rested on the seventh day from all his work which he had done. *3.* Elohim also blessed the seventh day, and hallowed it; because in it he rested from all his work which he, Elohim, had created and made.

It does not take an expert in language to notice, once the attention has been called to the fact, that in the first account of the Creation Story there is a formal, dignified and solemn style, regular and precise in its arrangement and full of oft-repeated phrases which create a literary atmosphere strikingly different from the second version with its picturesque and flowing words. Of course, the two accounts differ widely in details, that is evident. But what Simon wanted to show was that paralleling this conflict of details there was a wide difference in literary style. . . .

Simon also recognized that there were two contradictory accounts of the story of the "Flood" which are woven together in chapters six to nine of the Book of Genesis. A number of short passages taken alternately from two independent records are here dovetailed together to make a continuous story. Any one who reads this section of the Bible with a little care cannot fail to see this for himself. The two flood narratives are pieced together like patchwork, each having its own distinctive type of style. When the legend is carefully read it is seen that in one account the duration of the deluge is given as "forty days and forty nights," whereas in the other it is stated that "the waters prevailed upon the earth one hundred and fifty days." According to the nineteenth verse of the sixth chapter of Genesis, Noah is required by God to take into the ark one pair of each kind of animal. But in the second verse of the seventh chapter God directs him to divide the beasts into clean and unclean, taking seven pair of the former to one of the latter.

Simon did not attempt to reconcile these dual items of fact which are glaringly inconsistent with each other; the church and synagogue traditions had long ago attempted to do that by grotesque and impossible interpretations. Simon's scientific departure lay in his keen observation that what had been regarded as a single story was, in reality, two divergent and independent accounts which had been dovetailed together.

By segregating the obvious inconsistencies, the Flood Legend may be divided into separate and independent versions, each possessing its own distinct literary style. And just as in the Creation Epic where the difficulties vanished upon unravelling, so too they disappeared here.

5

The world is indebted to Father Simon for having proved what all scholarship to-day accepts as final: that diversity of style implies different authors. "The variety of style we meet with in the Books of Moses seems to be a convincing argument that one and the same man was not the author."

The scientific principle of style, now so firmly established, has helped innumerable investigators in their long search after the true story of how the Bible was composed. It proved to be one of the fundamental guides in unravelling documents that had been pieced together by unknown editors. What had long been regarded as a confused jumble began to assume order once the original writings were segregated and restored. For many centuries the whole Jewish and Christian world believed that the Hebrew Scriptures were an exact dictation from heaven and that the Hebrew language used in the Bible was God's own choice vocabulary. To-day, however, it is impossible to even talk of the Hebrew of the Old Testatment as if it were all of a piece, inasmuch as some writers used Palestinian-Hebrew, others Babylonian-Hebrew, and still others Aramaic-Hebrew, types that differ as widely as Chaucer from Shakespeare, and Shakespeare from Bernard Shaw.

Not dissimilar to the work of Simon were the labors of the other scholars searching out the analysis of Greek literature in practically the same manner that biblical investigators were severing the Hebrew texts. The long supposed unity of the Iliad and the Odyssey as the work of a single poet—called Homer—was finally broken up into a cycle of separate lays by different authors, collected, arranged and put together for the first time during the administration of Pisistratus. Here as elsewhere style proved to be one of the distinguishing characteristics of its many-sided authorship.

Now that the greater part of the thinking world has come to realize that all writing bears upon itself the traces of its own historic origin—which betrays the imprint of the age and the environment in which it was produced—the Bible is no longer regarded as an exception to this rule. Just as the different geological epochs have left their deep traces on the strata of the rocks so do various documents of Scripture reflect the history of the successive ages which gave them birth.

The Second Result

Different authors characterized by differences in diction and style wrote the Pentateuch—not Moses.

CHAPTER III

HOW JEAN ASTRUC, A FRENCH PHYSICIAN, FOUND
THE TRUE KEY TO UNLOCK THE DOCUMENTS OF
GENESIS, AND HOW PROF. J. G. EICHHORN, THE
GERMAN ORIENTALIST, APPLIED THIS NEW-
LY DISCOVERED KNOWLEDGE

THE works of Spinoza and Simon created an inter-
nationally popular interest in the Bible. Various writers throughout Europe now began to bring to light an
amazing number of valuable facts that demanded the
attention of scholars of all creeds.

For almost a hundred years a brilliant succession of
investigators, recognizing the differences of style, inconsistencies, contradictions, and chronological difficulties
of the Scriptures, added fresh confirmation to the ideas
advanced by the two great masters of Scientific Biblical Study. An immense amount of labor was expended
. . . but still the main puzzle continued unsolved, for
no one had as yet attempted a scientific analysis of the
text with a view of restoring the original sources from
which the Bible had been compiled.

If the Pentateuch is a composite work made up of
different documents from the hands of different writers
or schools of thought, how distinguish them? Of
course, there is "style"—but style itself in order to be
an accurate guide must possess distinctive guarantees.
Are there any such certainties? Even Spinoza and
Simon had declared the Bible to be a compilation from
different documents and went so far as to definitely
recognize the two accounts of Creation and the Flood

—but even these men were never able to suggest a method of accurately distinguishing one document from the other.

. . . And so the puzzle continued as a deep and dark riddle of the Sphinx.

For a long time many eminent scholars thought the problem was hopeless of solution, for the documents of Genesis seemed so inextricably mixed up as to defy disentanglement. Finally, from a wholly unexpected quarter the right clue was flashed to the world by the brilliant discovery of a French physician.

And this is how it was done.

2

While engaged in the study of skin diseases, of which he was perhaps the most prominent authority in France, Jean Astruc, consulting physician to Louis XV, was led to consider the Old Testament Laws of the clean and unclean. Bringing to the search of the Hebrew Scriptures a mind thoroughly trained in the methods of science he began making a series of independent investigations. After some hesitation and timidity, characteristic of such a man, this distinguished doctor of medicine published anonymously his findings in a little duodecimo volume entitled *Conjectures on the Original Memoirs Which it Appears that Moses Employed to Compose the Book of Genesis.*

Because of his scientific training Astruc was extremely modest and over-cautious, which largely explains why he refused to give his name out as the author of the *Conjectures.* "I decided to publish this work," he declared, "and submit it to the judgment of enlightened persons, to whose remarks I will gladly listen. I protest beforehand very sincerely, that if those who have the right to decide and whose decisions I should respect, find my conjectures either false or dangerous, I am ready to abandon them; or rather, I abandon them from the present moment. Never shall a preconception in favor of my own ideas prevail with me over the love of Truth and Religion." . . .

Astruc started from the observation that in some chapters of Genesis the Hebrew name for God was Yahweh, and in other sections it was Elohim. After dividing the Story of Creation into two narratives as Father Simon had done, Astruc—gifted with a penetrating and imaginative insight—proceeded to point out what no one before him had ever seen:—that each narrative in Genesis had a distinguishing mark in its peculiar use of either one name for the deity or the other.

"In the Hebrew text of Genesis," writes Astruc, "God is regularly designated by two different names. The first which presents itself is that of *Elohim* (God) אלהים. . . . The other name of God is that of *Yahweh* (Lord) יהוה. . . . It might be thought from those remarks, that these two names, *Elohim* and *Yahweh*, are employed without distinction in the same places in Genesis, as synonymous terms, and appropriate for varying style; but this would be an error. These names are never confounded; there are whole chapters, and the greater portions of chapters, where God is always named *Elohim*, and never *Yahweh*; there are others, at least as numerous, where the name of Yahweh alone is given to God, and never that of Elohim."

Now, if the reader will take the same two independent accounts of Creation as unravelled by Richard Simon he will notice that in the First Account the

Hebrew deity is called exclusively by the name of *Elohim* which is rendered into English "God." In the Second Account a different name appears—a name which is not used in the first at all, that is, *Yahweh* which is translated "Lord." The same phenomenon crops up in the Flood Legend (again illustrating Astruc's principles) where the First Account of the deluge uses the name of Yahweh, the Second employing the term Elohim. "This variation," observed Astruc, "is so striking and so often repeated that I defy any one ever to render a sufficient reason for supposing that all of Genesis came from the same hand, and that it was composed by the same person. This difficulty vanishes, however, if one admits my conjecture, and supposes that the memoir where God is called Elohim came from one hand, and that the other, where he is called Yahweh, came from another."

Brilliant as this discovery was, no one at that time seems to have grasped its epoch-making importance—nevertheless, an entirely new process had emerged, for here was something definite, concrete, and admitting of no juggling—moreover, it satisfactorily explained what no other analysis was able to do. The narratives of Creation and the Flood, being definitely stamped by the hallmark of the alternating use of two different names for the Hebrew deity, became a conclusive bit of evidence that opened for all time the path of biblical investigation.

With majestic devotion to the quest of truth Astruc now proceeded to submit to his readers the entire Book of Genesis with the text divided into separate columns, making an arrangement whereby those passages that belong to the Elohim record were segregated from those belonging to the Yahweh. It was a pretty picture that he presented, somewhat on the order of a modern business survey, with Exhibit A and Exhibit B so arranged as to afford an easy examination of his analysis.*

3

Although his information was too slight to give to his work anything approaching a final analysis, still to Astruc goes the undisputed and distinguished merit of having discovered the fundamental clew from which all scientific sifting of biblical documents has been carried on. Modest as he was, he received neither honor nor thanks for his epoch-making achievement. In fact, his book met with immediate contempt and was covered with slimy reproach.

Not only did the theologians of the day sneer at him as an ignoramus; but the politicians of Paris, despising his son-in-law, Etienne de Silhouette—a man of literary and financial ability in high office with the Dukes of Orleans—made capital of every unorthodox remark in the *Conjectures* to slander the Astruc influence. What right had a doctor of medicine to submit the Book of Genesis to an analysis? Wasn't it purposely designed to undermine Faith and subvert government? In his *Philosophical Dictionary*, Voltaire gives an interesting sidelight on the times when he tells us why the *Conjectures* has always been a rare volume to find in the library or bookstall. "It is sometimes very dan-

*Besides these two major records he segregated ten minor independent pieces which according to his plan could not be assigned to either the Elohim or Yahweh document. These minor parts of Genesis, Astruc supposed, were originally memoranda by different authors which Moses pieced together bit by bit.

gerous to make a book. Silhouette, before he could im-
agine that he would be controller-general of the
finances, had printed a book on the agreement between
religion and politics; and his father-in-law, Astruc, had
given to the public the memoranda from which the
author of the Pentateuch had taken all the wonderful
things that happened so long before him. The very
day Silhouette obtained his place, some good friend
sought out a copy of the books of father-in-law and
son-in-law, to place them before Parliament, that they
might be condemned to the flames according to custom. Both of them bought up all the copies in the kingdom; and that is the reason why they have become so
rare at present."

Notwithstanding the fact that Astruc had always
been a loyal churchman, the Catholics of France
flouted and denounced him as a heretic with such sys-
tematic ridicule and vicious slander that his book sank
into obscurity . . . pang-born and murdered.

4

It was not until thirty years after the publication of
the *Conjectures* that the world again heard about Astruc.
A German scholar of wide-ranging interests, who
seems to have known Astruc's work only at second-
hand, independently—more or less—arrived at the
same results reached by the abused physician in much
the same manner in which Charles Darwin independently reached the biological conclusions of Alfred Rus-
sel Wallace.

At the age of twenty-three Johann Gottfried Eichhorn, already distinguished by vigor and scientific acu-
men, was called to occupy the chair of oriental lan-

guages at Jena University. While he found time to write about forty-five books during a busy life of teaching, he is chiefly remembered to-day by his famous volume entitled *Introduction to the Old Testament* which first appeared in 1779.

In this book Eichhorn not only "rediscovered" the two main sources of Genesis but he went beyond Astruc by showing that the Yahweh and Elohim records each bear many characteristics other than the single difference in the divine names. He showed, for example, that linguistic differences regularly corresponded with the variation in the names of God. Thus, the narrative which uses Elohim speaks of God as *bara* "creating" the world, whereas the other narrative that uses Yahweh speaks of the Lord as *asah* "making" all things. When referring to the dry land the Elohim account uses the word *eretz*, meaning "earth"; but the Yahweh account uses *adamah*, "ground."

While he was perhaps the first scholar to draw up a list of the words peculiar to the Elohim and Yahweh records, Eichhorn did not stop short at linguistics. On reading the early chapters of Genesis he was quick to observe how the sudden change in the divine name coincides not only with differences in vocabulary, phraseology and style, but also with a different representation and spiritual atmosphere. In other words, certain religious ideas and conceptions tend to recur in similarities of language.

The precise and formal literary style of the first chapter of Genesis—which uses the name of Elohim exclusively—conveys a highly developed theological idea of God as a majestic and transcendent Being. In striking contrast, the second chapter of Genesis—which uses Yahweh and employs a picturesque and flowing style—describes God in naïve and primitive terms which make the deity almost human. There is nothing of the anthropomorphic in the Elohim account —but in the Second, Yahweh is spoken of with a certain vivid familiarity. One of the most delightful pictures of the Second Account is that in which Yahweh is described as first moulding man into shape, actually using his own hands as a potter would fashion a dish, and then breathing into his nostrils, thus transforming the hitherto lifeless clay into a living creature. Of course, this is a vastly different kind of creative process from that recorded in the first chapter where it plainly states that "male and female created He them,"—that is, in one act. Then again, the interest of the Elohim account of the Creation Story culminates in the sanctification of the Sabbath, while the most significant thing about the Yahweh record is the tree in the midst of Eden—the Tree of Knowledge of good and evil.

So, aside from the distinguishing marks of style, differences in divine names, and variations in vocabulary, Eichhorn proved the existence of decided differences in religious views between the two documents. In the hands of this scholar Genesis became known not only as a book based on pre-existing writings but it was now definitely shown that each section and paragraph and sentence still preserves its original style, vocabulary, and texture of ideas indicative of the source from which it came (and that by means of these criteria the book itself can be taken apart and its original sources reproduced). These variations in ideas, deeply embedded in the records of Genesis, opened up new paths of investigation which in time successfully answered the most baffling puzzles and led Biblical Criticism into the front rank of a world-wide scholarship. . . .

5

Unlike Astruc's *Conjectures*, which was badly abused, Eichhorn's *Introduction* turned out to be a best seller. Its popularity was so great that a new edition soon followed in 1787. This second printing is now memorable because of its historic preface wherein Eichhorn bestowed upon the science of biblical investigation the name by which it has come to be known throughout the world—"The Higher Criticism."

"I am obliged to give the most pains to a hitherto entirely unworked field, the investigation of the internal condition of the particular writings of the Old Testament by help of the Higher Criticism (a new name to no Humanist). Let any one think what they will of these efforts, my own consciousness tells me that they are the result of a very careful investigation."

. . . Unfortunately, however, the careful investigations of scholars are sometimes beyond the average person and so the term "Higher Criticism"—a clumsy and misleading name—stirred up needless prejudice, placing scholarly men at the mercy of a misuse of language.* It immediately became the source of considerable suspicion and hatred—many people, of course, deliberately misunderstanding the term and charging

---

*The use of the word "Higher" in connection with the Science of Biblical Criticism is to distinguish this department of knowledge from its sister branch already referred to as "textual" or "lower" criticism. Textual criticism looks no farther than the question: What did the final author, compiler or editor write? Higher Criticism goes beyond this and asks: How came he to write as he did?

those who used it with practising intellectual conceit.

While its meaning, in its technical sense, was always perfectly clear to honest investigators, to the untrained mind it was not. Eichhorn himself anticipated ingratitude and malice. "Party spirit will perhaps for a pair of decennials snort at the Higher Criticism instead of rewarding it with the full thanks that are due it." Perhaps he should have known that the very ambiguity of the term would have the tendency of subjecting the scientific investigation of the Bible to all sorts of distortions. The opponents of biblical science lost no time in denouncing "Criticism" as just another name for pernicious fault-finding; and, of course, the use of the word "Higher" in connection with it was made synonymous with egotistical pride and arrogance. Worse still, the sinister combination of the two words was scowled at as nothing short of a manufacture out of the Devil's own workshop! So, by playing upon popular fears the Bible alarmists succeeded (unfortunately even to this day) in causing many thousands of otherwise intelligent people to regard scientific investigation of the Scriptures as hostile to the spirit of religion.

Himself a theologian and a devout Christian, Eichhorn had no idea of criticising the Bible in the vulgar acceptance of that word. He had too much of the deep scholarly veneration for the Hebrew Scriptures to engage his talents in abusing it. To him, criticism meant an honest search after truth—and not an impertinent or flippant playing with a great subject. He wanted the world to learn from the Bible itself the correct story of its origin, in order to show how the Scriptures had been mistakenly blamed for things that could be easily explained. In former times the Scriptures

were not free to speak their mind in their own tongue
—the text being dominated and manipulated by dogma thrust upon it from the outside. The new process
must, therefore, be a reversal of the old method.
Whether actuated by love of truth, deep piety or just
ordinary curiosity, Eichhorn declared that men have a
moral right to learn everything it is humanly possible
to know about the Scriptures—its origin, language,
history and interpretation.

The organized and scientific pursuit of this desire
took shape in the mind of Eichhorn as a cross-examina-
tion which achieves its results by comparing book with
book, part with part, and by making a careful inquiry
into the manners and customs referred to in them.
Eichhorn therefore insisted that the real meaning of a
passage of Scripture must be determined not only by
the laws of language and grammar, but also by its
place and setting in history—and not, of course, by
the feeble and inadequate traditions of the church or
the synagogue.

"Higher Criticism" at the very outset of its growth
became known among leading thinkers as the process
by which the Bible is unveiled and its writings restored
to their original state—that is, before they were tampered with. "Most of the writings of the Hebrews have
passed through several hands"—and this, of course,
has been the fate of all ancient books. And inasmuch
as thought, like rock, is stratified it was soon recognized that an important function of criticism was to
accurately determine the different ages of the various
layers of composition.

By seeking to supply an intelligent answer to the
origin of the different books which make up the vast

writings of Scripture, the Higher Criticism became the only trustworthy instrument in the hands of truth seekers; and as a forward movement of human thought it now began to unfold itself with the inevitability of a great drama.

"Already long ago," declared Eichhorn, "scholars have sought to determine the age of anonymous Greek and Roman writings from their contents, since these are often insufficient for an investigation of this kind, from their language. They have also by the same means separated from ancient works pieces of later origin, which, by accidental circumstances, have become mingled with the older productions. And not until the writings of the Old Testament have been subjected to the same test can any one assert with confidence that the sections of a book all belong in reality to the author whose name is prefixed."

As a result of Eichhorn's colossal labors the Higher Criticism of the Bible has subjected the Hebrew Scriptures to a sifting process which no other writings—ancient or modern—have ever undergone. Beginning with the analysis of Astruc, which was largely confined to the Book of Genesis, a new method with startling results challenged the intelligent world. In the hands of Eichhorn—the master orientalist—the new method was greatly enlarged and immediately became the basis upon which all future investigation—as we shall soon see—established itself.

THE THIRD RESULT

The work of Astruc and Eichhorn may be summed up as follows: Genesis is composed of distinctive narratives which are distinguishable from each other (1)

*by the use of different names to designate the Divine
Being and (2) by vocabulary and representation which
regularly correspond with the variation in the names of
God.*

CHAPTER IV

HOW THE DISCOVERIES OF KARL DAVID ILGEN WERE LOST, AND AFTER FIFTY YEARS EMERGED THROUGH THE RESEARCHES OF HERMANN HUPFELD OF HALLE

ONE of the most interesting curiosities in the history of scientific research is the manner in which important discoveries finally emerge into the clear light of day after having been utterly lost and forgotten. . . .

Although it has no particular bearing on our subject, except to point an alluring parallel, there is, for instance, the strange story of Gregor Mendel—of Mendellian fame—that remarkable Austrian monk who rose from a peasant lad to the high office of abbot of Brunn. In his cloister garden, far from the noise of the world, this quiet and unassuming man devised and carried out a series of biological experiments that have since become the solid foundation of the new science of heredity. In 1865 Mendel published an account of his discoveries, but it made no impression and was politely buried away in the archives of the monastery. Not until the dust of thirty-five years had eaten its way into the folios was there any knowledge or appreciation of what Mendel had accomplished. When the time for rediscovery finally came (1900) his work was simultaneously exhumed by three distinguished botanists.

With the possible exception of the researches of Mendel perhaps no more striking example of "rediscovery" can be cited than the case of the almost forgotten name of Karl David Ilgen, whose contributions to biblical knowledge were overlooked for fifty years.

2

Like Eichhorn, whom he succeeded as head of the department of Oriental literature at the University of Jena, Ilgen was a great scholar. But unlike Eichhorn he was an extremely poor writer, which accounts for the little impression he made on his contemporaries. Not every discoverer is capable of presenting his thoughts in simple understandable language (a demand which the twentieth century has made so insistent that even the most pedantic of the pedants must modify their lumbering literary ways). Still, a discovery may be great in spite of the crude and puzzling manner in which it happens to be temporarily cast. For that reason we now turn to Ilgen's famous research, only too happy to forget his befuddling pen.

Every scholar must have a starting point notwithstanding the fact that some have tried to begin where there is no beginning and end where no end is in sight. With Ilgen we need not be lost. Starting out with the sound conviction that Hebrew history could not be properly studied until its sources had been completely unravelled, he published in 1798 his important book dealing with a "new" analysis of Genesis. It made its appearance under the fanciful title *Original Documents of the Temple Archives at Jerusalem in their Primitive Form*. In this volume the Jena professor accepted the results of both Astruc and Eichhorn as being perfectly good—that is, as far as they went. Only they did not go far enough! And so Ilgen sets out to improve upon them.

And this is how he does it.

Whereas Astruc and Eichhorn had discovered only two main documents in Genesis, Ilgen recognized and successfully demonstrated a third. How? By pointing out that the Elohim-document of Genesis was not all of one cast Ilgen showed that it could be severed into two distinct and independent sources,—that is, a First Elohist and a Second Elohist. "After a careful examination of the text of Genesis, in which I have faithfully followed the clews furnished by the headings, the frequent repetitions, the divergence in language and tone, and the varying and entirely contradictory contents, I have found that the documents . . . belong to three different authors, of whom two use the name Elohim, and the third Yahweh." In other words, stories that had been assigned, en bloc, by Astruc and Eichhorn to but one Elohim-document were now for the first time shown to belong to two. As dull as he was in writing, Ilgen was quick to see that in reality two altogether distinct documents were wrapped up in those narratives which were constantly using the word "Elohim" to designate the deity and that while these two documents were at one in their avoidance of the name of Yahweh they were in almost every other respect distinct.

Thus, under the name of the Elohim-document two different writers had previously been confused.

3

It was unfortunate that Ilgen's book was marked by too many eccentricities, a defect that caused it to fall into an unwarranted and unmerited obscurity. It was not until fifty years later that the "third" document of Genesis was again brought to light—this time rediscovered by Hermann Hupfeld, the brilliant orientalist of the University of Halle.

Hupfeld arrived at the same result, finding in Genesis—as Ilgen before him had found—three primary documents or sources (one Yahweh-document, and two Elohistic) which had been skilfully braided together. "I learnt to my great surprise among the many forced and apparently mistaken findings of Ilgen a variety of accurate and remarkable observations which I thought myself to have discovered first." . . .

Like his predecessor, to whom he made this generous acknowledgment, Hupfeld demonstrated that there were two independent writers in Genesis who used Elohim as a proper name to designate the Divine Being. This important fact Hupfeld placed before the world in a brief but masterly book entitled *The Sources of Genesis*. It appeared in 1853—exactly one hundred years after Astruc's ill-fated *Conjectures*. . . .

The story of how Hupfeld arrived at his conclusion can be easily illustrated by taking three important instances on which he relied to demonstrate the accuracy of his unravelling process.

On reading the twenty-eighth chapter of Genesis, Hupfeld noticed that the explanation therein given concerning the origin of the name "Beth-El" was altogether different from the explanation given in the thirty-fifth chapter of the same book. Yet both narratives giving these contradictory explanations designate God by the name of "Elohim." For example, in the former account the narrative says that Bethel got its name when Jacob was preparing to go on a trip to Mesopotamia. In the other account we are told that

Bethel got its name when Jacob returned from Mesopotamia after a long stay. It was on his return (not on
on his going) that God appeared unto him: "So Jacob
named the place where God had spoken with him
Bethel, that is House of God."

The other instance which Hupfeld used in his demonstration deals with the story of why Jacob had to
leave home. This is perhaps the first story in all literature, secular or sacred, dealing with the immortal
theme: "Why Boys Leave Home." And not unlike all
such stories, Hupfeld found in the Pentateuch two distinct accounts. According to the First Elohist, Jacob is
sent to Mesopotamia by his father that he may take a
wife from his own kindred. Jacob, therefore, leaves
home in quite a peaceable manner and is gone for many
years. On his return to his native land he helps his
brother Esau to bury the aged Isaac. After the burial,
Esau goes to Seir or Edom, leaving Jacob in Canaan.
. . . But according to the Second Elohist this is not
the true story at all! Jacob, so we are told, fled to
Mesopotamia at the suggestion of his mother, his
father having had nothing whatever to do with his
going. Rebecca sent Jacob away not to take a wife but
in order to escape the vengeance of Esau, who was out
to kill Jacob for having cheated him. After many years'
sojourn in Mesopotamia Jacob returns to Canaan. He
finds Esau already settled in Seir and to his great astonishment he learns that Esau is advancing against him
with an armed guard. But Jacob is a diplomat and so
he sends Esau rich gifts in order to make up for having
tricked him out of Isaac's blessing.

The third example that Hupfeld marshalled for his
demonstration deals with the two variant stories of

how the name Israel was bestowed upon the patriarch Jacob. In both accounts the term Elohim is used, yet each gives an entirely different reason for the origin of Israel (clearly indicating that they come from different sources).

Genesis 32:24-29

24 And Jacob was left alone and there wrestled a man with him until the breaking of the day. 25 And when he saw that he prevailed not against him, he touched the hollow of his thigh and the hollow of Jacob's thigh was strained, as he wrestled with him. 26 And he said, Let me go, for the day breaketh. And he said, I will not let thee go, except thou bless me. 27 And he said unto him, what is thy name? And he said, Jacob. 28 And he said, Thy name shall be called no more Jacob but Israel: for thou hast striven with God (Elohim) and with men, and hast prevailed.

Genesis 35:9-11

9 And God (Elohim) appeared unto Jacob again, when he came from Paddan-aram, and blessed him. 10 And God (Elohim) said unto him, Thy name is Jacob: thy name shall not be called any more Jacob, but Israel shall be thy name: and he called his name Israel.

4

Though Hupfeld's brief treatise was confined to the Book of Genesis, it had results of the utmost consequence. The two Elohistic documents which he recognized were soon found to run through the rest of the Pentateuch—and even beyond that! And—just as was to be expected from independent sources—the more they stretched themselves beyond Genesis into the other books of the Bible the more divergent they became in language, style, and point of view.

Even a very superficial familiarity with the two Elohim documents is enough to indicate to any alert-minded person the widely marked differences that exist between them. The oldest Elohim-record is characterized by deep human interests, charm of literary style, and delights to linger over tribal memories that cluster around the village shrines of the North, particularly Bethel and Shechem. The other Elohim-document possesses a distinctly "priestly cast" together with a rigid and formal style which makes it both dry and uninteresting; it is full of precise statistics and genealogical tables, inflexible ideas, and stereotyped expressions; it is devoid of human interest; and instead of speaking of the old shrines it purposely passes them by in utter silence as though they had never existed. Ecclesiasticism is the most noteworthy part of this priestly document in which everything that smacks of heathenism has been entirely dropped out. All references to the patriarchs as having worshipped local divinities in sacred monuments, stones, trees, and groves are expunged. The conception of God is loftier and more advanced, which largely accounts for a lack of picturesque words and an unusually dull literary style. Not only is this priestly document devoid of human interest but—and this is the most significant difference!—it speaks about institutions and customs altogether unknown to the first writer. If we are a bit patient we shall soon see what an epoch-making clew this difference turned out to be. It took scholars a long time to run it down, it evaded them at almost every turn in the road. But in the end its significance was completely captured. (That is why the Bible in the hands of modern scholars is no longer the kind of a book which the average person believes it to be.) . . .

The demonstrations of Hupfeld gave new life to biblical scholarship by whetting the exploratory appetite of investigators who were now encouraged to push on in their work. But in order to avoid confusion, it was necessary to properly designate the two Elohim documents by separate names. It was finally agreed to call the older one, the one with the human interest, the "Elohistic Narrative" because it consistently uses the name Elohim for the deity, even beyond Genesis. The other—or First Elohist—came eventually to be designated the "Priestly Document" because it expounds at length the priestly system of worship with an elaborate ritual.

When, after years of cumulative toil, scholars finally unravelled the whole of the Priestly Document and succeeded in setting it up as it originally existed as an independent work, many interesting facts long buried in the tomb of the past were brought out into the light of clear day. It was, for example, immediately noticeable that this document had marked similarities in expression and point of view with the writings of the priest-prophet Ezekiel who lived in far off Babylon. Upon closer investigation, it was even found that the Priestly Document had actually borrowed many of his ideas! . . . This fact became the historical clew which successfully dated the priestly legislation as a product of the age of Ezekiel—and not of Moses as people had supposed. In fact, Ezekiel is the true father of Hebrew sacerdotal law. It was he who sketched a plan of ritual reform in the year 571 B. C.—that is, about seven centuries after Moses. It soon became a demonstrable fact that the most striking points in the Priestly Document were unknown until Ezekiel gave them the emphasis of his powerful ceremonial programme.

5

Although it is not possible to give in this chapter an elaborate sketch of the long and sustained struggle of those scholars who worked with unwearying eyes to search for the true story of how the Priestly Document was written, still it will be of interest to set down here a very brief comparison illustrating the kind of inter-relation which is sometimes found in widely separated parts of the Bible. It might even be added that the resemblance between portions of the Book of Leviticus and parts of Ezekiel is so remarkably close that many scholars at first believed Ezekiel himself to be the real author of this long-supposed Mosaic Book. While it is now definitely known that Leviticus is not the work of Ezekiel there is no doubt that it embodies Ezekiel's spirit and essential teachings, differing only in details. Ezekiel was both a priest and a prophet, but foremost a priest. His stress upon ritual, his ideas, his elaboration, his priestly emphasis—yes, his very words bristle from the pages of Leviticus. One needs only a few instances like those to be given to see how closely akin they are.

It is not hard to understand why such a list of identities would cause a vast amount of uneasiness in orthodox circles. For it definitely showed that the very core of the Pentateuch, particularly the priestly Book of Leviticus, was written in the age of the Babylonian Exile, hundreds of years after Moses. Far from being the early ceremonial legislation of the primitive Hebrews given by Moses, scholars were compelled to regard this priestly system as a product of a much later period.

From the Book of Leviticus	*From the Book of Ezekiel*
17:8 . . . Whatsoever man there be of the house of Israel, or of the sojourners that sojourn among them.	14:7 For every one of the house of Israel, or of the sojourners that sojourn in Israel.
18:5 Ye shall keep my statutes and my judgments, which if a man do, he shall live in them.	20:11 . . . my statutes . . . which if a man do, he shall live in them.
26:4 Then will I give your rains (geshem) in their season.	34:26 . . . And I will cause the rain (geshem) to come down in its season.
26:4 And the land shall yield her increase, and the trees of the field shall yield their fruit.	34:27 And the tree of the field shall yield its fruit, and the land shall yield her increase.
26:5 . . . And ye shall eat your bread to the full and dwell therein safely.	39:19 And ye shall eat fat to the full. 28:26 And they shall dwell safely therein.
26:12 . . . I will be your God and ye shall be my people.	36:28 . . . and ye shall be my people and I will be your God.
26:17 And I will set my face against you.	14:8 And I will set my face against that man.
26:22 And I will send the beast of the field among you, which shall bereave you of your children.	5:17 I will send upon you . . . evil beasts, and they shall bereave you.
26:30 I will destroy your high places, and cut down your sun-images.	6:3-4 . . . I will destroy your high places . . . and your sun-images shall be broken.
26:40 . . . their trespass which they trespassed against me.	17:20 . . . his trespass that he trespassed against me.

This bit of information called for an entire over-hauling of Hebrew history. No one would have ever believed (even the majority of the scholars were slow in appreciating its significance) that such a radical re-construction of the true course of Hebrew development was about to follow. It seemed so natural, so time-hon-ored, and so true to speak of the "Law and the Prophets" meaning thereby, that in the evolution of the ancient

Hebrew religion the so-called Mosaic Laws preceded
the teachings of the Prophets. But in the light of the
newer knowledge, all this had to be completely reversed so that instead of the Law coming first and then
the Prophets, it now became the "Prophets first and
then the Law."

6

As long as these advanced ideas were confined between the covers of ponderous and learned volumes the
world-at-large was not at all disturbed. People had so
long been taught that Moses wrote the Book of Leviticus that no one in particular bothered his head trying
to get at the uncomfortable knowledge that it wasn't.
Anyhow, does the average man read the learned pro-
fessors' books? They may be good scholars but most of
them are poor writers. And so Moses continued to be
Moses and all was serene.

But things were not destined to remain that way.
There came a time when the whole matter was to be
brought out into the public forum, and at that in the
most popular fashion so as to be clearly understood by
everybody. . . . And then things went topsy turvy.
. . . It happened in England.

It came about that in 1862 Bishop John William
Colenso, an Anglican missionary to the Zulus in the
African Natal, published a book on the Pentateuch in
which, among the other iconoclastic things, he unwittingly showed up the late date of the Priestly Document. Unlike so many books written about the
Bible, which nobody reads (perhaps that's the reason
why it is the *Book Nobody Knows*) this volume from
the learned Bishop's pen proved immensely popular—

in fact, too much so! It was an instant success. Like night birds suddenly confronted with the sun, the theological leaders of England first blinked in bewilderment at Colenso's audacious book and then completely convulsed themselves with horror. The gentle breezes of uneasiness were suddenly turned into a howling storm. How dare any one, particularly a bishop in the employ of the Church of England, go out of his way to intimate that Moses did not write the Book of Leviticus!! . . . So loud and furious was the outcry against Colenso that a special convocation of the church had to be called where his book was solemnly condemned and its fearless and brilliant author excommunicated.*

But all the loud shoutings and all the anathemas could not stop the car of progress. The right to the freedom of thought had been paid for too dearly and, at least on the part of intelligent Englishmen, there was no disposition to go back to the persecutions and the trammels of the Dark Ages. Parliament finally intervened and upheld Colenso against the ecclesiastical powers that had excommunicated him. With the bishop's brave battle (it almost proved his martyrdom) a new era opened up for British scholarship, unyoked, untrammelled, and unafraid.

Dramatic as was Colenso's fight with the contemporary unreason of his day there were other men, equally brave, but fortunately not dragged out into

*Because he had discussed biblical matters with a Zulu the following bit of nonsense verse was used as a broadside of ridicule:

"A bishop there was of Natal,
Who had a Zulu for his pal;
Said the Zulu, 'my dear,
Don't you think Genesis queer?'
Which converted my lord of Natal."

the limelight, who worked with intense scientific zeal. The discoveries begun by Ilgen and Hupfeld and popularized by Colenso were carried on and elaborated by Graf, Noldeke, Kuenen, Wellhausen, and a host of brilliant scholars. They did not stop—nothing could make them stop, so determined they were—until they had succeeded in unravelling the entire Priestly Document, sketching its characteristics and defining its limits with great precision.

Yet all this had to be accomplished in the teeth of ugly hostility. It is one of the ironies of history that so much persecution and odium has been heaped upon those scholars whose only offense was their relentless search for truth. In the denunciation of such monumental achievements the height of vicious insult and deliberate misrepresentation was perhaps never so bumptiously achieved as in those contemptible words flung at Prof. Julius Wellhausen by an American theological pigmy: "The Old Testament is to him a corpse, the corpse of a criminal laid on his dissecting-table for the skill of his hand with knife and pincers, and the joy he derives from it is in discovering a new ganglion of contradictions."

7

Brushing aside all such crude and unwarranted attacks, the progress of scientific biblical study moved on apace. As a result of indefatigable labor of the most persevering kind the Priestly Document is to-day a familiar household acquaintance with every modern scholar.

In another section of this book we shall hear more about this great document and how it was written. For the present it is enough to say that as it now stands interwoven in the Bible this Priestly writing covers eighty-five chapters—eleven in Genesis, nineteen in Exodus, all Leviticus, twenty-eight chapters in Numbers, and parts of Joshua. It is a vast historico-legal work written and compiled by various groups of exiled Hebrew priests who lived in Babylonia during the fifth century before Christ. How it all came to be compiled and then skilfully transformed into a framework (what the German scholars called the "Grundschrift") into which the other documents of the Pentateuch were fitted is one of the most astonishing stories of antiquity. . . .

THE FOURTH RESULT

Genesis is made up of three major documents: Yahwistic, Elohistic, and Priestly. These were originally separate and independent records but were joined together. These three documents may also be found in several other books of the Old Testament.

CHAPTER V

THE EXCOMMUNICATION OF FATHER ALEXANDER GEDDES AND HOW W. M. L. DE WETTE FOUND THE ORIGIN OF THE BOOK OF DEUTERONOMY

DUE in no small measure to the stimulating work of Eichhorn, the last decade of the eighteenth century witnessed a flood of books dealing with every phase of the great biblical questions that were now pounding the citadels of tradition. While some of the books were written from the standpoint of the Higher Criticism, and were thus advancing the cause of scientific investigation, others were written in wild denunciation of the new progress.

At the Imperial University of Vienna, where in 1792 Father Johann Jahn, professor of oriental languages, published his *Introduction to the Old Testament*, a new storm centre arose. Although he was a devout Catholic priest and was considered one of the foremost scholars of his time, he did not escape being severely censured by his ecclesiastical superiors for his interest in scientific biblical investigation. Particularly what he had to say on the subject of "Inspiration" (denying that the Scriptures were the exact dictation of God) was just so much sandpaper rubbed on the sensitive flesh of holy tradition. Being in possession of a keen and methodical mind, not unlike that of Richard Simon whose opinions he frequently quoted, Jahn's views quickly assumed an heretical character which his superiors regarded as gravely dangerous. His book was accord-

ingly placed upon the Index, which is just another way
of saying that it was condemned by the church; and like
his fellow-priest Simon, who more than a hundred
years before was removed from his position in the
Oratory, Jahn's career as professor was terminated by
the cardinal-archbishop. . . .

2

In the same year that Jahn published his *Introduction* there appeared in Great Britain the first volume of
a "new" translation of the Bible with explanatory
notes, representing the life-work of Father Alexander
Geddes, one of the most colorful and interesting personalities in the history of biblical scholarship.

Although a native of Scotland and a priest of a Catholic Congregation near Aberdeen, this man had been
educated in Hebrew with brilliant success under Ladvocat, a professor in the Sorbonne at Paris. In spite of
his holy orders Geddes was essentially a liberal mind—
in fact, too liberal for the church. Moreover, he possessed firm and definite views that never swerved from
a relentless consistency. It was therefore inevitable that
sooner or later his intense scientific interest in the Bible
would bring him into serious trouble with the dogmatism of his superiors. That he clearly foresaw the
heavy price he would some day have to pay for his advanced ideas may be gathered from these remarkably
prophetic words: "The Hebrew Scriptures I have examined and appreciated, as I would any other writings of antiquity; and have bluntly and honestly delivered my sentiments of their merit and demerit; their
beauties or imperfections; as becomes a free and impartial examiner. I am well aware that this freedom

will, by the many, be considered as an audacious license; and the cry of heresy! infidelity! irreligion! will resound from shore to shore."

After the publication of the third volume in his series on the Bible, the inevitable actually happened in 1800. He had gone too far! and so was suspended from his ecclesiastical functions. But no sooner had he paid this price at the hands of his own church than another and more bitter one was exacted. The Protestants, who he thought would be more kindly disposed to scientific investigation of the Bible, now turned upon him and denounced his works as the wild yelpings of an infidel.

3

We have seen that the attempt to sever the documents of which the Book of Genesis is composed was begun by Astruc and Eichhorn. Geddes, however, deserves credit for having extended the investigations of these two men, for he not only analyzed the Book of Genesis but he brought the *whole* of the Pentateuch under the searchlight of scholarship. In addition to this he took one step more in advance by recognizing that the Book of Joshua is, from a literary and historical standpoint, an integral part of the first five books of the Hebrew Bible. In other words, Geddes claimed that the Book of Joshua was written by the same authors who wrote the Pentateuch. In this assertion he clearly anticipated the views of all the great scholars on this subject. For centuries, both Christians and Jews believed that the Book of Joshua was the work of a separate author—perhaps some man of inferior rank to Moses. But due to the investigations begun by Geddes, the Book of Joshua is now definitely known to be composed of the same documents that appear in the Pentateuch; consequently, the same men who are responsible for the authorship of the Five-Books of Moses must have also written the Book of Joshua.

Yet with all his remarkable acuteness and genuine flashes of insight, Geddes did not arrive at a true understanding of the literary structure of the Pentateuch. While he detected a great number of disconnected fragments he failed to combine them. His analysis, therefore, split the Pentateuch into a hodge-podge of unrelated documents—a lot of loose scraps, various in origin and pieced together. The resultant agglomeration came to be known as the "Fragmentary Theory."

Of course, Geddes was right in recognizing a variety of origins for the different documents. But he was utterly wrong in his denial of their unity. He did not fully comprehend that unity of plan may consist with diversity of origin. Not very long after Geddes wrote his books several able scholars demonstrated that many of his so-called "fragments" were nothing more than parts of one and the same document. So Geddes's Fragmentary Theory, romantic as it was, collapsed.

But even though his work was a bit fantastic, it was certainly not to the credit of England that Geddes's scholarship found little or no encouragement in the British Isles. He was ridiculed as having reduced the Mosaic authorship of the Pentateuch to a "mosaic" of fragments. And such was the odium connected with his work that in all probability it would have completely sunk into oblivion without so much as a trace left behind had not his views found a more hospitable soil across the sea. In Germany, where his ideas were finally transferred, Professor J. S. Vater of the University of Halle greatly elaborated upon what Geddes had begun. With much vigor and hard labor Vater carried the Geddes torch and continued the dissecting process. By translating this ex-priest's writings and incorporating much of the Scotsman's material into his own books, Vater succeeded in popularizing the fragmentary hypothesis throughout Europe.

Although Vater was once popular, having interested thousands of students in scientific biblical scholarship, his ponderous volumes are no longer read; they belong to that class of books that are now almost forgotten. But because of their influence upon the mind of a young man, the hero of this chapter, they are now chiefly remembered as the starting point in the career of a brilliant biblical investigator. . . .

4

It was in 1805 that Wilhelm M. L. De Wette, then only twenty-five years of age, published at Jena University a treatise he had offered for his graduation degree. It was entitled *Discourse on Deuteronomy* and represented a great deal of solid thinking and midnight oil. Like Lindbergh's flight across the ocean, this "Discourse" was the lone work of a solitary young man crossing the untrodden seas of research. When he finally landed on terra firma he boldly claimed that the Book of Deuteronomy was not written by Moses, but that some one altogether different from the writers of the other four books of the Pentateuch was its author! Of course, this was a very startling statement for a young man to make in a German University at that

time. How was De Wette led to this revolutionary conclusion?

This is the story:

Up to De Wette's time scholarly research dealt largely with the literary problems of the Scriptures. Spinoza
asked questions on authorship, Simon delved into problems of style, and Astruc, Eichhorn, and Geddes analyzed the materials from which Genesis was pieced together. With the arrival of De Wette a new line of
inquiry opens up, and a new angle to biblical study is
given to the world. This young scholar conceived the
problem of Scripture to be twofold: the literary side
and the historical side; and it was on the historical side
that De Wette showed a rare independence of judgment combined with singular insight.

By comparing certain basic social practices with each
other, De Wette saw that they could not have existed
at one and the same period of time, any more than the
institution of negro slavery in the United States which
was abolished in the middle of the nineteenth century
could be properly ascribed by some future historian to
the economic and social conditions of twentieth-century America. The Old Testament contains a collection of laws and histories, professing to tell the origin
of Israel's religion. A careful study of these collections
reveals that they do not agree with each other and the
stories they tell are not consistently represented. Practices which belong to a much later period are assigned
to an early one; and vice versa. De Wette recognized
this, and thus for the first time in the history of biblical study a well-trained scholar investigated the social
institutions and practices that underly the Pentateuch
with the result that a whole new field opened up, yielding amazing rich deposits of information.

De Wette began by a study of the ancient rite of sacrifice and found that there exists in the Pentateuch itself two different sets of laws flatly contradicting each other. Sacrifice was one of the most important customs of the Hebrews. Genesis relates that Cain, Abel, and Noah, as well as Abraham, Isaac, and Jacob, employed this form of religious homage. Moreover, a Hebrew did not have to be a member of the priestly caste in order to offer up an animal to Yahweh. Sacrifice was not limited to the priests: it was the paramount form of Hebrew worship—and everybody sacrificed.

When it is asked in what places and under what conditions the ancient Israelites engaged in this practice, the answer is found embodied in that early legislative rule of verse 24 of chapter 20 of the Book of Exodus:

An altar of earth shalt thou make unto Me, and shalt sacrifice thereon thy burnt-offerings, and thy peace-offerings, thy sheep and thine oxen: in every place where I cause my name to be remembered I will come unto thee and I will bless thee. And if thou make Me an altar of stone, thou shalt not build it of hewn stone.

A close study of this biblical law reveals at once a primitive mode of worship; an altar of earth or undressed stones, starkly bare and severely simple. It tacitly implies permission to erect such an altar in any place, for it conceives God as not being at all particular where He is worshipped. In fact, it is the assumption of this law that any place which had been a scene of a theophany may become a Hebrew altar and receive a blessing from the deity. In other words, according to this law no one place is sacred to the exclusion of all the others —Yahweh may be worshipped anywhere. (It is significant that in this Exodus passage no mention is made of a great temple of elaborate decoration—an altar of earth will serve.)

But, strange to say, this rule of sacrifice is not the view according to the book of Deuteronomy where a very different principle is laid down. Deuteronomy frowns upon the idea of a layman offering sacrifice, regarding it as the sole function of the priest. But more than this! Deuteronomy is opposed to the thought of a multiplicity of altars. It raises a hue and a cry against the village shrines by declaring them all illegitimate! According to the Deuteronomic law, as set forth in the 12th chapter of that book, only *one* shrine or altar constitutes the legitimate sanctuary of Yahweh. Therefore, in only *one* place may sacrifice be made: all other places are not accredited and consequently must be suppressed. In no uncertain language the law enjoins that:

Unto the place which Yahweh your God shall choose out of all your tribes to put His name there, even unto his habitation shall ye seek, and thither thou shalt come: and thither ye shall bring your burnt-offerings, and your sacrifices.*

Thus it is clearly seen that the permission granted in the law of Exodus for any one to sacrifice anywhere he chooses is flatly denied in Deuteronomy. The very essence of the Deuteronomic law is the uncompromising demand that all local sanctuaries be abolished and all sacrifice be restricted to a single place. "Ye shall surely destroy all the places wherein the nations which ye shall possess served their gods, upon the high mountains, and upon the hills, and under every green tree; and ye shall break down their altars, and break their

*Deuteronomy 12:5 ff.

pillars and burn their asherim with fire."* Constantly, over and over again with never wearying zeal, Deuteronomy repeats that no sacrifice may be offered save at one place, "the place which Yahweh thy God shall choose."

Now it was clear to De Wette that one and the same lawgiver would not have said to the people that they could sacrifice in any place and then tell them in the same breath they couldn't. Early Hebrew history made it clear to De Wette that the people continued to sacrifice in their village shrines hundreds of years after the death of Moses, which, of course, is valid proof that Moses was not the author of a drastic law forbidding such a practice. The important question therefore to be determined was this: when did the law of the single sanctuary arise?

5

With ample learning and irresistible logic De Wette answered this question by subjecting the twenty-second and twenty-third chapters of the Second Book of Kings to an exact and minute study. These chapters tell at length the story of a radical religious Reform carried out by a group of zealous prophets at Jerusalem in the reign of Josiah, the young king of Judah. The narratives relate that in the year 621 B. C., while making repairs in the Temple, a priest by the name of Hilkiah discovered a mysterious code of laws. Hilkiah announced his discovery to Shaphan, the king's secretary, who brought the code to the attention of Josiah. This

---

*Deuteronomy 12:2-3. All these local sanctuaries had originally been the sacred shrines of the Canaanites centuries before the Hebrew people took them over. Even to-day the Mohammedan population of Palestine regard these ancient sites as holy.

code was supposed to have been written by Moses himself, and it contained violent threats and curses that would be visited upon the land if its laws were not enforced. The young King Josiah was terrified when he heard the words of the newly found Book, and rent his garments in dismay. Hastily, he summoned members of the prophetic party, priests, and the people, and read it to them. It made an immediate impression. All the leaders of the people were deeply moved. Without losing any time the national assembly adopted it right on the spot. Thus the new-found Code, popularly ratified, became overnight the supreme authority of the kingdom.

What was the nature of the new law contained in this Code that created such a sensational religious revolution and immediate upheaval? The Book of Kings indicates that it was made the basis for one of the most sweeping and drastic reforms in the history of the Hebrew people and that it was carried out with much severity, cruelty, and bloodshed. The single purpose of the new-found Code was to wipe off the face of the kingdom every sanctuary except the temple at Jerusalem. Its regulations called for the ruthless abolition of all the village shrines that had dotted the country from time immemorial. With one fell stroke of the law they were all declared illegitimate and ordered to be torn down regardless of local pride or sentiment. Only the temple at Jerusalem was to remain as the sole and only God-ordained shrine of the Hebrew nation. It alone was to be the centre of worship and its altar the only altar where sacrifices could be made. Notwithstanding the fact that the Hebrews had sacrificed for hundreds of years in any place they chose to erect an altar, this ancient custom was now rigorously suppressed so that, as a result of the new-found Code, the concentration of sacrificial worship at the Jerusalem temple was made complete—and monopolistic!

6

On the basis of an accurate investigation, which has remained one of the assured results of scholarship, De Wette was able to identify Deuteronomy with the "Book of the Law" found by Hilkiah in the temple at Jerusalem. De Wette saw that by comparing the Book of Deuteronomy with the story of Josiah's reformation (as contained in the Second Book of Kings) one supplied the programme for the other! Point by point the account in the Book of Kings matches the injunctions in Deuteronomy and does not match the laws of any other book of the Pentateuch. Deuteronomy, therefore, declared De Wette, is the product of the age of Josiah and could not have been the composition of Moses.

How Josiah proceeded step by step to carry out the regulations of the new code can be seen in the comparison on page 72 which indicates that the reform measures are exactly those advocated in Deuteronomy.

The world owes young De Wette a well-deserved credit, for he was the first scholar to clearly understand that the creation of a God-ordained centre of the national religion was at variance with early Hebrew practice. The Bible itself teaches that the responsible leaders as well as the people did not confine their sacrifice in one place. Local worship was an acknowledged part of the established ordinance of the land. Solomon, for example, offered burnt-offering in the "high place" at Gibeon, and the prophet Elijah himself repaired the

	II Kings	*Deuteronomy*
	CARRIES OUT	
(1) Centralization of worship	23:8-20	12:2-6
(2) Abolition of the worship of the heavenly bodies	23:4, 5, 11	17:3
(3) Condemnation of high places, pillars, Asherahs, etc.	23:4, 5, 14, 15	16:21, 22
(4) Prohibition of religious prostitutes	23:7	23:17, 18
(5) Maintenance of priests ejected from the local sanctuaries	23:8, 9	18:8
(6) Abolition of Moloch worship	23:10	18:10
(7) Celebration of the Passover in a new style .	23:21-23	16:1-8
(8) Ejection of diviners and soothsayers	23:24	18:10, 11

altar on Mt. Carmel. Evidently neither of these celebrated leaders had any knowledge of the forbidden practice. From these examples it is very plain that the Deuteronomic law in no way controlled the early Hebrew nation, as can be easily learnt from further accounts in the Books of Judges, Samuel, and the Kings. Moreover, prophets like Amos, Hosea, Micah, and Isaiah never once declared the local shrines illegal. Being the great protagonists of the pure worship of Yahweh they of all men should have said something. Their complete silence and absence of protest impressed De Wette as it has every scholar since his day.

Instead of one great central Temple monopolizing the sacrifices of the people, early Hebrew history tells of a number of sanctuaries scattered throughout the country each one being regarded as legitimate for sacrificial purposes. For example, the Book of Judges mentions Mizpah, Bethel, and Shiloh as prominent centres where the ancient Israelites offered. The prophet Samuel as well as King Saul and King David are known to have sacrificed at many altars. It was at Shiloh that Samuel was dedicated to the service of Yahweh and, in after days, he ministered at the sanctuary in his own home town of Ramah. Thus the Deuteronomic restriction was unknown to Samuel and the early kings. In fact, no one in that far-off age had ever heard of a law limiting sacrifice to a single place.

De Wette therefore concluded that this restricted legislation utterly unknown to such representative men as Elijah, Hosea, Amos, Samuel, Saul, and David could not have been instituted by Moses. By the internal testimony of the Bible itself the Book of Deuteronomy must therefore have come into existence many hundreds of years after the death of the pioneer Lawgiver.

THE FIFTH RESULT

The Deuteronomic Code was unknown to Moses. It made its first "public" appearance in the reign of King Josiah, who proclaimed it the supreme law of the land.

PART II

THE STORY OF BIBLES WITHIN THE BIBLE, OR HOW
THE FOUR MOST IMPORTANT DOCUMENTS OF
THE OLD TESTAMENT WERE INDEPENDENTLY
WRITTEN AND THEN COMBINED INTO ONE
VOLUME CALLED THE PENTATEUCH (THE
FIVE BOOKS OF MOSES)

We are now ready to enter a strange land—full of surprises
and paradoxes. . . . But it would be impossible for us to step
into this region had not the great pioneer scholars of Biblical
Science charted the way through the footless mazes.

CHAPTER I

HOW THE MEN OF JERUSALEM WROTE THE YAHWISTIC DOCUMENT, OR THE BIBLE OF THE SOUTH KINGDOM

PALESTINE was old when the Hebrews began to beat their way into its territory, for it was already populated with civilized peoples dwelling in fortified cities. Thirty-five hundred years ago this tiny country—smaller than Belgium—was the seat of an ancient civilization and the highroad between the great empires stretched along the Nile and the Euphrates. But even at that early day caravans followed the wake of the setting sun and marauding tribes, swarming out of the Arabian Desert, sought for themselves new homes in that fertile crescent facing the western sea. Among these tribes came certain ancestors of the Hebrew race to contend in a life of destiny in this little strip of land pinched between Africa and Asia.

It was undoubtedly the land upon which they had squatted that gave the newcomers their start; for wherever they pitched their nomad tents they touched an ancient soil. Here they found a region already peopled with many nations and haunted by myth and legend trickling down from prehistoric ages. With remarkable adaptability they grew into the traditions they found and forthwith began to create charming traditions of their own. Just as the quaint legends of the Ainu people (the aboriginal inhabitants of Nippon) entered into the life of the Japanese when they

took possession of those volcanic islands; and just as
the legends of the Indians made their way into the literature of America and are responsible for many of the
names of American streets, parks, cities, and states; so
the ancient legends of pagan Palestine worked themselves into Hebrew life and literature.

Traditions of older peoples far and near—and fragments of peoples long forgotten—were associated with
hill and valley, waste places, and green groves. These,
the newcomers quickly absorbed. Being a deeply religious folk, the pagan aborigines of Palestine had already scattered over their land a multitude of sacred
shrines. Centuries in advance of Abraham such places
as Bethel, Dan, Shiloh, Hebron, and Beersheba had
witnessed the smoke of sacrifice. It was these ancient
sacrificial spots, marked by very ancient altars, that
became centres of priestly influence. Around these
shrines there clustered a wealth of local color; and
from these holy places—garnerhouses of rich folklore
deposits—the cause of a literature that was to be was
amply served. Such was the picturesque background
furnished by destiny to these Hebrew immigrants and
their fascinating history.

. . . But long before the Hebrews wrote down anything, stories lived from tongue to ear. The first step in
all literature is oral—and this was especially true in the
orient, where the sluggishness of many centuries created
no undue haste. For a thousand years the stories of the
early Hebrew heroes and patriarchs were recited by
the priests at their shrines or by wandering troubadors
who chanted at the firesides. And even though the outlines of these ancient stories and sayings are all but lost
in the mists of that far-off age, yet it is to them that hu-

manity is indebted for the beginnings of that imposing literature called the Bible.

With the progress of the arts of life came the impulse to put down in writing what had so long floated about in memory. It was this inspiration that started the Bible on the long course of its unique development. To properly tell the story of its growth we must begin at that time when Hebrew traditions were first transcribed from tongue to parchment. . . . And so, by the sweep of history this immediately takes us from the days of the semi-wild tribal life to the era of the kings. . . .

2

Among the famous empire-builders of the Orient no name is better known than the warrior-musician David, the son of Jesse. And no one quite like him ever sat on a self-made throne. He not only conquered the Philistines, those immemorial enemies of his people, but he succeeded in capturing the powerful fortress of Jerusalem from the Jebusites and transforming it into his own capital city. Above all, he did what all others before him, even Moses, failed to do: he welded into a single united nation the fragmentary Hebrew tribes. Under his organizing genius a new life was breathed into these rude herdsmen of the Judæan highlands who, but recently, had suffered several ignoble and crushing military defeats.

Peace and prosperity—which were greatly increased during the reign of King Solomon—were now brought to a land that had known little else than incessant poverty and bloody war. Along with these new and changed conditions there came the first really great opportunity for rest and reflection such as the Hebrew peoples had never before experienced. And so a new era of national life began to dawn and its rising sun smiled upon the first golden age of Hebrew literature. Before then literature of the true sort had no opportunity. The Hebrew people were struggling for existence, or feeling their way to nationality. It was David who really gave his people a sense of strength and superiority, an outlook and a future, and hence an impulse to survey their origins. It was in his day that the prophetic order assumed importance and dignity, developing ultimately a class of trained men with leisure for literary pursuits.

It is therefore not at all surprising to find in the accounts of this prosperous period frequent mention of the names of scribes—for a nation begins to write when it doesn't fight. Keeping the records of important events became a point of pride with newly consolidated Hebrew national government. And just because the common people had little knowledge of writing, the art, therefore, was great in their eyes. Oriental monarchs toyed with it as fondly as the heads of modern governments play with the airplane. Babylonian, Assyrian, and Egyptian rulers were very careful in having themselves written up by their own publicity men on clay tablets or on imposing monuments.

Not wishing to be outdone by their neighbors, both David and Solomon placed scribes in charge of their royal annals to show that they too could have their own literary courtiers. So, in creating his Cabinet, David appointed a recorder; and Solomon after building the Temple chose certain priests to act as scribes. Among those who were destined to play a long and

important rôle in the making of the Bible were these
priestly writers of the Jerusalem Temple. They not
only prepared the official records of the Sanctuary but
they wrote, arranged, and elaborated its ceremonial
laws. From this primitive nucleus there grew up a
strong ritual development which, centuries later, became the starting point of Ezekiel's programme and
the origin of that immense document known as the
"Priest Code." . . . Although it will be spoken of later
on, it is interesting to remark at this point that much
of the historical material that underlies the Books of
Samuel and the Books of Kings was originally taken
from the early writings of royal court recorders and
priestly scribes. . . .

3

It was during this same David-Solomon period that
a group of writers living in or about Jerusalem began
to collect the old folk songs and tales which had been
current among the people for many generations. (It
was about the same time that Homer was assembling
the traditions of the Greeks.) We do not know the
exact names of these men but it is certain that they
were neither royal scribes nor priests. All that we know
about them is that they had a burning passion to put
into writing a large body of tradition which had been
handed down from father to son from time immemorial. It was an immense undertaking which they
carried on with intense zeal; for it was their desire to
kindle a flame of religious patriotism in the hearts of
their countrymen by setting before them the inspiring
history of their past as Yahweh their God had devel-

oped it.* Of course, there was at hand an abundance of material in songs, folk-poetry, traditions, and tribal records. Some of these traditions were inherited from the Semitic past; others were the reflection or record of historical facts in the experience of the Hebrew people. Some explained historical movements; others, existing customs; still others, proper names of persons or places. Some were associated with great and well-known leaders; others, with shrines, or landmarks.

Like the minnesingers and troubadours of mediæval Europe, these Yahwistic men went up and down the country gathering the various legends and scattered stories about Yahweh's dealings with their ancestors. Important events of early tribal life strangely stirred their blood: History they loved and they were bent on collecting every scrap of it whether oral or written.

From the priests at the various local village shrines they learnt much about such things as primitive beliefs, ritual practices, and the relation of Yahweh to their patriarchs. From around Sechem they heard stories about Abraham's Sojourn. The district of Beersheba supplied them with materials about Isaac. From Bethel and Shiloh they gathered legends of Jacob. From the shepherds among the craggy hills of Judæa they collected tales of pastoral life. The farmers filled them with agricultural lore and daring accounts of the achievements of their ancestral heroes. From the city-

*Because these writings were written by men who employed the name *Yahweh* to designate God, their narratives have come to be known collectively as the "Yahwistic Document." This document is, of course, none other than the one originally detected by Jean Astruc when he pointed out that its distinguishing and characteristic mark was the use of the term "Yahweh" for the Hebrew deity. Like many of the other documents of the Bible, as we shall soon see, this Yahwistic narrative was combined with other histories which obscured its astounding unity until completely unravelled by a host of brilliant and fearless scholars. . . .

dwellers they collected proverbs, anecdotes, and wise sayings.

But even more than this! They not only gathered oral materials long treasured by wandering minstrels and story-tellers but they also laid their hands on various scattered codes of tribal law already written down in crude form. One whole block of primitive legislation, known as the "Little Book of the Covenant,"* and originally comprising a very ancient form of a worship-decalogue, was gathered up by these collectors and bodily incorporated in their writings. Several of these laws are very quaint, as, for example, the injunction "Thou shalt not seethe a kid in its mother's milk." . . .

Wherever ten Hebrews got together there must have been at least twenty stories! Doubtlessly these men picked up a great deal of material. Of course, the better and more worthwhile part of what they collected they reshaped and rewrote, transforming simple tribal memories into legends with a deep underlying ethical significance. They took the fragmentary and disjointed accounts of the distant past and welded them into narratives with a fair degree of coherence and so arranged the whole as to tell a connected story. They began their narrative with no less a theme than the creation of the World and step by step brought it up, in reference to their own people, to the sumptuous reign of King Solomon. History, they let it be known in no uncertain terms, is nothing more than the medium through which Yahweh works out His grand and glorious purposes—therefore this world and all its belongings is only a sort of proscenium before which a preparatory

*Exodus 34:11-27.

piece or prologue is enacted, while the curtain is getting ready to rise on the real drama—Yahweh's relation to his chosen people.

Having drawn material from many sources it was only natural that the writings of these men would be full of variant accounts, or different versions of the same thing. However, they were not troubled by incongruities—especially when their chief desire was to breathe into the glorious tales of their nation's past a profoundly religious spirit. Yet it is astonishing to think that these men, away back in that far-off age, produced the first comprehensive history of mankind that had ever been written. Taking nothing less than the whole world as their framework they cleverly began with the Story of Creation and connected it with the story of their own people. Insignificant as they were in numbers, they made up for it in an enormous self projection. Like little Steinmetz working in a cosmic laboratory, they commanded spiritual thunderbolts. Not until centuries later did other writers of antiquity —not even the Greeks—achieve anything quite like the grandeur and universal sweep of their method. Little did these Yahwistic men think that they were laying the foundations of a mighty literature that some day would have universal significance. The very idea of what we understand by the word "Scriptures" was utterly unknown to them. They wrote because of a deep urge—and yet they unwittingly produced the first Bible.

When their document is unravelled out of the heart of the Old Testament and set up in approximately its original form we realize what superb historians and wonderful literary artists these old writers really were.

They knew how to tell a story with great charm and forcible art. There is nothing aimless, nothing tossed off without reflection. The pictures they draw are as fresh and lifelike to-day as when they first wrote. With flowing style and picturesque vocabulary they make us share the antique world in which they lived. No wonder people are still delighted by the sweet poetic fragrance that trails through these old legends—in them heaven and earth are magically blended into one.

But these men were no mere collectors or historians. While one of their aims was to glorify the establishment of David's monarchy, their chief purpose was religious, for they were prophets, men of Yahweh. Yahweh was to them the one great God; and although at times He had unaccountable moods, still He had gone out of His way to fight for their ancestors. Not only was Yahweh the God of their heroes but He was also the Creator of their country. Therefore, their chief concern in writing was to prove that Yahweh alone had protected the Hebrews from the beginning. In fact, one of the reasons why He created the world was because He wanted a special people to love and worship Him. For this reason stress is laid throughout all their writings on faith and trust in Yahweh. . . .

Besides this patriotic feeling toward their deity they made it plain that Yahweh is a moral God who demands righteousness and punishes wickedness and only by keeping His holy commandments would He continue His divine protection for the present and extend it to the future. . . .

4

Fortunately, a large part of the writings of these Yahweh-prophet-men have come down to us, notwithstanding the mutilation and the wear and tear of the centuries. Like huge blocks of fossil embedded in the rock they have been preserved in several books of the Old Testament, although their "remains" have been greatly scattered and disarranged. In fact, they are among the earliest and most primitive portions of the Bible. This, of course, explains why the modern reader of the Scriptures frequently comes across crude, and sometimes even half-savage, ideas. No writing can utterly escape the age in which it was born; and when it is kept in mind that these Yahweh-prophet-men wrote about eight or nine hundred years before the birth of Christ much allowance will be made for them in not having reached, what we delight to call, the higher planes of "modern" morality (conveniently forgetting the barbarism of the last World War).

Notwithstanding much of their crudity these Yahwistic men were interested in moral questions; and their stories clearly show how much thought they gave to speculating on the origin and growth of the Power of Evil. They wrote about the Garden of Eden and Adam's fall, the subsequent corruption of mankind and the penalty of the Flood, and the wilful pride of those Babel men who arrogantly tried to build a tower reaching to Heaven and were punished by a confusion of tongues. Disobedience to Yahweh, they wanted to show, causes sin—the ugly barrier that keeps man from his Paradise.

Besides speculation on the power of evil, all these tales served another purpose: they answered with naïve simplicity certain curious questions which always interested the primitive as well as the modern mind. How did sin enter the world? The Yahwistic story answers it impressively by telling how Adam and Eve ate fruit from a forbidden tree. The account of the Deluge answers why rainbows appear in the sky: For is it not Yahweh's promise that he will not send another flood? The Tower of Babel legend satisfactorily explained to the primitive Hebrews why there were so many different languages among men.

Compared with the grotesque stories of other oriental peoples these narratives of the Yahwistic men are remarkable for the simplicity of the style in which they are written as well as the simplicity of ideas about such complex subjects as God, creation and man. While the legends of other nations reeked with the vulgarity of many deities who had mingled with women, the Hebrews were breathing into their narratives the spirit of the rightful worship of only one God. They did not, it is true, deny the existence of the gods of the surrounding peoples but they emphatically stated that for the Hebrews there was only one God—Yahweh. (This emphasis upon one god without denying the existence of others is called "monolatry.") It was their belief that no other deity could be lawfully worshipped in Judæa: for Yahweh's province begins and ends with Israel's borders. That is why they were intolerant of idolatry. Of course, outside of Yahweh's province there are other nations, but these nations are regarded as being out of Yahweh's sphere. Therefore, the nations have their own gods who in every respect are looked upon as the peer of Yahweh. For example, there is Chemosh, god of Moab; or Milcom, god of Ammon. But Chemosh is for Moab, whereas Yahweh is *exclusively* for Israel.

This stage of Hebrew thought cannot be called pure

monotheism (which stands for the recognition and worship of only one universal God). It may be somewhat of a shocking surprise to learn for the first time that the ancient Hebrews were not originally a purely monotheistic people. Actually, real monotheism did not appear until hundreds of years after Moses, and even then it was not sharply defined. On the contrary, it was trembling into full consciousness through the various stages of monolatry. But it is significant that these Yahwistic stories contained the germ of the universal *God* idea. Monolatry had to proceed monotheism, and the Yahwistic narratives are monolatrous. It was from this level of thought that the pure and exalted conception of later times was developed.

That the Yahwistic view of God is, at times, grossly childish and anthropomorphic is due to the crude age in which it was born. Nevertheless, the Yahwistic documents are full of charming simplicity and quaint naïveté, for Yahweh is intensely human to these men. Whenever we come across passages in the Pentateuch which make the Deity very intimate with these old Hebrews we can be pretty sure that the thought belongs to these old writings. They make it very clear that their God is not supercilious or far away beyond the clouds. Yahweh gets about without too much dignity and He accomplishes His desires in His own natural and homely way. For example, He puts Adam in a mythical garden where a serpent speaks and where a tree supplies the means of escaping death. With a great deal of primitive curiosity He brings all the animals to Adam to see what he will call them. Then we see Yahweh walking in the Garden of Eden during the cool of the day calling to Adam and Eve to ask where they are. When they have sinned it is this same Yahweh, as angry and ruthless as a bedouin sheik, who drives Adam out into the cold world and bars the way to Paradise. But this is not all. He closes the door on Noah when he goes into the ark; He is jealous and apprehensive of the men who build the Tower of Babel and He actually goes down from Heaven to investigate the enterprise and confound their speech; He appears in human form to Abraham and eats with him butter, milk and veal; He goes to make inquiries about the iniquity of Sodom to see for Himself whether it is as bad as represented; He wrestles with Jacob; He meets Moses and comes close to the point of killing him; and later on He actually stoops to remove the wheels from the chariots of the Egyptians.

5

Yet it is most significant that this God is ethical. Yahweh is a deity of righteousness, even though it is a crude and half-developed kind. While it is true that these Yahwistic men give us a morality of a distinctly rudimentary type, this should not dim the glory of their narratives or diminish their value to humanity. With equal faithfulness they reflect the primitive morality of the times with which they deal and record the vices as well as the virtues of their heroes. They contain many childish ideas—yet modern man has climbed to his present outlook by them. When, for example, these Yahweh men tell us with evident joy how Abraham passed off his wife as his sister without regarding his duplicity as a sin, we must remember that we are here face to face with a quaint primitive morality. Or, when they tell of Jacob's deception of his father and his subsequent fraudulent tricks upon Laban it is because these stories come from the earliest period of the nation's moral development and, apparently at that time, supplied a good laugh and much comic amusement when told around the fireside. (The ancient Hebrews, let us not forget, had a sense of humor!)

One of the most interesting traits of the Yahwistic stories is the manner in which natural instead of supernatural agencies cause things to happen. These Yahweh men show that their God exhibits Himself not in occasional supernaturalness but in the continuity of the actual experience of the Hebrew nation; not here and there in fleeting glimpses, but everywhere in broad sunlight. This feature of naturalism is particularly deserving of attention because later writers reversed the process, assigning supernatural causes to natural events. There is, for instance, the account of the Egyptian plagues. The Yahwistic narrative simply states that it was an east wind which brought the locusts into Egypt, and a west wind which swept them into the Red Sea. According to the Yahwistic way of thinking the marvel of the plagues lay not so much in the events themselves, which were natural, as in the fact that they were predicted by Moses and therefore came with lightning-like rapidity. So, also, it is a natural east wind which blows all night, drives the Red Sea back, and enables the Hebrews to cross. . . . Later on, however, as we shall see, these simple facts were changed: supernatural ideas crept into the stories and completely transformed them so that the natural and unsophisticated events they relate finally emerged into stupendous oriental miracles!

CHAPTER II

HOW THE MEN OF EPHRAIM WROTE THE ELOHISTIC DOCUMENT, OR THE BIBLE OF THE NORTH KINGDOM

THE pages of oriental history are strewn with the wreckage of empires. . . .

Shortly after Solomon died a split-up completely dissevered the United Hebrew Commonwealth which King David had fought so desperately hard to create. The North tribes broke away from the South with as much hostility and bitterness as the Confederate States of America exhibited against the Union during those frightful years of the Civil War.

About a hundred years after the North Kingdom had won its independence a group of enthusiasts, inspired by local pride, began to collect the stories and sayings current among their own people. Maybe they just wanted to imitate the example set by their southern rivals. Whatever their motive, they possessed a passionate desire to write a new history of the Hebrew traditions from their own point of view. So they set about somewhat in the same manner as the Yahwistic men had done many years before to arrange their material in order to tell a connected story. After much hard work they finally brought into existence a set of documents which bear many resemblances to the Yahwistic narrative written in the South; in several other ways, however, it is strikingly different and represents an advancement in thought and feeling.

In all probability these younger authors were the

companions of Amos, Hosea, and Isaiah, the great reform leaders of the North Kingdom. While these
prophets were preaching their sermons with eloquent
voice, their friends of the writers' guild, with equally
eloquent pens, were framing the new history. And because their documents, as Astruc first pointed out, are
distinguishable by the use of the name Elohim, instead
of Yahweh, to designate the Divine Being these men
are known to us as the "Elohistic School."*

2

Writing many years after the Yahwistic accounts it
is no wonder that the Elohistic men spoke of God in
more elevated language. One of their main reasons in
producing a new set of narratives was just this very desire to improve upon the ideas and stories of the older
Yahwistic records. Thus, for example, these Elohistic
men scrupulously avoided speaking of God in terms of
the old fancies that pictured Him walking with man, or
sitting at the door of Abraham's tent or eating food from
tables—that was too grossly material and unedifying
for the deity. Accordingly, they spiritualized God by
making Him more dignified so that He no longer visits
men directly; He appears to them in dreams or visions

*The points of difference between the Yahwistic and Elohistic documents
are very numerous in vocabulary and style; and for this reason scholars
were able to unravel the two sources notwithstanding the closely knitted
manner in which they had been interwoven. For example, the Elohistic
men prefer names different from those used by the Yahwistic writers. They
never use the word "Sinai," but prefer to call that mountain "Horeb."
They never speak of the inhabitants of Palestine as the "Canaanites"—
these people are called "Amorites." Then again, the Elohistic men call
the third Patriarch "Jacob" and never refer to him as "Israel." The Yahwistic documents call a female slave "Shiphhah" whereas the Elohistic
writers use "Amah." . . . Although it would be entirely too long to
enumerate here, there is a vast mass of such characteristic differences which
separate the two documents.

or through the ministry of angels. That is why in the story about Jacob's dream there was need for a step-ladder: the communication between Elohim and His mortal child had to be carried on by the aid of celestial messengers ascending and descending. The Jacob legend is a good example of the extreme care exercised by the Elohistic writers in not letting God be seen by human eyes, for does not Elohim dwell in secret majesty in the high Heavens far above and far away from men?

But although Elohim cannot be seen physically by the eye yet men may communicate with Him in visions or catch His revelations through heavenly voices. It stands to reason that the more spiritual the man the more attuned he will be to such divine visitations. Consequently there was closely associated with this finer view of God the idea of the prophet—that is, the man through whom the Deity speaks. Abraham was a prophet. So were Moses and his sister Miriam. Prophets were the prominent heroes of the North Kingdom and it is therefore not at all strange that these Elohistic men should place a strong emphasis on this spiritual quality. By the rôle of his holy office the prophet saves the Divine Being from too close a contact with man—in fact, he is God's oracle; and any person wishing to know the divine Will has only to "inquire of the prophet."

3

Now that their God is farther removed from mundane things, the Elohistic authors seized upon this cleavage as a wide opening for the play of supernatural activities. Scattered throughout the Pentateuch are

stories of miracles and signs and marvellous experiences, for the deity is now a God who "works in a
mysterious way His wonders to perform." And it is not
only through the manipulation of the huge forces of
nature that the Divine Being expresses Himself. There
is the prophet—Elohim's representative—through
whom history is moulded. The prophet is the medium.
For instance, the Elohistic writers make Moses a mere
mouthpiece for the divine message; and it is because of
supernatural agencies working through him that the
old Legislator is able to bring plagues upon Egypt by
the use of his miracle-working rod. The Yahwistic
writers are careful to give natural causes for the wonders wrought in Egypt—but not these Elohistic men.
To them, Moses is a master magician—an enchanter—
who by the mere waving of the magic wand governs
the winds and the waves. Did he not change his wand
into a serpent? and was it not at Horeb (Sinai) that
he took his rod in hand and smote the rock out of
which there suddenly gushed a fountain of flowing
water? And did he not win the battle at Rephidim
against his arch-enemies, those terrible Amalekites, because he held this same magic rod in his hand? Like
some mystic giant in fairy-land Moses is pictured by
the Elohistic writers as commanding the huge forces of
nature—all for the glory of God.

That there is a natural love among nomadic peoples
for the magic and the splendor of the supernatural is a
familiar fact to every thinking person, and so when we
remember that these stories were told in Bedouin tents
by public entertainers or elaborated upon by teachers in
religious meetings we can readily appreciate how many
a glamorous halo grew up around the cold facts. From

this same oriental world have come those enchanting
and delightful stories of the Arabian Nights and this,
of course, helps us to acount for the fairy-like character
of many of these Elohistic tales. Still there is a marked
difference in these Hebrew legends, and it lies in this:
the Elohistic men did not write a story for its own sake.
They had a definite theological motive; they endeavored to show that all happenings and events connected
with their ancestral history were vehicles for religious
truth. By investing each story with a distinctly religious character they wanted to show that Elohim
guided and guarded their heroes with mighty works,
miracles, and wonders. And in order to prove their
point they brought into play a vivid imagination that
believed in nothing less than "Bigger and Better Miracles."

4

There is also a difference in the moral level between
the Elohistic and Yahwistic schools of writers. The
ethics of the Elohistic men were far more developed
than the Yahwists of the South; and their laws, too,
were more elaborate and more humane. They stressed
new conceptions of duty and went so far as to teach
that kindness be shown to one's enemy. The century
intervening between the preparation of the Yahwistic
document and the literary production of the Elohistic
school were years of progressive religious thinking of
which the northern writers reaped full benefit. With
their advanced views they would hardly have dared to
speak of God as "walking in the garden in the cool of
the day," or as taking food under a tree in front of
Abraham's tent.

An interesting contrast between the two documents is easily illustrated by the distinctive treatment each group gives to the story of Abraham and Hagar. The Yahwistic authors described Abraham as rudely turning out of his home the mother of his yet unborn son, Ishmael. Hagar, his natural wife, is pictured as an outcast alone in the desert awaiting there the birth of her child. To the Elohistic writers this treatment of Hagar seemed downright crude; they felt that it was dishonorable for the head of the Hebrew tribe to act so inconsiderately toward a woman. Now, when they came to tell this same story they purposely gave it a different moral twist because they were anxious to tone down the objectionable features portrayed in the Yahwistic account. Their version was therefore quite different. According to them, Sarah's demand to expel Hagar and her son actually pained Abraham. Being softhearted and kind, the Patriarch did not really send Hagar away until Ishmael grew up and was able to learn something of the occupation of the desert. Moreover, when Hagar and Ishmael left, Abraham did not put them out empty-handed—he provided a bottle of water and bread.

The finer feeling of the Elohistic men also shows itself in the story of how Sarah got into Pharoah's harem. It is the old story of a woman in a man's apartment, and like all such stories there are different versions—then as now. As recorded by the Yahwistic authors it left an unfavorable impression upon the patriarch, for Abraham, according to this version, had deliberately told a lie when he palmed off Sarah as his sister. In correcting this story, the Elohistic men placed Sarah in the harem of King Abimelech of Gerar and emphasized that nothing had happened to her because God warned the king in a dream! But this is not all. They had to whitewash still more by showing that Abraham really did not lie in speaking about his brotherly relationship to Sarah (because Sarah was indeed his sister—that is, the daughter of Abraham's father, though not of his mother). And thus the First Patriarch was cleared of stain!

Because they were sensitive and refined in their feelings, these Elohistic men corrected many of the older and more offensive stories. One of their strongest motives in writing was not only to present the Hebrew ancestors in the purest light but to supersede crude and popular beliefs by their own advanced and higher views. For this reason they held together a number of traditions that the Yahwistic men did not preserve, and deliberately amplified several of the old ones in order to give them a different moral twist. . . .

Not only do the Elohistic narratives show a more refined outlook but they also exhibit a more learned and antiquarian interest in things than the older Yahwistic documents. They linger fondly over long and difficult words, like a group of college sophomores just becoming conscious of the delights of etymology. It is they who call Laban, the father-in-law of Jacob, an "Aramaic-Syrian"; and designate his boundary cairn as "Jegarsahadutha" (an awfully hard name to pronounce, which means in Aramaic "The Heap of Stone Witness"). But it is one thing for a father-in-law to bestow a name, and another matter for his son-in-law to change it. And that is just exactly what Jacob did. The Elohistic writers tell us that Jacob changed the name of the place to "Galeed" (Gilead), which in Hebrew means just the same as Jegarsahadutha.

Besides noting various Aramaic origins, all sorts of Egyptian names and titles are sprinkled through the Elohistic narratives which are entirely lacking in the Yahwistic records. Evidently these men were well informed on the customs and manners of the Land of the Pharoahs, for they give a number of concrete facts which are not to be found elsewhere, and in other ways indicate that they were well acquainted with Egyptian folklore which abounds in miracles. Perhaps this very intimate knowledge of Egypt is one of the chief reasons why the famous story of Joseph is their masterpiece.

5

But it was not only in the writing of History that these Elohistic men left their influence on the Bible. They were intensely interested in Law—especially those older codes that contained an ancient Mosaic nucleus. Such primitive digests, whether oral or written, usually circulated in decalogue fashion, an easy tenfold arrangement so that people could quickly remember them.

Embedded in the Book of Exodus there are three quaint chapters which taken together form a definite body of legislation that the Elohistic men had carefully gathered up and edited.* Because this legislation is described as having been written in a book marking a covenant between God and man, it is known as the "Book of the Covenant."

A single glance through these chapters enables one to see that this ancient "Book" contains several layers of very old Palestinian laws of singular primitive character. Agglomerate as these statutes are, they undoubt-

*Exodus 20:22 to 23:19.

edly reflect different periods of those far-off days of the Judges and the early Monarchy when cattle and crops were the main wealth of the people, thereby indicating a settled, agricultural mode of life.

Because of their antiquity these laws were embodied in later codes and quoted over and over again. That is why we find various prohibitions and injunctions repeated four or five times within the Pentateuch. However, the undeniable indebtedness of later Hebrew legislators to the Book of the Covenant may be matched in turn by an indebtedness which the Covenant Code owes to ancient Semitic laws that were already extremely old when it was young.

Several comparisons, for instance, have been made between this Book of the Covenant and the famous law code of early Babylonia known as the Code of Hammurabi (which was cut in stone a thousand years before Moses was born).* The many resemblances between them seem to imply that the Elohistic men had knowledge of this older legislation, for Hammurabi was not only King of Babylonia, but "King of Amurru," that is, the land of the Amorites, and his Code of course ruled in Palestine as well as Babylonia centuries before the Hebrews settled in the land. The many similarities in literary form and in the identical wording of parallel laws is sufficient to indicate that one influenced the other—or, that each in its own way drew upon that ancient body of Semitic law which antedates both. Of course, there are some legal points that will always remain uncertain, but there can be no dispute that Ham-

*Hammurabi, King of Babylon, reigned from 2123–2081 B. C. By his order a code was prepared. It represents a revision and expansion of several older and previously existing codes. French excavators at Susa in 1901–1902 found it carved on a great stone column of black diorite.

murabi's Code is better developed than that of the early Hebrews, particularly on the subject of social relations; however, in matters of religion and ideals of righteousness the Book of the Covenant is on a much higher plane.

But far more interesting than abstract considerations is the pleasure of comparison. In both these codes, for example, there is to be found that stern rule of primitive justice, "red in tooth and claw," which the legal world styles Lex Talionis "Eye-for-Eye"—that is, the judgment of Like for Like. A simple comparison between the Hebrew and Babylonian law reveals this striking similarity:

Hammurabi Code	Book of the Covenant
196, 200:	Exodus 21:23-25:
If a man hath caused the loss of another's eye then some one shall cause his eye to be lost. If he hath broken another's limb (or tooth) some one shall break his limb (or tooth).	If any mischief follow, then thou shalt give life for life, eye for eye, tooth for tooth, hand for hand, foot for foot.

To the student of history the presence of the law of retaliation in both these ancient codes is nothing more than the presence of a fossil thought jutting out from a rudimentary stage of literal justice. It harks back to the primitive promptings of revenge whose gesture is the upraised fist. Yet it is from such crude concepts, representing the dawning sense of justice, that mankind has painfully lifted itself to those higher ideals of a social order that still awaits fulfillment and realization. The Lex Talionis may be nothing more than the echo of the caveman's voice—still it was spoken by a human tongue. Like a crude tool of the Stone Age it tells a valuable chapter in the deathless struggle of the human spirit.

From a photograph by Underwood & Underwood.

STONE COLUMN ON WHICH HAMMURABI'S LAW CODE IS INSCRIBED.

"Comparisons between Hebrew and Babylonian law reveal many striking similarities—both are pervaded by a remarkably humanitarian spirit, especially
when one considers the age in which they were written."

On the whole, however, both the Code of Hammurabi and the Book of the Covenant are pervaded by a remarkably humanitarian spirit, especially when one considers the age in which they were written. They have much to say on the subject of justice between man and man; and crude and quaint as it is, fundamental jurisprudence is enforced. Murder, man-stealing, and offenses against parents are strongly opposed. Toward the poor and defenseless they exhibit a fine regard. Among the many humane regulations taught by the Elohistic documents is that every seventh day was to be given to the servants and the beasts of burden as a holiday; and every seventh year the crops of the field were to be left for the poor to harvest. In matters of slavery it goes a long way to mitigate the lot of the bondsman. It even commanded that kindness be shown to one's enemy, although in the same breath it said "Thou shalt not suffer a witch to live!"

6

Besides this group of eighty or ninety injunctions which the Book of the Covenant has preserved for us, we are further indebted to the Elohistic men for the first version of the Ten Commandments—that majestic decalogue of elemental morality which has never ceased to interest mankind at large.* What we now have of the Ten Commandments in the Bible is the result of several changes, amplifications, and revisions extending over a period of many hundreds of years.

*It is surprising how few people know that the Old Testament contains two versions of the Ten Commandments. The Elohistic version is to be found in the Book of Exodus 20:1-14. This is quite different from the one given in the Book of Deuteronomy 5:6-18.

Originally, the Ten Words were pithy one-line prohibitions, like the present form of the sixth, seventh and eighth commandments. The arrangement of these terse sentences, ten in number, seems to have had the practical aim of aiding the memory by associating a brief law with each finger, thereby making it exceptionally easy for a semi-civilized people to recall them. Later generations, however, with more advanced ideas kept on elaborating, making additions here and there, so that in their present form and character these commandments are extremely complex, having been welded together in the blazing fires of successive developments.

In what form then did the Ten Commandments leave Moses' hand? It is impossible to say. But this much is fairly certain: Moses' original Ten Words— (whatever they were)—must have contained a strong moral and uplifting element which served as a nucleus around which the subsequent revisions took place. Many modern biblical scholars think that the Decalogue, in what would presumably be its original form, contains post-Mosaic elements. On the other hand, there are others who think that the original must have read substantially as follows:

Thou shalt have no other gods in front of Me.
Thou shalt not make to thyself any molten image.
Thou shalt not pronounce the name of thy God in vain.
Remember the Sabbath day to keep it holy.
Honor thy father and thy mother.
Thou shalt not kill.
Thou shalt not steal.

Thou shalt not commit adultery.

Thou shalt not bear false witness against thy neighbor.

Thou shalt not covet.

Impossible as it may be to recover the original, still
we know that by the time the Elohistic men arrived on
the stage of Hebrew history—already several hundred
years after the death of Moses—many changes had
crept in. Consequently, in the Elohistic version of the
Ten Commandments we find many highly developed
ideas of conduct and high-pitched conceptions of prop-
erty rights which could not have been the social code of
nomadic bedouins moving about the desert with their
half-starved cattle. When, for example, the commandments enjoin the observance of the Sabbath day and
then go on to say that even the "stranger that is within
thy gates" shall rest, it is clear that the very idea of
"gates" implies a settled community—which, of course,
was not the social condition of the Hebrews under
Moses. Also, the use of the word "house" in the last of
the Ten Commandments is a fingerprint of an era long
after the people had given up living a roving life in
tents. It would even seem that the whole idea of the
Sabbath was impractical for bands of herdsmen mainly
in charge of live stock; and for this very cogent reason
many scholars date the Sabbath law hundreds of years
after Moses.

Yet, from the very earliest times the persistent tradition of the orient ascribed not only a Mosaic date but
also a *divine* origin to these ten laws. So it was only
natural that when it came to weaving their own account of how the Commandments were delivered to
their ancestors these Elohistic men repeated that tradi-

tion. Having a keen sense of dramatic values they told the old story with magnificent effect, for these Elohistic men were literary artists with superb powers to stir the emotions of their fellow tribesmen. And even after a lapse of almost three thousand years their descriptions have lost none of the old-time appeal. In fact, one of the most successful photoplays ever produced by the motion picture industry—and one of the very few which by its universal interest thrilled the entire world —was built around the story told by these Elohistic men!

At bottom, of course, there is nothing unique even in this, for all ancient peoples ascribed to their laws a divine origin. On that black diorite slab which gives the Babylonian Code there is carved a bas-relief representing the sun god Shamash handing a new set of laws to Hammurabi so that judgment might shine in the land. The Egyptians always pictured the great god Toth with a writing tablet in one hand and a stylus or pencil in the other, because they regarded him as the deity who had written the laws laid down by the scholars and priests. Numa Pompilius, the wise king and legendary lawgiver of Rome, is said to have received all of his wisdom from the nymph, Egeria. Greek tradition traces back the laws of Sparta to the venerable Lycurgus, who was described as receiving them from Apollo. Mythology represents Minos, King of the Cretans, ascending to the sacred cave on Mount Dicte, where he found the laws which Zeus had prepared for him. In the same way in which other ancient peoples looked back upon the origin of their laws the Israelites looked back upon Moses as the wise lawgiver who enjoyed direct communion with God. . . .

One of the most astonishing facts in the spiritual history of the western world has been its ready recognition of the legendary character of all those stories relating to the divine origin of laws from Egyptian, Babylonian, Greek, and Roman sources and at the same time its persistent refusal to so regard the origin of the Ten Commandments. Why? Perhaps the answer is to be found in the high character of the Hebrew injunctions. The Decalogue stands on a loftier plane than any other short set of laws known to mankind, and because of its intrinsic excellence and universal appeal it won its way into the heart of civilization as the voice of God. At any rate, the Ten Commandments are to-day the best-known laws in all the wide world. It may be that the ancient Hebrews, simple as they were in some things, were in other respects wiser than our modern legislators. At least they gave the people a handful of moral fundamentals which they could understand and use in a practical way. And the people knew them—right on their finger tips! Can the average American voter name ten laws of his native State or any other State? Or, can any citizen of Chicago, Philadelphia or Los Angeles enumerate a decalogue of civic virtues?

CHAPTER III

HOW THE BOOK OF DEUTERONOMY CAME INTO EXISTENCE, OR THE RADICAL REFORM OF JOSIAH

ONE of the most corrupt periods in oriental history is responsible for having brought into existence the Deuteronomic School of writers and the creation of a legal code that bears this same name. For the Book of Deuteronomy, even as we now have it in the Bible with many accretions, is essentially a legal document— a rigid code of laws by which its authors sought to regulate not only the religious life of the whole nation but the whole life of the nation upon the basis of religion. . . . And just because of its legal nature Deuteronomy stands in a markedly different position from the Yahwistic and Elohistic documents which are largely historical narratives.

2

The fascinating story of how Deuteronomy was written takes us back to the year 685 B. C. when the Hebrew people fell under the political control and demoralizing influence of Assyria. It was in the reign of King Manasseh, one of the cruellest and most unscrupulous rulers of antiquity, that the vile practices of Assyrian heathenism became rampant throughout Judæa. All the hard work which had been accomplished by such reforming prophets as Amos, Hosea, and Isaiah, and the pure worship of Yahweh which they had long advocated was suddenly swept away in an awful frenzy of paganism. It came as a terrific blow dealt by the mailed fist of an irresponsible tyrant.

Although he was only a vassal of Assyria, Manasseh and his henchmen of the anti-prophetic party acted with a high hand. Not content with restoring the social evils which the prophetic party had denounced, they introduced and revised old forms of superstition, witchcraft, and necromancy. Lewd and coarse practices now began to fill the villages of the country with their licentious abominations and superstitious corruptions. Even so ghastly a rite as the sacrifice of human beings sprang into popularity. Just outside of Jerusalem, in the valley of Hinnom, they built an altar upon which little children were sacrificed to Yahweh in imitation of the blood-thirsty services to the heathen god Moloch. It is recorded that Manasseh himself caused his own son to pass through fire, apparently on the principle that nothing succeeds like excess. His reign was a vile and wild orgy—one of the worst blots on Hebrew history.

But there were vigorous protests! Not everybody was a weakling ready to sell out to Assyrian ideas; and in spite of his strength Manasseh was not suffered to take his mad course unopposed. From the members of the loyal Yahweh-party there came thunderous opposition and stout resistance: particularly, the prophets and their followers were loud in denouncing the introduction of foreign practices. Tradition has it that the prophet Isaiah was cruelly murdered during this turmoil of resistance, and his body sawed into pieces. Whatever may be the particular truth about Isaiah there is no doubt as to the nature of Manasseh's hostility toward the prophetic party. Hundreds of their leaders and disciples were hunted down and savagely slaughtered. Those who were fortunate enough to escape the sword fled to the waste places, the high hills or far into the forests. . . .

That a reaction was some day sure to follow, the prophets were confident. So during the years of their hiding these men began to prepare in secret for the day of assault. They could not preach in public. Then the next best thing to do was to write and get ready. Immediately they set about collecting and editing the documents of their great leaders so as to properly preserve these prophetic messages from the cruel fate of wilful destruction. Then they put their heads together as revolutionists, and in the spirit of their masters mapped out a complete programme of anticipated reform.

3

Because of the grossness of Manasseh's corruption their zeal was all the more intensified. With superb courage and daring they agreed to do something very bold and very original: they wrote a whole new code of laws which they planned to put into effect the moment the day of reaction set in. The earlier collections of Hebrew law had all been too inadequate. What the people needed now was an effectual body of legislation that would be comprehensive enough to guide and regulate the whole life of the nation, individually as well as collectively. These men were determined to formulate the demands of the Yahweh religion with such exactitude that a sweeping upheaval such as Manasseh had brought about would be forever impossible. Like the framers of the revolutionary Constitution of the United States, these men had definite conceptions for the well-being of their people and their land. Their

VALLEY OF HINNOM.

This is the valley, just outside of Jerusalem, where little children were sacrificed to Yahweh in imitation of heathen worship. It is recorded that Manasseh himself caused his own son to pass through fire. This valley was polluted by King Josiah so that it might never again serve as a place of worship. Its name was changed to Ge-henna (Hell).

principal theory was the grand and exalted idea of uni-
fication: *One God, One Altar, One People.*

By one God they meant that Yahweh alone must be
worshipped as the sole and only deity of the Hebrew
nation. Yahweh is exclusive—therefore, all foreign
gods must go and their cults, altars, abominations and
corruptions, together with all the paraphernalia of their
ceremonies and rituals, must be exterminated and utterly destroyed.

As an integral part of their theory these Deuteronomic men demanded the abolition of the village
shrines—even those places that had been erected long
ago by their ancestral heroes—for they had all become
breeding spots of the worst forms of idolatry. Yahweh
is *One*, therefore—so they argued—there must be only
one sanctuary. It is this emphatic demand that Hebrew
worship be concentrated in one place that constitutes
the most revolutionary element as well as the most important feature of their code. These men were convinced that only by a strict centralization of worship
could theological ideas be supervised and kept pure,
and political interests be controlled. That—and nothing less than that—would satisfy. And no matter what
the cost, they felt the price had to be paid.

It was a very bold and singular reform these men
mapped out. What led them to believe they could put
it over?

It was their stern faith in Yahweh and their high
consciousness of duty. They wanted to regulate the life
of the nation by certain fundamental principles of law
and religion which they honestly believed were the un-
expressed intentions of Moses. Therefore they did not
hesitate to ascribe their code to the Great Lawgiver. It

was no case of pious fraud on their part when they made their laws imply Mosaic authorship. They did not wish to deceive either the people or themselves. But inasmuch as Manasseh's idolatry imperilled the purity of Mosaic religion, they felt it was necessary for them to speak in the person of Moses, rightly believing that they were called upon to expound in modern form the pure worship of Yahweh which their hero-Lawgiver himself would advocate were he alive. . . . And so they prepared themselves with plenty of legal safeguards and patiently awaited their opportunity. . . .

4

At last the great day of Reform dawned, although it was no rosy fingered morn o'er the hilltops. Manasseh died in 642 B. C. and his son, Amon, ruled only two years when he was slain by a conspiracy of his nobles. A new king now sat on the Judæan throne. His name was Josiah, and from what little we know of him he had probably been under the secret influence of the prophets from his early childhood. Consequently, the new régime gave these Deuteronomic men the long hoped for opportunity of emerging from their hiding places. At first cautiously and then boldly they drifted back to Jerusalem and once more they began to preach in the open. Prominent among these agitators for a reform was Zephaniah, a cousin of the king. There was also among them Jeremiah, a young man of aristocratic family. The need for a thorough house-cleaning must have been felt in widely different circles, for even the powerful priests in Jerusalem began taking an active hand in the movement. . . .

What actually hastened the coming of the reform

was the terrifying news of a savage invasion of Scythian hordes who had suddenly made their appearance out of the dark forests of Europe. Crossing the Caucasus, they poured down into the Mediterranean coast lands spreading destruction and terror in every direction. By dealing several severe blows to Assyria they sent that ancient empire into a headlong descent of chaos and ultimate death. It is not surprising to read that the neighboring peoples were panic-stricken and that the inhabitants of Judæa feared the worst, for the Scythian hordes were bound for Egypt and woe to anything that lay in their path!

This unusual state of things gave the prophets the one great chance of launching their reform policies; and they lost no time in seizing the opportunity. Up and down the land they went, calling on the people to heed the dread warning and immediately repent. With wild shrieks and cries they declared that the awful Day of Yahweh's judgment was at hand—"the day of wrath, of terror and distress, of wasting and desolation, of darkness and gloom." To a people conscience-stricken and trembling with fright they shouted only one thing—*Repent, Repent, Repent*. How? There was only one way—"Return unto Yahweh or be destroyed."

Luckily, the barbarians passed Jerusalem by and left the city unmolested. No greater piece of good luck could have befallen the Hebrew highlanders, for had the Scythians made for Jerusalem their ravenous claws would not have left one stone on top of the other. It was a hairbreadth escape that left the people weak from the awful scare.

5

Horrified by the death and desolation which the wild Scythian hordes had spread on the coast plains the Hebrews, in their mountain villages, knelt in gratitude for their fortunate escape. The hour of repentance had struck! They now returned to Yahweh by the thousands, forsaking their idolatrous practices, for they now believed that Yahweh had delivered them! Led by the terrified young king Josiah they renounced the Assyrian gods and utterly foreswore the vile and wicked rites that had drenched their land with paganism.

With this sudden change of the national heart the prophetic party gained the upper hand. Realizing their immense power they deemed it expedient at this time to bring into the clear light of day the secret Code of laws they had prepared while hiding from the persecutions of Manasseh. Their method of bringing this Code to the attention of the King was rather unique in its arrangement, for they must have prudently placed the document in the Temple where it would certainly be found—but not too easily, since they wanted the finders to believe that the Code had come out of the sacred past. The story of how the document made its public appearance is related in the twenty-second chapter of the Second Book of Kings. In this account we are told that it happened in the eighteenth year of Josiah's reign —621 B. C. to be exact—that while some repairs were being made in the Jerusalem Temple the chief-priest, Hilkiah, discovered a mysterious code of laws supposed to have been written by Moses himself. Hilkiah announced his discovery to Shaphan, the king's secretary, who hurriedly took the scroll to Josiah.

When the young king read the newly found document with its harrowing detail of curses and threats that would be visited upon his land if its instructions were not obeyed, he rent his clothes in fear and anguish. Immediately he set about getting counsel in order to find out if the new Code represented the real will of God. Upon being assured that its threats would be executed if obedience to its laws were not immediately enforced, Josiah quickly summoned the people of Jerusalem to the Temple. In the presence of the prophetic party, nobles, priests, and the people, the King himself read the newly discovered law-book, and right there and then he made a solemn promise to enforce it, and at the same time exacted from the people their pledge to do likewise. Everybody vowed to make the new Code the supreme law of the land.

Led by their King and the prophetic party, the people now began a series of sweeping reforms which were carried out in the full light of day. The Jerusalem Temple was immediately cleansed of everything connected with foreign worship—all the symbols of the Assyrian deities were destroyed and every unclean and cruel element of paganism suppressed. Altars which had witnessed the sacrificing of children were torn down; idols, pagan shrines, pillars and groves—everything connected with heathenism was pulverized into dust. Yahweh, and Yahweh alone, was proclaimed the only god of the Hebrews. From one end of the country to the other every altar of every description was reduced to ashes.*

*Many of these old altar sites are still considered as sacred places by present-day Mohammedans who live near them.

6

It was the most radical reformation imaginable, and in the world of antiquity can only be compared to the amazing changes brought to Egypt by Iknaton (1375-1350 B. C.), father-in-law of King Tut. Like all drastic measures it was carried on with relentless zeal, and even cruelty. The abolition of these shrines was a revolution as radical as would be involved to-day in the burning of all the country churches. When one remembers that from the very beginning of their history up to Josiah's time the Hebrew people sacrificed at their village shrines, the enormity of the Deuteronomic change can be comprehended. Peoples of antiquity did not quickly let go of their age-old attachments. It was therefore all the more amazing that Josiah's reformation could prove so sweeping, for the Hebrews dearly loved those old sanctuaries which dotted the land from Dan to Beersheba.

One might compare the Deuteronomic edict with the American Prohibition Act which wiped out the saloons over the country notwithstanding many fond local attachments to these places. By stringently prohibiting all sacrifice at village shrines, Josiah's ukase forced the country priests to go out of business: even the fixtures had to be destroyed. For the new law made sacrifice permissible in only one place, namely: the temple built by Solomon. Thus with a single, sledge-hammer blow the village shrines crumbled into dust, and overnight the worship of Yahweh became centralized at Jerusalem.

Just as Prohibition destroyed the saloon and threw people out of employment, so the drastic enforcement

of the Deuteronomic law threw the village priests out
of their jobs. They now had to come to Jerusalem to
find work, or starve. Of course, the Deuteronomic law
tried hard to mitigate their lot, and even went so far
as to advocate admitting these country priests to equal
standing with the powerful Jerusalem ecclesiastics. But
the law miscarried. When it actually came to applying
it the rich priests of the central Sanctuary (the Zado-
kites) were too arrogant to welcome their rural col-
leagues to equal participation. Consequently, the somewhat fair expedient suggested by Deuteronomy for
dealing with the dispossessed priests of the local sanctuaries proved a flat failure. So without power, without
jobs, without their old altars, and without their regular
income these out-of-town men presented a grave problem. Caught in the clutch of circumstances beyond
their control they were socially degraded and had to
accept menial tasks, subordinating themselves to those
in control of the Jerusalem situation. . . .

In many respects the new law was a wise ruling although a bit harsh. The village shrines were as bad as
the old saloons. They had become vilely corrupted and
had always been the starting points of debasing practices. Then again, the village priests were an ignorant
and superstitious lot, and seldom did they prevent their
altars from becoming the centres of the crudest idolatry. It was therefore the intention of the new law to
centralize Yahweh worship so that it could be guarded
and kept pure.

7

And thus the Code of law which Josiah read to the
people—although it has long since been greatly en-

larged and modified—is none other than the Book of Deuteronomy containing the legislation which the prophetic party had secretly prepared while in hiding. Various men of this party spoke out their ideas: consequently their code represents a combination of many utterances welded together into a single document. In all probability this is one of the chief reasons why Deuteronomy is decidedly a radical book. Yet it could never have succeeded had its legislation not grown out of older documents and codes. And the same is true of the Constitution of the United States. Radical as that document may be called, every student of law knows that it is based upon governmental principles as old as Anglo-Saxon civilization. When Gladstone spoke of the American Constitution as the greatest instrument "struck off" by the mind of man he perhaps knew that in a truer sense it was not at all struck off as something entirely original. Law is amazingly evolutionary; and the Deuteronomic men used ancient codes with remarkable freedom of adaptation, rejection, combination, and addition.

That the authors of Deuteronomy felt that they were in no sense breaking with the past may be gathered from the fact that they made their code imply a Mosaic authorship. They honestly believed that they were writing in the spirit of the great pioneer Lawgiver and that is the reason they did not hesitate to effectively place the new legislation in Moses' mouth. To allege, as some have done, that this was a case of pious fraud is to miss the whole spirit of ancient Hebrew law which always speaks through the person of Moses. Perhaps the story of the making of the Bible could never be told had these men failed to invent this "fiction" as one of their most important safeguards. Even modern law, with all its advantages, is not without its "fictions" which, to be sure, rest upon some measure of truth. But however harsh we may choose to be with the legal thinking of antiquity, still it must be admitted that the Deuteronomic authors were right to this extent: that all Hebrew law springs from Mosaic roots—and that is no fiction.

In our story of the scientific investigation of the Bible we must be prepared to meet this interesting phenomenon over and over again. Ancient peoples always ascribed their sacred writings to great personalities. In the case of the Deuteronomic authors they rightly felt that Manasseh's idolatry imperilled the Mosaic religion. Only by destroying everything that confused and misled the people could the pure worship of Yahweh be restored. And so in writing a new set of laws these men regarded themselves as carrying out and developing the intention of Moses—projected, of course, to fit the needs of their own particular age.

Then again: it must always be remembered that the literary etiquette of the ancient world was different from ours in that it permitted certain practices which we of the twentieth century regard as nothing short of curious. The Babylonians ascribed their laws to Hammurabi, the Greeks to Solon, just as the Hebrews made all legislation imply a Mosaic origin. Essentially all new legislation is based upon older laws and inasmuch as these in turn run back to time immemorial it was most natural for the Deuteronomic men to feel that their ideals were implicit in the teachings of Moses. For Hebrew tradition had already established the fact that Moses had proclaimed certain fundamental prin-

ciples. As judge, leader, organizer, and prophet he rendered decisions and taught the people the rudiments of
their social and religious institutions. It was therefore
only natural that when the oral laws were committed
to writing, they should be attributed to him.

8

But it would be a mistake to regard Deuteronomy as
mere legislation. It is much more than that. Having
been written by men of deep religious convictions it is
animated with a spirit of nobility and idealism together
with a superbly beautiful insistence upon justice, holiness, and humanity. It is not a code of law in the ordinary sense, for it subordinates everything to religion.
It teaches that only the pure worship of Yahweh can
save the people from the evils of heathenism; therefore,
Yahweh must be worshipped with absolute devotion of
heart and soul. Other gods are forbidden, and so is
every attempt to represent Yahweh in a material form.
The supreme utterance of Deuteronomy centres in one
mighty, absolute declaration: "Hear, O Israel, Yahweh
thy God, Yahweh alone." This means that the Hebrew
people must know that there is no other god for them
beside Yahweh: He is the one and only. Consequently,
the Deuteronomists conceived the supreme duty of
every Hebrew to love his God because Yahweh Himself is Love: "Thou shalt love Yahweh thy God with
all thy heart, and with all thy soul, and with all thy
might."*

Next to devotion to Yahweh comes pride in the nation: Israel the one people. The Deuteronomic Code
is very patriotic. Perhaps the chief cause of its immedi-

*Deuteronomy 6:4-6.

ate acceptance by Josiah and the people was its insistence upon the integrity of the national soul. In Deuteronomy the Hebrew people are alone legislated for. They are conceived as a free nation recognizing no foreign king and bowing to no foreign deity. Only the revealed Will of Yahweh as contained in the Code was regarded as sufficient for all individual and national needs.

Thus, Deuteronomy treats the nation as a moral unit and enforces justice between man and man. There are many humane regulations in it like the law which enjoins the freeing of all slaves at the end of every six years. Charitable provisions are made for the poor who are to have some share in the crops. Servants, foreigners, widows, and orphans are to partake of the Thanksgiving dinner which was held in the fall when the grape harvest was gathered. Deuteronomy lifts woman to a higher position than was ever accorded her in the past, and by exhorting the people to educate their children it attempted to create "a righteous people and wise above all others."

The fact that Deuteronomy was brought forward as though it were a divine command made it the first instance in Hebrew history of a book which was regarded as "sacred"—that is, professing to have divine authority. Deuteronomy is, consequently, a turning point in the history of religion, for it gave religion an authoritative book. As time went on, other Hebrew books were placed in the same category and came to be regarded equally as holy. Once the idea of "book-sanctity" got started it grew by leaps and bounds so that a large body of writings eventually grew up possessing this quality distinct from all others. And that's how the ancient Hebrews got their holy books into one collection which we call the Old Testament. Centuries later, the writings that now make up the New Testament and the Koran were accorded, by their devotees, a position like that which Deuteronomy occupied before them. Deuteronomy is therefore responsible for having begun the movement by which the Hebrew religion became the religion of a sacred Book—and in this respect it has left its influence on Christianity and Mohammedanism.

CHAPTER IV

HOW THE HEBREW PRIESTS WROTE A NEW VER-SION OF THEIR PEOPLE'S LAW AND HISTORY, THEREBY CREATING THE PRIESTLY BOOK OF RITUAL

WITHIN an incredibly short space of time, after Josiah had made the Deuteronomic Code the supreme law of his land, the kingdom of Judah was brutally besieged by the Babylonians under Nebuchadrezzar. When the bitter fight of unimaginable horrors finally ended in the year 586 B. C. Jerusalem was captured and destroyed, the Temple of Solomon demolished, and the very best elements of the people mercilessly dragged off as slaves into exile. It was a wholesale deportation, an unexampled humiliation.

In their strange surroundings in far-away Babylonia the Hebrews underwent many profound changes. Suffering and bitterness always does that. Uprooted from their soil, torn from their native homes, unable to sacrifice to Yahweh, their God, because His temple lay in ruins hundreds of miles across the desert, no wonder these Hebrew captives sat by the waters of Babylon and wept. They were homesick, bitter and bedraggled. What a sorry and disheartened lot they must have constituted as they hung their harps on the willows and sat down in gloomy silence to despise the gods of their conquerors. How lonesome they were for Jerusalem, and yet how utterly alienated they felt themselves to be from their own Yahweh!

2

To those who are defeated and dejected a word of comforting encouragement is the best first-aid. "Seek ye the peace of the city whither I have caused you to be carried away captive, and pray unto the Lord for it," was the remarkable advice which the prophet Jeremiah addressed to his distressed compatriots; and wretched as they were in the face of all their shattered hopes they turned a willing ear to his letter of good counsel.

But Jeremiah was not the only one to help heal the fresh wounds. Among the very first to have been deported was an aristocratic priest of Jerusalem whom the people called Ezekiel. Possessed of a dynamic personality and splendid leadership his bracing words of faith constantly roused their flagging spirits and stirred within them new longings and new ambitions. He met every jeer of the captors with a challenging cheer, every taunt with a renewed trust in Yahweh. And while around him the harps were still hanging on the willows he could see Hope as an archangel with her foot on the dragon of disappointment. . . .

Yet with all this encouragement it is still a miracle how those Hebrew captives pulled themselves together. Within a remarkably short space of time they grew into an organized and flourishing community. Some of its members even rose to high positions in business and in the imperial court, for the policy of Babylonia made foreign birth no bar to advancement under the empire. But more remarkable than their material prosperity was their spiritual and literary progress. The exiled priests now had the leisure to write, and so the captivity turned out to be a blessing in the way of a prolific literary activity. In fact, it would be impossible to tell this wonderful story of the making of the Bible had not the deported Hebrews taken to the gentle art and amenities of book collecting. They eagerly gathered together all their old writings that managed to survive the cataclysm—the Yahwistic and Elohistic narratives, the Deuteronomic Code, the sermons of the prophets, the songs of their minstrels and poets, their cultic hymns, fragments of the royal annals and many of their laws. These they edited by recasting the older material into newer forms and toning down crude expressions that jarred their ethical sense. Nor did they hesitate to mingle their own advanced and more humane ideas with those of older times, so that as a result of this process much of the Hebrew Scriptures comes to us reshaped and revamped by the editorial revisions of this period.

Babylonia—splendid and opulent—where writing was nearly universal and employed in every-day affairs, is responsible for having stimulated the literary activities of these exiled Hebrew priests. She was not only rich in commerce and industry but she was the university of Asia possessing an elaborate religion and a vast and varied literature. It is, therefore, not at all surprising that the Jerusalem priests began to write down and systematize what they had formerly practised. They were the chief depositaries of the ancient Hebrew laws—and they now had the necessary leisure to work in an atmosphere that was conducive to their new task. We are greatly indebted to them for having preserved the old ritual and usages of the Temple which they doubtless did out of fear that their sacred traditions might be lost if they were not committed to writing.

At first they began in a rather small and fragmentary way to preserve these memorials of the past, but as their economic condition became more settled and secure their work grew enormously by fresh additions and clever modifications. Later on, their writings were taken up by a group of younger men who used them as the basis for creating a vast Priest Code which in time overshadowed in importance any legislation the Hebrews had ever known. Before one can fully appreciate the enormous significance of this Priest Code it is necessary to understand a little more fully what was happening among these exiles—particularly what thoughts were disturbing the heads of their leaders.

3

Deprived of their centralizing Temple at Jerusalem it became urgent for the captive community to reorganize itself in conformity with the entire change in its situation. So, in the various places of their dispersion these exiles established for themselves houses of prayer (a prototype of the synagogue) where for the first time it was learned that Yahweh could be worshipped without sacrifice and without Temple; and here they gathered for common worship and study. Among their chief leaders were men of the former priesthood who had ministered in the glorious Temple of Solomon; they now came forward to guide and direct the destinies of their flock. The most prominent of them all was Ezekiel, a rare individual who possessed that blessed nuisance—a theory and a vision. And perhaps it is just because of this combination that Ezekiel became (with the possible exception of Moses) the most influential man in the whole course of Hebrew history.

It is strange to say of him, and yet it is true, that he was born into the priesthood in Jerusalem and died as a prophet in Babylon. But when he became a prophet to his people in Babylon he did not cease to be a priest in spirit, for Jerusalem and Babylon were curiously mixed within him.

Although he is commonly known as a prophet (because he foretold the doom of Jerusalem and later predicted its restoration) still his prophecies were outweighed by his practical work. Like the other seers of his day he had a deep mystical temperament and many visions; but unlike most of them he had a definite theory of religious organization which eventually became the basis of the new Jewish community when it was finally restored. Here was a man who saw no hope for the Jews without transforming the state into a church and regulating its life through elaborate ritual, laws, and ordinances. This spirit eventually gave rise to a huge body of legislation known as the Priests' Code. Of course, it did not embody an entirely new spirit, for the Hebrew peoples had always observed some form of ritual. But with Ezekiel a new interpretation of the past arose and with it a new emphasis upon religion, ritual, and ceremony as the supreme and authoritative powers. Although he lived in deportation in far-away Babylonia, Ezekiel's chief interest was centred in mapping out a reconstruction programme which he hoped would be put into effect just as soon as Jerusalem and the Temple were restored to his people.

In the year 572 B. C. this man Ezekiel issued a unique code which is found in the Bible bound up with his other writings.* In this document he drew up a

*Ezekiel 40-48.

blueprint of a new social order—a priestly Utopia—to
be set up on the return of the exiles to Palestine. Like
all utopias it is filled with many impossible schemes.
But his main idea was not beyond accomplishment:
that the re-establishment of the Jerusalem Temple
must make that sanctuary the Centre of all things Jewish and the supreme authority over the Holy Land.

To Ezekiel, the future Temple was to be the all in
all: dignified by history, enriched by tradition, sancti-
fied by Yahweh, glorified by sacrifices and idealized by
holiness. In his visions he described the new building
and its altar with the measurements of an architect's
plan, giving full details of how everything should be
done. He also laid down minute regulations for the
Priests through whom the sanctity of the shrine was to
be maintained. All these instructions (and this is the
significant thing to keep in mind) provided for a more
elaborate priestly organization than had ever been
known before the exile.

4

While the dominating thought of Ezekiel's code was
the idea of the Holiness of Yahweh, the outstanding
working principle was priest-control over everything.
Himself a Jerusalem temple-priest and educated in the
priests' training college, it is not at all astonishing that
this creative theologian and original thinker should
dogmatically emphasize ecclesiastical control as the
only security for political and moral restoration. What
Augustine's "City of God" was to the mediæval Catholic Church, that Ezekiel's Church-state idea was to the
Jewish restoration programme.* The perfect, ideal state

*In Ezekiel's Utopia, Jerusalem will become the centre of the Universe
and the new name of the city will be: "God is There" (see the last words
of his book).

must not simply take account of religion—it must be religious! The question of church and state might not enter; the church was to be the state, and the state was to be the church. Plainly put, Ezekiel's theory may be summed up in one overtopping sentence: Yahweh is Holy, and Yahweh is above all—therefore, Yahweh's representatives, the Jerusalem priests, must be above all and rule all.

As a result of this closely knitted reasoning, the future Temple must be not merely Yahweh's sanctuary— it had been that before the exile—it must now become nothing less than the external and visible form of Divine Government. Upon the return of his people to Jerusalem, Ezekiel planned that the Hebrews would no longer be a nation like other peoples ruled by a secular king—upon being restored they will automatically be transformed into a church ruled by the priests who are to be regarded as God's Representatives. And that is just exactly what happened in less than a century after Ezekiel's death. . . .

Ezekiel laid down many laws which are not in harmony with corresponding laws of the Old Testament. In fact, some of his laws are so extremely different that at one time the right of Ezekiel's book to a place in the Bible was hotly disputed by the rabbis. For example, Deuteronomy gives the Jewish king supreme authority over the State and over the Temple. But Ezekiel took this power away and placed it in the hands of the men of his own caste, the hereditary Jerusalem priests. Consequently, the king was retained as a political head but reduced to a very colorless figure with limited functions. The only value a king possesses in Ezekiel's Church-State is to guarantee the regular performance of Temple worship and safeguard priestly legislation! In other words, the entire political machinery had to be subordinated to Religion.

But it was not only the king who suffered in Ezekiel's programme. The country priests came off equally as bad! It will be recalled that Deuteronomy had provided that after the destruction of the village shrines these rural men (the Levites) should be on an equality with the Jerusalem priests. Ezekiel flatly opposed this. Being a Jerusalem priest he demanded that only members of his own order (the Sons of Zadok) hold the priestly office—and thereby, of course, the power and the revenue. It is interesting to see what sort of subterfuge Ezekiel played upon in order to put over his point against the Levites. By charging them with having seduced the people to idolatrous worship Ezekiel felt justified in forcing them into a subordinate position, unfit to be the equals of the Jerusalem men. Thus for the first time in Hebrew history a clear-cut distinction was drawn between Priests and Levites. And that's how Ezekiel threw the plans of Deuteronomy to the winds.

5

Ezekiel was not the only one to attempt the writing of a code. His grandiose scheme for regulating worship was soon followed by another, likewise written in the priestly spirit, with priestly thought and priestly expression. This other author must have been a close spiritual kinsman of Ezekiel, but his name, unfortunately, is not known. He wrote that short code—partly ceremonial, partly moral—which is preserved in the Book of Leviticus from the beginning of the seventeenth chapter to the end of the twenty-sixth. It is called the "Holiness Legislation" because it is marked by an intense feeling of reverence for the "holiness" of God, and everything connected with His service. Holiness is, indeed, a duty laid upon the Hebrews in other codes earlier than this; but while elsewhere it appears merely as one injunction among many, it is here insisted on with a striking emphasis. Its keynote is found in a single phrase, occurring with a frequency which constitutes it the leading motive: "Ye shall be holy, for I, the Lord your God, am holy."

Originally the Holiness code was a small independent document. As it now stands in the Bible it is incorporated in a more elaborate and developed legislation of the same general character. Like all Hebrew law, the Holiness Legislation is a collection compiled from older materials. Some of its proposals, like certain laws of Deuteronomy and Ezekiel, proved impossible —others needed still further revision. Yet, notwithstanding its shortcomings, it managed to survive and was incorporated in the Bible because there was something more in it than a group of ritual laws. It stresses social and ethical interests of universal value. For example, it contains laws which forbid the rich from taking unfair advantage of the poor, and it thoughtfully requires the well-to-do classes to aid their impoverished fellow Jews and to charge no interest on loans made to them. Embodied in the very heart of its moral principles is the highest ethical note of the Pentateuch which Jesus quoted as the basis of his teaching: "Thou shalt love thy neighbor as thyself."*

*See Leviticus 19:18. From this same code the founders of the American Republic took the famous text inscribed on the Liberty Bell—"Proclaim liberty throughout the land unto all the inhabitants thereof" (Lev. 25:10).

6

Chiefly because the Holiness Code needed further elaboration and development, and because many of the details of Ezekiel's plan were not workable, there arose a younger group of priest-writers whose object was to draw up a code which would be fuller, more explicit, and more consistent with itself. They wanted a body of law that would not only harmonize with the ritualistic spirit of the age but would be practical enough to go into effect just as soon as the exile should end and the Restoration become a reality. By making use of the material that had already been reduced to writing by the older men, these younger priests set about compiling, systematizing, and reforming the sacred laws and usages in accordance with their own advanced thinking.

They did not hesitate to use any good suggestion that came their way. For example, they took several important ideas directly from Ezekiel and merged them with their own. Then they took the Holiness Code and, after having made several interpolations in its text, bodily incorporated it. By transforming ancient practices and working them over into an up-to-date authoritative system they had to force new meanings and interpretations into old ideas so that what had once belonged to a previous age could be freely applied as a means to organize newer methods.

They also invented a Mosaic dress for their writings, sincerely believing that they were justified in attributing all law to Moses (in fact they knew of no indirect way of expressing Mosaic principles). Therefore, old and new alike were thrown back into the age of the pioneer Lawgiver and were honestly represented as having originated at the time Moses was leading their ancestors in the wilderness. When it is remembered that all codes are essentially combinations of new and old legislation the idea of pious fraud is dismissed, for it does not account for the mental attitude of these men who honestly incorporated in their writings enough of the old to justify a Mosaic fiction according to the literary standards of antiquity. Furthermore, it was not their way to be too original. They did not wish to break with the past or strike out into an untracked, open country. In this respect these younger priests acted in accordance with Jewish tradition which in every age of its long history has taught an indebtedness to the wisdom of former generations. Instinctively the Jew seemed to know that progress does not outgrow the past, rather does it grow out of it.

And quite as extraordinary as his consciousness of the past is the unique capacity of the Jew to absorb the environment into which he is placed, no matter how alien or strange, without losing his identity. No finer illustration of the working of this principle can be found in the whole course of Hebrew history than in the age of the exile. For example, the highly developed Babylonian temple services with their stately pomp and vast slaughter made a deep impression on these younger Hebrews who, after all, may be compared to the sons of backwoods farmers suddenly placed in the heart of a great metropolis. They were profoundly stirred by the ceremonial magnificence of their masters' religion but they were not carried off their feet by it. For after all, underneath the showy tinsel and costly parade, Babylon was nothing more than a remorseless, cruel, and arrogant power.

When it came to the task of re-writing their own Temple Code it is true that they colored it with the ritualistic zeal of their overlords, clearly showing how much of their strange environment they soaked up. It has been carefully figured out that the legislation these younger priests codified called for an annual slaughter of 1093 lambs, 113 bulls, 37 rams, and 32 goats—this together with a vast paraphernalia of Sacrifice including fine flour, oil, and incense in huge quantities. . . . But while they superadded to the simple Jerusalem ritual some of the more seductive features of the elaborate Babylonian religion they did not substitute the one for the other.

While they borrowed much from Babylonian paganism it must not be forgotten that they modified what they borrowed, and it is in that small margin of difference—the result of modification—that the ancient Hebrew genius lies. There is no doubt that the Creation Story, the Flood Legend, and the institution of the Sabbath had their earliest origins among the Babylonians. But these borrowings were so vastly reshaped by the Hebrews that in time they came to differ from their Babylonian counterparts as much as the civilization of modern America differs from that of mediæval Europe. The spiritual realities of the Creation myth of Genesis appear even greater when compared with the polytheistic Babylonian version where the gods and goddesses fight among themselves. The Hebrews purified what they borrowed and made their stories carry a high spiritual message which stands alone in a unique position among the writings of ancient peoples.

Although these younger Hebrew priests borrowed many ideas which they incorporated into their sacrificial system, still when compared with the sacrificial cults of the pagan religions it stands in quite a striking contrast. The slaughter of human beings so universal throughout antiquity is utterly unknown to the Hebrew Codes. While other peoples were burning the flesh of men and women in order to win favor from their gods the Hebrews were writing a story about Abraham and his son Isaac in order to definitely protest against the practice, to prove that Yahweh did not wish human life offered to Him.

While it is true that the total cost of the sacrificial system was an expensive and heavy economic burden on the people, still the individual spiritual value of a sacrifice was never measured by its costliness, for something far more deeply ethical was interfused in the Hebrew ritual. In its highest form (and we must be liberal enough to judge it at its best) the system emphasized not the elaborateness of the offering but its moral significance: it conceived sacrifice to stand for repentance on the part of the worshipper and for forgiveness on the side of God. Thus, it was "sin-offering" when the worshipper sought to express penitence; "burnt-offering" when he desired to renew his consecration to God; "thank-offering" when he came with a heart full of gladness and was eager to express his gratitude and joy. In other words, sacrifice did not take the place of righteousness. Before sin-offering could be conscientiously brought to the altar reparation must be made to the one who had been wronged.*

Many centuries after these young priests had written their code it was reported (Matt. 5:24) that Jesus said to his disciples, "If thou bring thy gift to the

*See, for example, Leviticus 5:21-26.

altar, and there rememberest that thy brother hath
aught against thee, leave there thy gift before the
altar, and go thy way; first be reconciled to thy brother
and then come and offer thy gift." No utterance of the
lowly Nazarene could more genuinely set forth this
principle of the new code: that all restoration must
precede sacrifice.

. . . In quite another sense, too, it might be said
that "restoration must precede sacrifice" for it was a
cardinal point in the theology of these priests that
there could be no resumption of an authorized sacrificial cult at Jerusalem until the national Hebrew Restoration became a reality. When would this happen?
—that was the question uppermost in the minds of the
exiles. . . .

7

The great dream of Restoration which the Judæan
Colony had cherished did not prove an illusion. At
last, in the year 538 B. C., within half a century of
the captivity, the long looked-for day dawned. It was
in that year that the huge Babylonian Empire was
brought to a sudden and dramatic fall by Cyrus, king
of the Persians. Entering the city of Babylon he succeeded in incorporating the old empire into his own
new kingdom. Cyrus was not only an able soldier;
he was a shrewd statesman and an exceedingly subtle
diplomat. Instead of showing harshness to his subjects
he exhibited understanding and patience. One of his
very first acts was an edict permitting the Hebrew
exiles to return to their own country and rebuild the
Temple. He even promised to contribute to the cost
of its erection!

This sudden good turn in their fortune filled the Hebrews with wild enthusiasm and rejoicing. Cyrus was loudly proclaimed "Savior," "anointed one," "messenger of Yahweh." But soon after the heated celebration cooled down, the enthusiasm quickly ebbed away so that only a small number of the exiles actually availed themselves of the privileges. The majority looked upon Zionism as Utopian. There was no rush to pull up stakes and move out. Why give up lucrative positions in order to go back to live in poverty? Had not Babylonia proved a permanent home? Then why leave? Doubtless they were familiar with the deplorable conditions existing in Palestine and preferred Babylonian business prosperity to Jerusalem sentiment and starvation.

A small band of loyal patriots, however, were of another frame of mind and they were determined to return to their homeland, no matter what difficulties lay in their path. Motivated by intense religious zeal and led by Sheshbazzar and Zerubbabel they cut loose from their friends and marched out, crusaders before the Crusades, bound for the Holy City.

It was no rainbow adventure, this hot and dusty trek across nine hundred weary miles of desert and plain. And at the end of their dreary trail neither joy nor a pot of gold awaited them. In fact, these exiles found on their return to Jerusalem a most deplorable state of affairs. There was not only internal dissension among the Jews themselves, but envy and hostility from surrounding peoples. The wretched conditions of the country were utterly disheartening, the struggle for existence exposing them to all the hardships of new settlers.

Yet these men and women were of unusual fibre—
heroic souls enduring awful strain with tremendous
fortitude. Amid the fallen and overgrown débris they
slowly began the job of rearing their houses, which
were nothing more than mere shacks. Worn and tired
out, they still found enough strength to hold on to
their ruined sanctuary. They seemed to be possessed of
an almost superhuman tenacity, for although the Temple was in desolate confusion they finally raised it
stone by stone from the dust. It was only after a long
and bitter struggle with terrific handicaps, tossed about
by many ups and downs, that they finally succeeded
in rebuilding it. This was in the year 516 B. C.

Of course, the rebuilt Temple was nothing more
than a rude reproduction of Solomon's beautiful shrine
possessing little of the majesty and grandeur of the
old. It represented the crude efforts of a poverty-
stricken people who had long been alienated from their
soil. While many of the younger generation rejoiced to
witness the re-establishment of the sacred edifice, the
old men who had seen the former Temple "wept with
a loud voice." But unpretentious as it was the new
Temple nevertheless stood out as an important achievement. It became the symbol of unity and the rallying
point for all Hebrews; and its personnel contained the
very elements out of which a new commonwealth was
to be built.

8

Now that there was a Temple how were the regular
services to be conducted? There was much confusion
and discussion about this. Some wanted one way,
others preferred still another. Of course, they finally

had to fall back on the old Deuteronomic laws and such meagre codes as contained the practices and usages of the first Temple. But new occasions teach new duties and the old practices stood badly in need of serious revision.

The confusion in the Temple was but a reflex of the conditions of the new community. Things were not prospering well even after the Temple was rebuilt. The people were thoroughly discouraged. The few who were rich cared only for themselves—they were greedy and violent. Oppression, fraud and injustice stalked almost unashamed. Jerusalem, somewhat like a wild western town in the old frontier days, had a mixed population that practised all types of intermarriage, and "companionate" marriage too. The Jews were fast losing their racial purity and peculiar identity—everything was ramshackle. Even the ancient walls of the city, left in ruins by the Babylonians, were still dismantled—an open invitation to marauding bands of hostile peoples. This deplorable state of things, going from bad to worse, made them feel that the long looked for Return was not the glorious Golden Age predicted by the prophets. Try as hard as they might to adjust themselves, still everything seemed insecure. Instead of feeling rooted to their ancestral soil they now saw themselves hanging over a wild precipice.

Thus both the city of Jerusalem and the Temple were in need of an immediate change to hold things from plunging headlong into utter chaos. It is hard telling what would have happened to the Judæan Community had not two men appeared at the right time to save the situation. . . .

9

It was in the year 458 B. C. that there arrived in Jerusalem a scribe of high priestly family. His name was Ezra and he was a rigorist of the first order. He came to Palestine as a representative of the Persian king, bringing with him large administrative powers and a caravan of patriotic Jews anxious to participate in the upbuilding of their ancestral home.

Ezra began at once the strenuous work of reform, but despite his moral earnestness and ardent zeal he managed to make but little headway. He was hampered by politics on the inside and hostility on the outside. Fortunately for Ezra, his hands were greatly strengthened by the arrival in Jerusalem of a Jewish layman possessing an exceptionally strong personality and executive ability. This was Nehemiah, a cup-bearer to King Artaxerxes. He came to Jerusalem directly from the royal Persian Court at Susa where he had been in high favor. Through his personal request the king had granted him permission to proceed to Jerusalem as Governor and to rebuild the walls of the Holy City.

Escorted by a Persian military guard which was provided by the king, Nehemiah entered Jerusalem with high prestige. However, he lost no time in ceremonies but immediately began to steer his way amid difficulties which would have appalled the ordinary man. With characteristic energy and resolution he set about to rebuild the walls of the Holy City; and although he was vehemently opposed by the neighboring Samaritans nothing could divert him from the set determination of his purpose. Within the extraordinary short space of fifty-two days the work was finished. What had long seemed to be an impossible task was now an actual accomplishment! Perhaps no event in the history of antiquity is comparable to it as an instance of patriotic fervor—except it be the completion of the Long Walls of Athens. A solemn service of dedication marked the conclusion of the work, so that with the Walls rebuilt Nehemiah and the people felt that Jerusalem was safeguarded from her outside foes—and there were plenty of them.

It was unfortunate for the struggling community that in 433 B. C., shortly after the rebuilding of the walls, Nehemiah was recalled to Persia. The people sorely needed his dynamic leadership. No sooner had he gone, opposition and reaction raised their ugly heads. Rather than have his efforts chopped to pieces Nehemiah secured from the court permission to return to Jerusalem, where now an infinitely harder task awaited him. Having rebuilt the physical walls of Jerusalem on his first visit, his task now was to rebuild its spiritual walls, to safeguard the Temple and Judaism from corruption and disintegration from within and paganism from without. With the aid of Ezra, Nehemiah immediately set about the reformation of the priesthood and the Temple service. He enforced the strict observance of the sabbath by keeping the city gates closed to all trading. Then he went about forcibly stopping all intermarriage, thereby creating a high wall that henceforth separated Jew and Gentile. With one mighty stroke the entire Jewish community was reorganized, converting what was left of the old nation into a strictly disciplined church under the Highpriest as its king and the priests as his assessors. By the promulgation of a code of laws Nehemiah stripped the secular nobility of most of the authority which it had possessed and transferred it to the priests.

It was a herculean task.

How was it so speedily accomplished?

10

A graphic account of the way in which these two Persian Jews created a new basis for both the Jewish State and the Jewish Religion is given in the eighth chapter of the memoirs of Nehemiah. Here it is told that in the year 444 B. C. both Ezra and Nehemiah hand in hand introduced a new "Book of Law." We saw how Josiah in 621 B. C. publicly proclaimed Deuteronomy as a divine book, thereby enabling it to become at once the supreme authority of the land.

The case of Ezra and Nehemiah is almost an exact parallel.

On the first day of the seventh month—so the memoir states—a public assembly was arranged by Nehemiah and held in one of the open squares in Jerusalem. Standing upon a pulpit of wood which had been expressly erected for him, Ezra the scribe opened the new Book in the sight of the people and in their hearing read it to them. By declaring the Priest Code to be the authoritative Will of Yahweh it did not take long before the people solemnly accepted it as such. The memoir tells us that the impression made upon the hearers by Ezra's reading was one of gloom: "the people wept" as they listened to the divine commandments of Yahweh for they were shocked and horrified to hear how much they had sinned by their utter ignorance of this legislation. So they all pledged themselves by solemn oath "To walk in God's Law, which was given by Moses, the servant of God."

II

If the Priest Code was written in Babylonia who brought it to Palestine?

In all probability Nehemiah himself brought the document with him directly from the far East awaiting, of course, the right opportunity to proclaim it to his fellow Jews in Jerusalem who were still living under the old Deuteronomic laws and apparently knew nothing of the very different demands of the new code.

In its original form the Priestly Legislation was completed in Babylonia about 500 B. C. or a little later, but like Deuteronomy it underwent various revisions. Many additions were incorporated in it from time to time because circumstances necessitated changes; consequently, laws regulating these various changes were inserted in the code. Frequently the old legislation lies side by side with the newer, and this, of course, accounts for conflicting statements. When in the Book of Numbers, for example, one passage defines the age of Levitical service from 30 to 50 years, and another from 25 to 50, we can readily understand the reason for the two statements.

Not only did this great Code receive various modifications in the course of its practical application but something far more interesting happened to it once it became supreme in the land. All of its laws were put into a framework of history in order to show that each piece of legislation fits into a definite historical situation. A brand-new version of Hebrew history had to be invented in order to accomplish this clever feat—

yet it was immediately and skilfully done. Just how it was manipulated constitutes an important factor in the story of the making of the Bible which will be explained later on. . . .

12

That the Priests' Code was read to the people shows that it was not intended solely for the ecclesiastics. In fact, it was the purpose of the new law to separate all the Jews, priests as well as the laymen, from the Gentile world in order to unite the Hebrews to their God by obedience to a rigidly constituted ritual. The Code literally became the Magna Charta for the entire community; and not for the priests alone. Appropriate as the name is, still it would be misleading not to fully appreciate the fact that the Priest Code was written to benefit the masses. In fact, the Hebrew script now in vogue was then introduced for the first time by Ezra and Nehemiah who, in order to make these laws more accessible to the people, changed them into Aramaic Characters whose square-lettered alphabet was dominant in the country at that time. It was certainly a great victory for these two Persian Jews to have been able to get the people of Jerusalem to accept a new code of laws and at the same time adopt a new way of writing.*

The Priest Code with its stress on Jewish exclusiveness may be regarded as an historic necessity for the age in which it was promulgated. There is no doubt but that its provisions to utterly isolate the Jews saved the little colony of returned exiles from being completely

---

*The old Hebrew Alphabet used Canaanite characters (see Moabite Stone illustration). The "modern" Hebrew Alphabet adopted the square-lettered or the Aramaic type.

א	אג	אֿ	ᚷᚷᚦᚦᚩ
ב	בכ	פ	ᎶᎶᎶ
ג		ᴛ	ᴧᴧᴧ
ד	דר	ᕁ	ᕁᕁᕁᕁ
ה	ה ח	ᴂ	ᴣᴣᴲᴲ
ו	ו ו ι	ᴪ	ᚷᚦᚦᚦ
ז	ι (	ᴕ	ᴢ=(ᴣ)
ח	ᕁᕁ	ᴃᴃ	ᴃᴃᴾᴃ
ט		ᴳᴳ	6
י	ᴧᴧ	ᴪᴪ	ᴢᴴᴢᴢ
ד כ	כב	ᴣᴣ	ᴊᴧᴧ
ל	ᴊᴊ	ᴧ	ᴧᴧᴵᴧ
ם מ	ᴧᴧ	ᴃᴃᴃ	ᴪᴪᴪᴪ
ן נ	ᴊ	ᴊᴊ	ᴧᴧᴧᴧ
ס	ᴠᴠ	ᴪ	ᴤᴤ
ע	ᴛᴛ	ᴼᴼ	ᴼᴼᴼᴼ
ף פ	ᴧᴧ	ᴃᴃ	ᴣ
ץ צ	ᴧ	ᴹᴹ	ᴾᴧᴣᴤ
ק	ᴾ	ᴠᴧ	ᴾᴾᴾᴾ
ר	ᴧᴧ	ᴧᴧ	ᴧᴧᴧ
שׁ שׂ	ᴪᴪ	ᴓ�”ᴡ	ᴡᴪᴡᴪ
ת	ᴧᴧ	ᴧᴧ	ᴧᴪᴧ

The column at the right illustrates the style of writing in use before the times of Ezra and Nehemiah. The column at the extreme left illustrates the "square-letter" style made official by these two men.

absorbed into the surrounding nations. As rigid and cold as these forms may seem to us in this far-off age, it must nevertheless be remembered that had they not been called into existence the legacy of Hebrew thought could not have been preserved. If this is so, then the modern world owes the Jewish priesthood a great debt, since whatever the means used they did keep alive the immortal genius of the race. . . .

Practically all the ritual and sacred ordinances which the Jews possessed may be closely paralleled by those of other oriental peoples. What was peculiar to the Jew was not his religion but his religiousness—his intensity of religious feeling. It is this feeling that the Priest Code preserved. Under its sway the Jews pulled themselves together with an amazing spiritual cohesiveness. While it was rigid and in places even excessively strict and gave rise to a narrow particularism, still plenty of room was left for the most varied types of expression; for the Code contained within itself many beautiful elements of which we, living in the twentieth century, have little knowledge and less appreciation.

For this very cogent reason it would be a vast mistake to believe that the rule of the priests crushed the spirit of the Jew under a gloomy legalism. One glance at the richness and manifoldness of the literature produced under its sway (—many of the most beautiful Psalms are from this period—) is enough to dissipate the false notion of the so-called "barrenness of the Law." It may be paradoxical, and yet it is true, that when the Law was most rigid and apparently under its narrowest construction it was nevertheless giving rise to the broadest and most spiritual types of religious expression. When animals were being slain by thousands and when washings and purifications were engaging the attention of the priests—yes at this same time, hard as it may be to believe it—the Hebrew religion was furnishing in the Psalms the highest spiritual contemplation and communion with God which has ever been given to man. . . . How exceedingly varied, complex, and strange this priestly element was!

CHAPTER V

HOW THE FOUR DOCUMENTS WERE WOVEN TOGETHER

It has been an interesting story to trace step by step the various stages out of which the great documents of the Pentateuch sprang up. What is equally as fascinating is the maner of their preservation, how these diversified writings were woven together into one organic body popularly called by the Jews "Torah," which may be roughly translated into English by the word "Law."

Had these documents continued to exist separately it is certain that there would have been no Bible to write about, for they would have perished in the vast sea of oriental decay. What kept them afloat was the fortunate circumstance that they were joined together at different times and thereby grew into strength and importance.

The story of the first fusion of the documents takes us back to the seventh century before Christ. It was at that time that the fighting Kings of Assyria took it into their heads to make trouble for the North Hebrew Kingdom. Hardly had the Elohistic men finished writing their narratives when these ancient warlords invaded their country, destroyed their towns, deported the inhabitants of the open cities and laid siege to Samaria, their great fortress-capital and rival of Jerusalem. The siege which lasted three years was full of horrors—and then Samaria fell. With the sad loss of

the capital the whole northern Kingdom of these Elohistic writers came to an abrupt end in 722 B. C. The
leading men of their tribes, the "Ten Lost Tribes,"
were led into captivity and no trace of them has ever
been found. . . .

However, many of these northern Hebrews managed to escape the iron hand of Assyria and by secretly
crossing the border stole their way into Jerusalem. As
refugees they carried south the Elohistic writings, and
that is how the people of Jerusalem fell heir to the
literary remains of their misfortunate brethren of the
North.

Although the people of Jerusalem had their own
Yahwistic writings they were quick to see that the Elohistic narratives contained a lot of good historical and
religious material; consequently, they felt a deep reverence for these stories despite the fact that they had been
written up in the North. For after all did they not
deal with common Hebrew traditions? So, eager that
nothing of real value be lost, it wasn't very long before
a group of zealous Jerusalem prophets got together and
combined the two—giving the Yahwistic document
the preference.

Because their stories were originally drawn from a
common stock of Hebrew tradition, both the Yahwistic
and Elohistic documents contained parallel versions of
important tribal events. Where these were similar, the
Yahwistic account was quoted more fully, with the result that the Elohistic narratives were greatly curtailed
so that much of its material perished in the process of
union. (This explains why the Elohistic narratives have
come down to us as the most fragmentary of the four
distinct groups of narratives of the Pentateuch.) It is

quite possible, for example, that the Elohistic narrative began with an account of the Creation and that this part was entirely cut out and displaced by the corresponding section in the Yahwistic. In the combining process various changes were made by the Yahwistic men. Sentences and words that seemed desirable were added; and what did not suit the taste of the new editors was suppressed. And finally, in order to harmonize the two versions a few words—finger-prints of editorial revision—were added here and there in the interest of smooth reading.

Thus, what had once been the independent and separate documents of the South and North were now cleverly brought together by a close interweaving. And that is how they emerged as one book!

Very often the independent sources may be easily disentangled; but sometimes the documents having been so neatly pieced together make it utterly impossible for scholars to sunder them into the originals. Occasionally, here and there, some valuable clew may be picked up by which it is possible to track the ancient compilers. But frequently the harmonizing of two versions has been done with such skill that it defies the most careful analysis.

One of the best examples of the oriental practice of weaving and interweaving of documents is clearly seen in the 37th chapter of Genesis where the story is told of how Joseph disclosed his dreams to his brothers and the experiences that followed. In combining the two records the editors retained the two names Jacob and Israel—knowing that the Yahwistic account always uses the name Israel and the Elohim account Jacob. But this is not the only tell-tale evidence! Judah is made the spokesman for his brethren (indicating the Yahwistic source) in the same story where Reuben (the hero of the Elohistic) is given the identical honor. Perhaps the best illustration—and one that has caused plenty of grief to those who have rigidly adhered to the Mosaic authorship of Genesis—may be found in the duplicate story (a twice-told tale) of how Joseph was sold. The following verses present the contradiction between the Yahwistic record that tells of Joseph being carried into Egypt by the "Ishmaelites" and the altogether different story told by the Elohistic authors who emphatically declare that it was the "Midianites."

—from Yahwistic Account in Genesis

Chapter 37:

25 And they lifted up their eyes and looked, and, behold, a travelling company of Ishmaelites came from Gilead, with their camels bearing spicery and balm and myrrh, going to carry it down to Egypt. 26 And Judah said unto his brethren, what profit is it if we slay our brother and conceal his blood? 27 Come, and let us sell him to the Ishmaelites, and let not our hand be upon him; for he is our brother, our flesh. And his brethren harkened unto him. . . . *28* . . . And sold joseph to the Ishmaelites for twenty pieces of silver.

—from Elohistic Account in Genesis

Chapter 37:

23 And it came to pass, when Joseph was come unto his brethren, that they stripped Joseph of his coat, the coat of many colors that was on him. 24 And they took him and cast him into the pit—and the pit was empty, there was no water in it. 25 And they sat down to eat bread. . . . 28 And there passed by Midianites, merchantmen, and they drew and lifted up Joseph out of the pit . . . and they brought Joseph into Egypt.

2

This fusion process, or the compacting of different writings, is the most remarkable literary fact of the Bible, being exhibited on almost every page of its multiform books. And, of course, it is just because of this that the writings of Scripture are so composite and bristle with so many repetitions and contradictions.

And for this reason too it may be rightly said that there is not a single book in the Bible which is original in the sense of having been written by one man, for all the books are made up of older documents or pre-existing sources which were combined with later materials, undergoing in this way several revisions and editings at the hands of different scribes or compilers. Deep traces have therefore been left upon the text of the Bible by these several stages of expansions, additions, modifications, revisions and incorporations—they appear to the scholar of biblical literature much like the striations grooved in the rocks by huge glaciers to the student of geology.

It was a common oriental practice—not altogether confined to the Hebrews—for various compilers to piece narratives together, taking a bit from one source and a little from another. Of course, the compilers had to be exceedingly tolerant of incongruity in order to do this. Frequently, they did not even trouble to smooth down the whole into compact form; that is why the points of juncture are often clearly evident—(and the sources are, in consequence, capable of being separated from one another).

In some cases the various versions are given in succession lying side by side in continuous pieces—as in the opening chapters of Genesis. Sometimes, however, only a part of one document is used, and the corresponding or parallel version contained in the other is omitted. And still another method was employed as in the Flood Story where the original sources were cut up and the fragments dovetailed together (but even here the seams are still plainly traceable).

A great deal of valuable material always perished

by these methods of handling the old sources. What we now have preserved in the Pentateuch of the Yah- wistic and Elohistic documents are just those portions which, by having been pieced together, escaped the fate of oblivion. We saw, for example, that nothing of the Elohistic narratives was preserved prior to the stories of Abraham.

Yet this much we may be thankful for: that while vast sections of these old documents of the Bible have been irrecoverably lost, what has managed to survive is treasurable.

3

The next stage in the making of the Pentateuch occurred shortly after the promulgation of the Book of Deuteronomy which introduced into Hebrew think- ing a new order: the dominant influence of written law to be placed into the hands of the people. With Deuter- onomy began the movement by which the Hebrew reli- gion became the religion of a book.

But long before Deuteronomy became the popular rule of the people's life and worship there existed a Deuteronomic school of writers who now, under the protection of Josiah, were encouraged to go forward with their work. These Deuteronomic men not only set the religious ideals of their age but they moulded the phraseology in which those ideals were expressed.

Of vital importance to the Deuteronomic men was the conservation of the knowledge of their people's glorious past; and they were anxious to preserve every memorial of it. While their own law book gave a new interpretation of Hebrew history they did not feel that on that account it was necessary to destroy documents coming from other sources and presenting a different point of view. On the contrary, the old documents were to be zealously guarded and preserved—it being only necessary to re-edit them from the newer standpoint in order to have them harmonize with Deuteronomic teaching.

So it was that in the seventh century B. C., or shortly thereafter, the Deuteronomic School of writers took the combined Yahwistic-Elohistic Record and added it to their own Book of Deuteronomy. Only here and there was it necessary to retouch the old documents and they did so by making several changes and substitutions, clearly shown on many pages of the Pentateuch which bear the fingerprints of their editorial revision.*

Of course, it is frequently difficult to detect the hand that has tampered with the original writings, particularly when the editorial revisions have been done so deftly. But the style and language of Deuteronomy are easily tracked by any Hebrew scholar who is familiar with its distinctive phraseology and set dogmas. One brilliant biblical investigator by the name of Riehm successfully enumerated sixty-four words or phrases characteristic of the Deuteronomic School.

If—as some scholars have been fond of telling us— there existed bibles before the Bible, then it may be unhesitatingly said that this new fusion represented the first real bible of the Hebrew people. Of course, Deuteronomy continued to overshadow in importance the Yahwistic-Elohistic Record but it was essentially in this triple form that the books circulated for several gener-

---

*Traces of Deuteronomic touching up occur in Genesis 26:1-5 and in Exodus 15:26 as well as in the Decalogue given in Exodus 22.

ations—that is, until the curtain rose on the next grand performance.

4

Shortly after Ezra and Nehemiah succeeded in getting the ecclesiastical Code adopted as the supreme law of the land, a group of zealous priestly authors proceeded to assemble materials for a new history of the Hebrew people in keeping with the ritualism and priestliness of the age. They felt that full justice had not been done to the institutional side of the Hebrew nation. They aimed, therefore, to indicate the origin of the development of Israel's institutions and the historical origin of the law. They also wanted to show that each law found in their Code fits into a definite historical situation so that the new legislation could be backed up by time-honored and sacred authority. By combining History with Law they aimed to teach the people the importance of the origin of their sacred institutions together with those rites, ceremonies, and traditions they deemed necessary to safeguard the nation.

Accordingly, they began their ecclesiastical history by going as far back as the story of Creation. This they did, not primarily because they wanted to tell how God made heaven and earth and all things therein. What concerned them most was to give an adequate explanation of the origin of the Sabbath by telling how God made the world in six days and how He Himself rested on the seventh. Thus they felt that they had graphically presented the divine sanctity of this weekly institution.

Once having established the divine origin of the Sabbath they next proceeded to sketch a short and dry his-

But did these writers invent this story or did they simply record what had long been a tradition?

tory of the ten generations leading up to the big Flood and culminating in the famous covenant between God and Noah which embodies the command that the blood of sacrificed animals shall not be eaten. After still another decade of generations the story of Abraham is told in order to give patriarchical significance to circumcision as a holy rite. Then follow long genealogies broken by the stories of various experience which befell the Hebrews in the wilderness and how everything worked forward to that one superdivine event when Yahweh made a covenant with all their ancestors by giving them the great Law at Sinai.

No outline could be a more cut and dried affair than the one which these priests wrote. They pinned down the elusive pages of Hebrew History with the finality of a taxidermist transfixing a butterfly. They so artificially shaped Hebrew history that at each step they presume to accurately tell the progress of revelation, or the exact degrees by which God made Himself known to their ancestral heroes. For example, they wrote it down in their history that not until Moses' time did God reveal Himself as "Yahweh." Unto all the generations before Moses they assumed the name of the Hebrew Deity was "Elohim." For this reason they were very careful to use only the name of Elohim from Genesis down to Exodus 6:2 but from that point on they used the name "Yahweh" exclusively.*

*The name "Elohim" employed by the Priestly historians in the opening chapter of Genesis was one of the most baffling problems that confronted biblical investigators. For a long time it confused the Priestly writings with the Elohistic narratives. It was not until the middle of the nineteenth century that the solution was finally reached when it was clearly shown that these two documents use the name "Elohim" throughout Genesis. Such scholars as Hupfeld, Colenso, Graf, Riehm, Noldeke, Kuenen, Duhm, and Wellhausen deserve special mention in the halls of Science for their masterly and indefatigable labors.

By dressing up the old naïve traditions with learned patches, and by giving long lists of chronologies, names, and places, they produced a history that had the smell of the lamp and the air of authoritative documents. Of course, that is just the impression they wanted to give. History was just so much wax in their hands ready to be set by a highly artificial scheme. Accordingly, they grouped their materials to fit a well-defined plan, making it so uniform in character as to be easily recognized. It was not a popular story they were writing but an outline of history treating all events from their own priestly point of view.

It was characteristic of these ecclesiastical historians that they read back into the life of Moses, customs, traditions and institutions existing in their own day. Neither did they scruple to place into earlier times the ideas and enactments of their own age, thereby making it appear that what they themselves believed had always been the fixed creed from time immemorial. They strangely intermingled old and new conceptions. If some modern historian were to ascribe the League of Nations to the age of George Washington, or the Federal Reserve System to Abraham Lincoln he would shock his readers by gross inaccuracy. But modern ideas of history were unknown to these ancients and it would be unfair to judge them by our advanced standards. With no desire to deceive, but with nothing of the modern historical spirit, they felt a glow of satisfaction in freely projecting the ideas of their own day into the dim and distant past.

By referring to Moses what was of recent origin they were able to marshal the whole movement of Hebrew history under one great idea—ritualism. The result is that they did not write an exact or reliable history, but they did do this: they gave their own conception of the way in which the course of history should have been unfolded. This was, to be sure, a distinct advantage, for they were able to use a definitely constructed plan; and although it was extremely artificial still it served their purposes admirably well. When they finished writing their history they had it so cut and dried that they were able to take the Priest Code and set it down bodily into their work much as a skilled jeweler sets precious stones into platinum. And that is how the Priest Code was linked up with the winding course of Pentateuchal development.

5

Within a very short time after this combination of priestly Laws with priestly History was made, another group of men were quick to see that the new book afforded an excellent framework into which could be placed the Yahwistic-Elohistic Record and the Deuteronomic Document which were now in danger of being neglected and lost.

This far-sighted coterie of priests, called Redactors, dearly loved these older writings, and so in order to preserve them from being destroyed they conceived the idea of incorporating them into their new Historico-Legal Book. But in order to do this without violence to the integrity of their own writings and their own advanced theological ideas it became necessary to re-set the ancient documents—not of course in their entirety but only here and there in spots. Consequently, if they thought they could improve matters, they did not hesitate to take out certain sections and insert some of their own. Nobody thought this method of handling old documents wrong—it was merely their way of editing so as to make it possible that the older material could be fitted into the new framework. In this way, they figured, all the versions together when properly re-shaped and smoothed out would fall into a consecutive whole and tell a connected story.

And that is just what these Redactors did. Taking the Priestly Book with its orderly succession of institutional origins they fitted in—here and there—parts of the Yahwistic-Elohistic Book and by patching up the loose joints with their own editorial additions they produced a single book—with, of course, the bodily addition of Deuteronomy. The relative completeness of each narrative when segregated shows the care that was taken by these Redactors to preserve everything of distinctive value. The resulting history of the Hebrew people was better balanced and more comprehensive, while at the same time retaining all those notable characteristics which had already given value to each separate document.

By working in such a conservative spirit as this, the Redactors were able to hold intact the essential integrity of each document and—what interests us most —they allowed these documents to speak for themselves. That is how a superficial unity came to be established; and that is why it is possible to undo their labors and separate the materials they joined. In addition to combining the various documents they undertook to revise and edit them in accordance with their own views. Deep traces have therefore been left upon the text of the Bible by these revisions. Like striations grooved on the rocks by huge glaciers they are unmistakable.

When the Priestly Redactors Had Finished Their
Work the Pentateuch As We Now Know It Became
a Reality for the First Time!

6

Unfortunately we do not know the exact date when
this redaction was made final but the year 400 B. C.,
when Plato's brilliant intellect was beginning to illumi-
nate the philosophy of Greece, may be regarded as a
fairly accurate assumption. However, that is not nearly
so important as the fact that immediately following its
completion the Pentateuch acquired a sacrosanct character beyond that which was given to any other writings.

As it is read by us to-day, it represents the final
combination of four distinguishable groups of narratives, each existing previously in an independent form.
Looking at these facts, biblical scholars have made it
easy to understand the story of the fusion of the documents by using symbols to represent each group. The
Yahwistic writings were designated by the letter J (because they were written in Judah of the South). The
Elohistic writings received the designation E (because
they were from Ephraim of the North). Now, when
these two were combined they became JE. Later on,
when Deuteronomic men added their own book to the
Yahwistic-Elohistic Record it became JE + D. Still
later when the Priestly writers added their own accounts it became JED + P. Now, if R is made to stand
for the work of the Redactors, the Pentateuch in its
final form may be symbolized as Rjedp.

The welding together of four distinct documents is
significant of the Jewish spirit. That such independent

writings so wide apart in style, thought, and date could have been pieced together in one organic whole is amazing particularly when we can see for ourselves their mutually inconsistent facts set down beside each other with little attempt at harmonizing them. But it is because the Hebrew trait is essentially simple and incoherent that it could harbor wide differences without being jarred. Yet, strange as it sounds, herein lies its strength for it could consistently hold within itself inconsistent minds! . . .

7

When the Pentateuch was completed it was divided into five books. We know them to-day under the titles: Genesis, Exodus, Leviticus, Numbers, and Deuteronomy. Although these books tell a connected story, and because of many editorial revisions present a certain organic whole, still the ancient Jews did not hesitate to divide them into five volumes. The reason for the division is not far to seek. Strips of parchment upon which books of antiquity were written were of limited length and necessitated the cutting up of longer documents into shorter ones. Many Greek and Roman writers, like Homer and Virgil, have been similarly broken up into more convenient sizes.

Once completed the Pentateuch was accepted by the Jews of Palestine as their supreme guide—the revealed Will of Yahweh. In other words, the Pentateuch became a Bible—which means, a sacred and authorized book whose writings are regarded as too holy to be changed. It was this deep veneration for these five-volume documents that earned for the Hebrews the name given to them by Mohammed—Ahl Ulkitab—The People of the Book.

PART III

THE BIBLE KEEPS ON GROWING—AND THEN SUDDENLY STOPS

Here is told the growth and the final shaping of that remarkable record of a remarkable people. Like an oriental rug . . . it is woven of many colors, each one warm with the luxury of feeling.

CHAPTER I

THE ORIENTAL METHOD OF WRITING HISTORY AND HOW THE ANCIENT HEBREW HIS-TORIANS WROTE THEIR BOOKS

In the long course of Jewish history no other writings ever occupied as holy and as sublime an eminence as the Pentateuch. To its sacrosanct character the Hebrews poured out their highest veneration. While other books were, from time to time, accorded much reverence and devotion still the Pentateuch remained supereminent in its inviolable sacredness as the first and foremost Jewish Bible; for the ancient Jews felt that in the Pentateuch God had spoken to their ancestors with an immediateness and fulness of teaching not found in any other set of books.

But the literary activities of the Hebrew people were not confined to the writing of merely five books. For many centuries the prophets of Yahweh had preached great sermons which they either wrote down themselves or preserved from notes taken by their faithful disciples; historians wrote biographical sketches and dramatic stories firing the imagination of the people; chroniclers set down the annals of state; poets wrote their epics; singers composed their hymns; and philosophers compiled their wisdom teachings. Gradually, the best elements in all these varied types of literary expression were picked up and gathered together and then put into book form. The ancient Hebrews dearly loved the art of writing and many of their noted men were honorably called "Scribes." Being a people of books they would most naturally preserve the best. So, in time, those books that contained within themselves "survival values" came to be recognized as possessing a degree of sanctity—not, of course, as holy as the Pentateuch which was unique in that it purported to come directly from God to Moses—but holy in the sense that they had been preserved out of the nation's glorious past, which always appeared "golden" when viewed in retrospect.

When all the various books had been collected into a Bibliotheca Divina, a divine library, a three-fold title was bestowed upon them: They were called by the ancient rabbis *TaNaK*—an abbreviated name which stands for Torah-Neviim-Ketubim, meaning "Pentateuch-Prophets-Writings." It is this TaNaK that has come to be commonly styled the Old Testament but which in reality is not a single testament but a library of thirty-nine books grouped into three sections.

Now, what interests us most is just this triple arrangement—for thereby hangs the next part of the story of the making of the Bible.

We will get on the inside of things once it is understood that this triple division of the Old Testament is of the utmost significance: it indicates three definite stages of the process which finally resulted in the completed Hebrew Scriptures.

Just a brief survey of this interesting development will prove illuminating.

2

Let us begin with the Pentateuch.

As the first Jewish Bible the Pentateuch was accorded the highest degree of sacred recognition shortly after Ezra and Nehemiah had rounded out their great reform work. A few generations later a second group of books were assembled together and added to the Five-Books of Moses: this new addition was called Neviim or "Prophets." Later on, a further enlargement was made by appending a third group called Ketubim or "Writings."

In other words, the completed Hebrew Bible as it now stands represents a process of consecutive addition comprising three distinct sections each completed in a particular age and carrying its own rank of holiness just one step or degree above the other:

1. *The Pentateuch: most Holy*, made up of five books and completed about 444 B. C.
2. *The Prophets: sacred*, made up of twenty-one books and completed about 200 B. C.
3. *The Writings: inspired*, made up of thirteen books and completed about 100 B. C.

We have already traced the story of the origin and the compilation of the various documents of the Pentateuch and how they were finally combined into a single huge volume made up of five separate books. Once it is understood how this first section of the Hebrew Bible grew up it is comparatively easy to understand the development of the second section and the third, for they all follow a somewhat similar process.

And just to show that this is the case let us take a peep into that set of books called "The Prophets."

3

The old Hebrew tradition divided "The Prophets" into two sections: *The Former Prophets* including the books of Joshua, Judges, Samuel, and Kings; and *The Latter Prophets* consisting of material grouped into four sections: Isaiah, Jeremiah, Ezekiel, and the Twelve Minor Prophets.

In reality the so-called "Former Prophets" represent the history books of the ancient Hebrews. They were associated with the prophetic writings under the mistaken supposition that they had been written by certain of the prophets. Of course, prophetic teaching had a great deal to do with the moulding and the shaping of the national history, and so in that sense it is not difficult to understand why these books joined hands with the various collections of sermons written by the prophets and their disciples.

Unique as the Hebrew prophets were in their own way (and we shall talk about them later on), the Hebrew historians ran them a close second; for these historians were men of a deeply religious turn of mind having an eye to the significance of events in relation to the Will of God. Political history for its own sake they did not write. But because they had definite religious convictions they undertook the task of authorship with specific moral aims. For this reason, the Hebrew historical books do not simply relate facts but interpret them—that is, they endeavor to show that behind the experiences of the individual as well as the nation spiritual realities operate.

4

Because they wrote for edification rather than for information these historians were not so much concerned with the details of history as with its solemn lessons. Consequently, only those facts that illustrated their themes were selected and those things they felt were irrelevant were purposely left out. Of course, that is not the manner in which the modern historian treats his materials (but we must remember that these ancient Hebrews were not at all concerned about our modern scientific methods—in fact, strange as it may seem to some people, the ancient Hebrews actually died before modern history was born!).

Not only were their ideas about history different from ours but their methods of writing it were distinctly oriental.

We have nothing quite like it to-day.

The ancient Hebrew historian dovetailed his sources together thereby producing a literary patchwork-quilt. When a modern writer is about to produce a history he collects all available material and after a careful study and sifting rewrites the story in his own language. Not so the ancients. They produced history by a compilatory process—and just because they frequently preserved the exact language of each source it is possible to unravel the original documents they used.*

In the braiding process these Hebrew historians had much to do, for it was not a mere haphazard jumbling together of records (even a patchwork-quilt requires skill). They had to trim the materials at their disposal, making adjustments here and there and weaving together words, clauses, sentences and even whole paragraphs in order to harmonize them with more ad-

*Mr. Cecil B. DeMille, the famous motion-picture director, curiously enough employed this patchwork method in the production of "The Ten Commandments." Although it is considered as one film, in reality it contains three separate stories cleverly dovetailed into each other. First there is the biblical account of the Exodus, then there is the modern story into which the scenarist incorporated an originally independent and separate yarn about an Eurasian woman.

vanced ideas or bring them into the framework of certain theological concepts.

If modern readers were to find bound together in one volume, without regard to age and historical sequence, such diverse writers as Chaucer, Shakespeare and Tennyson he could, by his knowledge of the English language, readily separate the three yoke-mates of the binder's fancy. And so it is with these Hebrew historians. They are compilers of pre-existing documents and only add to their books such matter as suits their purposes and plans. Differences in literary characteristics, or variations in historical fact which would naturally abound in documents of diverse origins, did not trouble these men. They interest us, for we are of an analytical turn of mind.

Because of our dissecting itch these old biblical compilations have been subjected to an enormous amount of careful, scientific scratching—at times very irritating but always extremely comforting. Investigation has its disagreeable elements that suddenly crop up as well as its overtones of pleasantness that soothe our fears. But one who has his mind prepared for both will be eager to know not simply one part of the story but the entire account of how the documents of the Bible were unravelled.

So we will now continue the process.

5

After the death of Moses, which properly brings the narratives of the Pentateuch to a solemn close, Joshua became captain-in-chief of the tribes.

It has always taken a strong man to lead the Hebrew people, and so it was only natural that there

THE MOABITE STONE

Specimen of writing employed by the ancient Hebrews. In all probability
the Yahwistic and Elohistic Records were written in characters just like
this. Modern Hebrew writing (introduced by Ezra) uses another style.
This Stone is now in the **Louvre, Paris.**

should grow up a collection of stories, war-ballads, and poems dealing with the adventures of this hero. Consequently, the Book of Joshua, like the Pentateuch, is a compilation of several records woven together and finally touched up and edited.

It would be a mistake to treat the Book of Joshua as a collection of bald historical annals, particularly when so much of its prose has a poetic basis. The famous apostrophe to the sun and moon, which foolish people unfortunately have taken in a literal sense, is nothing more than a fine poetic conception—an appeal addressed to the forces of nature to lend help to the Hebrew clans:

> Sun, stand thou still upon Gibeon;
> And thou, Moon, in the valley of Aijalon.*

There are two important instances given in Greek literature that parallel this biblical event: The Iliad tells of Agamemnon praying to Zeus that the sun may not set before Priam's dwelling is overthrown; and in the Odyssey the sunset was delayed for the sake of Ulysses. That is the way things happened, poetically speaking, in those far-off days when there were no associated-press reports to give a prosaic account of what actually transpired. . . .

What interests us in the Book of Joshua is the version it gives of the conquest of Canaan which is quite different from the story told in the Book of Judges.

---

*This fragment of a poem was taken from the Book of Jashar which was an ancient collection of poetry. The following is a partial list of books mentioned in the Old Testament, all of them unfortunately lost. Much of this lost material existed long before a single chapter of the Bible was written:
(1) Book of Jashar. (2) Book of the Wars of Yahweh. (3) Book of Nathan. (4) Book of Gad. (5) Book of Jehu. (6) Book of Shemiah. (7) Book of Iddo the Seer, etc.

There is no doubt that the Book of Judges contains much older material than Joshua and therefore gives a more accurate picture of what happened in those blood and thunder days when the Hebrew tribes, just emerging out of the desert, had to match their wits against the old Canaanitish population of Palestine.

In Joshua, the picture is presented of the united armies of Israel under the command of one general conquering all of Palestine from Lebanon to the southern desert. This account relates that the conquest was a comparatively simple task speedily accomplished, for we are told that the land was partitioned among the tribes who had only to enter and take possession of the territory.

In Judges, however, a contrasting picture is painted in which we see that the struggle was not the work of a single dramatic campaign. The Hebrew tribes appear upon the scene of action as a half-civilized horde of straggling, quarrelling, nomadic clans and not a finely disciplined and united army under the banner of one leader. Neither do they make a collective invasion of the country but they are compelled to fight their way singly, tribe by tribe, getting a toe-hold here and there and holding their place by brute force. Instead of having an easy or speedy job of it, it took several hundred years of slow penetration for these desert men to entrench themselves in the new soil. And the price they paid for every inch of footing was terrific, for it was an age of half-barbarism and social chaos. With no national unity, with no established law, these scattered Hebrew clans fought desperately hard to maintain themselves against the native Canaanites. If we did not have the Book of Judges it would be difficult to get this true portrait of affairs which is really a huge canvas filled with assassinations, violence, and treachery.

We are also indebted to the Book of Judges for having preserved for us some of the oldest fragments of Hebrew literary composition—the choicest of all being the famous song of Deborah, almost contemporaneous with the event it describes. As a primitive Hebrew poem it is full of force and passion sweeping across storm and battle. Its rude verse stands as much in striking contrast to the finished and stately poetry of later Hebrew centuries as the irregular form of the early English ballads when compared to the polished measures of Tennyson.

It is this old material—songs, legends, scraps of history, poems and folklore—that we find set up in the Book of Judges. And if we look carefully into its arrangement it will be found that the ancient historian had a definite theological framework into which he carefully fitted his sources in order to illustrate his religious philosophy of history. This is clearly seen in his continually recurring formula, the peg around which the perpetual backsliding of the people is stoutly tied:

> The Children of Israel sinned against Yahweh,
> And Yahweh sold them into the hand of . . .
>
> Then the Children of Israel cried unto Yahweh,
> And Yahweh raised up for them a deliverer.

Story after story is told in terms of the above formula: a see-saw of national apostasies and repentances. First, we are told how bad the people became: by sinning against Yahweh they sank into terrible bogs of suffering and oppression—and then when they returned to their true senses and repented, Yahweh had compassion on their misery and raised up for them a real hero who crushed the enemy. Over and over again this tale is told, and thus the kaleidoscope passes before us wherein the picture of every judge is put into this framework of a sinning and suffering people that finally gets tired of sinning and repents (only to sin again).

But with repentance always comes delivery from their enemies—and that constitutes the moral that the ancient historian is trying to drive home. (It is the old story of the Stars and the Stripes: if you are good you get the stars, but if you are bad you get the stripes.) So, in reality, the Book of Judges is nothing more than a continuous cycle of naughty pictures of a wicked people whom Yahweh had to be constantly helping. Every time they got into trouble Yahweh had to pull their chestnuts out of the fire by raising up tribal heroes (judges). It was through this framework that the ancient Hebrew historian endeavored to prove to his fellow men that God is behind the wheels of human events, for the moment Yahweh is forsaken trouble always begins to brew.

6

The same noble purpose of providing religious instruction through the lessons of history is equally apparent in the books of Samuel and the Kings. Every scrap of material seemed to have some meaning for these pious authors. That is why they gathered up and shaped into connected form all kinds of independent and divergent documents including court records, royal annals, biographical sketches, and folklore. Like the histories of other ancient peoples these Hebrew records grew from age to age. It is known that the Arab historians worked in a somewhat similar fashion. They, too, took older sources and dovetailed them, interspersing here and there their own ideas. Even the Hindu compiler of the great Law-book of Manu adopted this method of skilful weaving: extensive extracts were made from older sources which were fitted together, and in this manner all that was good in the writings of the past was preserved.

As they now stand the historical sources that underlie the Books of Kings have been revamped, edited, reshaped, and revised at several different times in several different ages so that in their present form they represent a very interesting as well as a vast amount of accretive compilation. For this reason, their composite quality could hardly fail to strike the most careless observer. For example, there are two accounts of Saul's death: according to the one he committed suicide, according to the other he was slain by an Amalekite. Even so well known a story as David's encounter with the giant Goliath is made uncertain when we find in one and the same book a record that says that Goliath was slain not by David but by Elhanan.*

The Books of Kings (they were originally one) expressly mention three important sources from which their editors gathered the material to form a history of the Hebrew monarchs: The Book of the Acts of Solomon, The Book of the Chronicles of the Kings of

---

*The story in II Samuel 21:19 contradicts I Samuel 17:49. Realizing the need of getting over this difficulty some Bible translators have dishonestly inserted the words "The brother of Goliath." But these words are not found in the Hebrew text or in any of the ancient versions.

Judah, and The Book of the Chronicles of the Kings of Israel. The nature of these older documents may be inferred from the information they supplied. They contained long accounts of wars, revolutions, conspiracies, conquests, reforms, Temple affairs, and facts about various building operations. All these jumbled records were finally joined together in a rather loose historical sequence and then edited by disciples of the Deuteronomic School who set the various kings and their reigns into a cut and dried framework. In other words, the Deuteronomic disciples shaped the material at hand into an ecclesiastical history in order to illustrate the religious teachings of their school. (And inasmuch as their outstanding dogma was the centralization of worship at Jerusalem they utterly condemned all those kings who, before Josiah, had sacrificed at the old shrines!)

But despite their evident moralizings these old histories recreate the past for us with crisp simplicity and naïveté, for they tell an unvarnished story reflecting the national character with all its undisciplined passions. In fact, the biographies of Saul and David are here presented with an intimacy of detail combined with a detachment that is rare in the literature of mankind. Because the careers of these two men run the gamut of experience the stories of their lives have always been invaluable to the student of human nature. No less a person than Robert Browning knew the pricelessness of his sources when he wrote his masterpiece "Saul," re-immortalizing the first Hebrew King in a form more monumental than bronze.

CHAPTER II

THE LITERATURE OF RADICALISM IN WHICH IS TOLD THE STORY OF THE GROWTH OF THE BOOKS OF THE HEBREW PROPHETS

WHILE the historians were perfecting their histories certain prophets were beginning to commit their sermons to writing.

And what masters of language they were!

When we remember that these prophets were not bent on producing best sellers for the book market or making immortal contributions to the world's literature it is all the more amazing that they should have laid hold of such exquisite felicities of style in which to denounce the iniquities of their fellow-Hebrews. What politician in America would dare to say the things they said, or granted that he had the courage to plead for justice could he then use the majestic strength of diction employed by these ancient men? They wrote unconscious of what later ages would think—in fact, they did not care a snap of their fingers about popular approval or disapproval. They felt a sense of partnership with Yahweh, their God, and so they poured themselves forth as unconscious as a mountain torrent lashing its rocky walls. Seldom did these men hold an official position, yet they had an indefinite amount of power, sometimes enough to change the reigning dynasty.

Never has the world seen so earnest, so original, so unselfish a group of reformers. They not only went to the roots of things but they tore things up by the roots. They were Radicals—and the things they wrote were radically different from what can be found among the prophets of any other nation of antiquity; for the Hebrews were unique in that the poor and oppressed found champions. Not one of the prophets—from the greatest even unto the least—was an ambitious demagogue. At a time when all other peoples, civilized or barbarian, were steeped in superstition, these same prophets were proclaiming the recognition of one God, Creator of the World, and Father of all mankind.

But these prophets were no dried-up spouters of the old-time religion. As radicals they moved along with progress—mostly a few jumps ahead of their kinsmen. They were liberals in all things. Each prophet retained his own individuality of outlook and was not afraid to differ on vital questions. They were a courageous and original lot. Only upon one principle of their work were they obstinately dogmatic and that was their cardinal teaching that *Religion is Righteousness*. Never before or since has this fundamental truth been thundered into the ears of people with such persistency and reiteration. Nothing else mattered much to these men: Religion is Righteousness, and with this cry they lashed the iniquities of their age into fury.

Because this radical literature of the prophets covers a period of many hundreds of years it deals most naturally with ideas, situations, national and individual experiences, hopes, ambitions and disillusionments of widely separated ages.

Perhaps the oldest recorded address to be found in the Hebrew Bible is contained in that little pamphlet called the Book of Amos. Sometimes complete sermons have been preserved for us almost as fresh as though they had been spoken but yesterday, but more often only short extracts or epitomes are given. The deep interest felt by various disciples in their masters' works is evident on almost every page of this prophetic literature; for while the disciples preserved a certain nucleus of the original utterances they added many new ideas of their own and did not hesitate to put them in the mouths of their leaders. Sometimes men of prophetic gift wrote in the name of a distinguished teacher, being perfectly content to obliterate themselves. Sometimes they took an original utterance, adopted it and then wrote it over after a new fashion or dressed it up in changed clothing. Many a new book used an old title. And just because the writers of antiquity did not refrain from changing original scripts or inserting fresh matter into them, that is why the whole field of prophetic literature is extremely complex. Consequently, each book presents its own series of knotty problems as to variety of authorship, date of composition and style, together with important differences in theological and political ideas. For this reason it is not easy to enjoy the prophetic books in their present form. The modern reader who demands a connected sequence of thought is apt to be greatly disturbed when the thread he is holding in his mind suddenly breaks. Because of so many fractures and leaps in the original text he must frequently be prepared to look for the continuation of the paragraph he is reading in quite another part of the book. Most people are greatly disturbed by the very loose manner in which the individual chapters hang together. But once the reader is aware of the compilatory process by which these books have been built up he will understand that the material in his hand has been grafted upon an original nucleus—then the dislocations will be less troublesome.

2

The composite character of these prophetic writings in their present form can be seen to the best advantage when one follows the careful analysis and dissection of the Book of Isaiah.

Here is a single volume made up of no less than two (and maybe as many as a dozen) distinct contributions coming from different men living in different ages. The First and original Isaiah, he of the Judæan aristocracy in the days of King Hezekiah (720-692), has given us his work in the first thirty-three chapters of the book that bears his name.* In the remaining chapters of this same volume (with the exception of 36-39) there have been preserved the writings of another man, an unknown prophet who lived two hundred years after the original Isaiah. That this "Unknown" prophet was a product of later times, may be gleaned from two allusions to Cyrus who conquered Babylon and became its king in 538 B. C. In fact, the name of this monarch is actually mentioned in the first verse of the forty-fifth chapter—clearly indicating to the investigators that the document bearing it was not written by the same man who served under Hezekiah.

If, for example, in a sonnet attributed to Shakespeare we found unmistakable reference to Abraham Lincoln, we should be decidedly correct in our knowledge that the poem in question was not composed until after the

---

*But even in these chapters there are embedded many insertions coming from different hands.

middle of the nineteenth century. Similarly, when in a writing attributed to Isaiah who lived in the eighth century B. C. we find mention made of Cyrus, who reigned two hundred years later, it would be folly to relate the one to the other.*

Yet, notwithstanding the fact that these later sermons were appended to the First-Isaiah, the old traditions naïvely taught that they had all come from the pen of one man. It was assumed that because Isaiah was a prophet he could look down the corridors of the centuries and foresee the events of two hundred years —yes, and by divine clairvoyance easily name the very king who would conquer Babylonia. Others again declared that he may have been lifted out of his surroundings and transported into the midst of a state of affairs which did not exist until many years later!

It was a long and bitter fight that scholars waged against this medley of dogmatism and error. Even the wily old Ibn Ezra, he who detected signs of post-Mosaic documents in the Pentateuch, knew full well that many of the later chapters of this book did not belong to the original Isaiah. To biblical investigators there was no difficulty in recognizing that these later chapters came from a different hand: their language, style, background, political and theological ideas are not at all alike. The whole coloring is so utterly different that one and the same man could not have written both sections. Once these chapters of the Second-Isaiah are interpreted in the light of their true historical setting they take on real meaning and purpose—but as a

---

*Even if the Cyrus-allusions are regarded as interpolations (see Professor C. C. Torrey's latest book, "The Second Isaiah," New York, 1928) still the evidence for separating the writings of the First Isaiah from the Second is exceedingly large.

part of the "First" Isaiah they are nothing more than a complex and confusing jumble.

So it became abundantly plain to thinking people that the old synagogue and church tradition that had taught their faithful adherents to regard these books of the prophets as having been wholly written by the men whose names they now bear is without any accurate foundation. Even toward the close of the eleventh century a wise old Jewish commentator living in Cordova by the name of Moses Ibn Gikitilla had to break with the time-honored assurance when he suggested that the second-half of the Book of Isaiah was the work of a prophet near the end of the Babylonian exile.

Since Gikitilla's day biblical investigators have extended the process of scientific analysis to all the other books of the Prophetic set so that our knowledge of their composite nature is clearly established. There is not a single book devoted to the utterances and orations of the prophets but what contains a considerable amount of additional matter from outside sources.

They are all compilations.

3

The story of how the other prophetic writings were pieced together is about the same as that of the Book of Isaiah. Yet there was no one exclusive way in which these books were written and compiled. Perhaps some of the prophets possessed only condensed summaries of what they had originally said in public; others in all probability jotted down notes or fragments of notes which were preserved by their faithful disciples: and some prophets never troubled themselves to write any-

thing. Men like Amos, Hosea, and Micah spoke to the
people as the opportunity presented itself and it is very
doubtful if they ever wrote a single word. This fact
should not surprise us when we remember that many
of the great leaders of antiquity are to be placed in the
same category. Socrates, for example, wrote nothing.
Neither did Jesus. Yet all these great men left a profound impression on their audiences. Those who heard
them immediately became responsible for an "oral"
tradition which, temporarily at least, served as the
chief means of preserving the recollection of events and
utterances. Later on, perhaps in the next generation
after the prophet was dead and his voice could be heard
no more, some faithful disciple or some especially interested person would put down on parchment what
he thought best represented the original utterances.
From such scrappy materials as these the various documents of the various books were grafted on each other.

Essentially the prophet was a preacher: he spoke to
men directly. Consequently, it is often a mere accident
that his words have been preserved. As a matter of fact,
the prophetic literature as we now have it in the Hebrew Bible is a survival of a much larger activity than
we realize. Only in rare cases would the oral message
get itself on parchment. Even to-day not every preacher
has his lectures published. So it goes almost without
saying that there were prophets in Israel whose messages have been entirely lost. In the case of Jeremiah,
who survived the destruction of Jerusalem, there is a
tradition incorporated in his book which represents
him as dictating his utterances to a scribe: "Then Jeremiah called Baruch the son of Neriah; and Baruch
wrote from the mouth of Jeremiah all the words of the

Lord, which He had spoken unto him, upon a roll of a book."* But Jeremiah must not be taken as an example. He represents a transition period from the "speaking" prophets to the "writing" prophets. Later on, when we come to Ezekiel, we have the completed evolution, for here is a prophet concerning whom it is doubtful if he ever spoke. His chief activity consisted in getting his thoughts in written form and circulating the copies. For this reason his book shows more unity than any other book in the prophetic collection.

Great men always left an impression so that even in their lifetime certain pamphlets setting forth their main ideas must have found a limited circulation. And particularly after the death of the prophet his disciples would most naturally be eager to supplement his teachings, or in some way strive to hold together a permanent memorial of his work. It was this burning desire to preserve the fragments, even amid the cruellest vicissitudes of the ages, that constitutes one of the most amazing facts of Hebrew history. While they were alive the prophets were hated, taunted, despised, stoned and persecuted—yet what they said somehow never died:

> Truth crushed to earth shall rise again,—
> The eternal years of God are hers;
> But Error, wounded, writhes in pain,
> And dies among his worshippers.

4

How were all these prophetic books and pamphlets massed together in one volume?

Unfortunately no one knows the exact answer and

*Jeremiah 36:1-5.

the old traditions on this point are vague and unreliable so that all that can be told is a bare and fragmentary outline, most of which is lost in the haze of antiquity. The best reconstruction of the story would run somewhat like this.

About two hundred years after the Pentateuch had been given a rigid and sacrosanct form there came over the Jewish people an intense desire to preserve the works of the prophets. So, around the year 200 B. C.* these various prophetic documents were collected into a single volume where they were grouped according to certain notions. It is evident, for example, that these prophetic books were not arranged in the order of their historical sequence. The men who planned this classification (whoever they were) certainly were not especially concerned with chronological problems or the question of correct dates. What mostly interested them was the greatness of the "message," and not whether one prophet lived three hundred years before the other. And because the work of such men as Isaiah, Jeremiah and Ezekiel bulked larger in size than the pamphlets of Amos or Hosea they were given first position as "major" prophets.

When these books were finally brought together they were put into circulation as one completed volume (which meant that no more writings could be added). The Prophetic Books now became rigid and fixed; or, to use an ancient expression: "They were sealed."

And now that the writings of the accredited prophets were stamped with the hallmark of recognition they became available in convenient form to the masses

*Proof that the Prophetic collection was complete by 200 B. C. is supplied by a reference in the original work of Ben Sirach which dates from 180 B. C. This reference in Sirach enumerates the Twelve Prophets.

of the people who read their noble utterances with great delight and with deep religious fervor. There was something in these messages that touched the hearts of men and women. Next in importance to his written law the Jew placed the books of those wondrous men who had prefaced their utterances with, "Thus saith the Lord." And although many of the prophets had lived in an old and far-away world yet they had said things strangely near to the needs, sorrows, hopes and temptations of every age. So it was only natural that the completed volume began to take on a certain degree of "holiness" which grew from year to year until, by popular esteem and veneration, it came to be regarded as "sacred" literature, second only to the authority and solemnity of the Pentateuch.

CHAPTER III

THE ZIGZAG ORIGIN OF THOSE MISCELLANEOUS
DOCUMENTS CALLED "THE WRITINGS" AND
HOW THE PEOPLE CAME TO REGARD
THEM AS INSPIRED

HEBREW history may be represented by an unbroken
series of books piled on top of each other with monumental grandeur.

Other peoples of antiquity immortalized themselves
in stone: the Pyramids of Egypt, the Temple of Diana
at Ephesus, the Coliseum at Rome. But the Jew just
wrote. He carved no statues in marble but he carved a
place for his thoughts. And the more he wrote the
more prolific he became. For hardly had the Prophetic
Books settled down to a rigid and fixed collection when
the making of a new set got started.

It is to the formation of this new group of books that
we now turn our attention, for many of them stirred up
quite a hot and dusty discussion before the ancient
rabbis were willing to admit them to a place of sanctity alongside of the older sacred volumes. Of course,
both the Pentateuch and the Prophetic Books were already regarded as unique in that one collection represented mainly the legal side of Hebrew literature and
the other the direct oracle of inspiration through the
gift of prophecy. Should or should not the Scriptures
be limited to just these two sections, or should it be

expanded to embrace a third?—that was the question the Bible makers had to face.

Just because a good book could not be compressed into the categories of Law and Prophecy was no reason why it should perish. If Yahweh spoke to men through these two already acknowledged mediums, of Law and Prophecy, did He not also speak just as truly through a proverb, a psalm, a memoir, or a piece of fiction? Then why shut out those meritorious books that were just miscellaneous in character simply because they were not fortunate enough to have secured a place for themselves in the two older collections?

That the ancient Hebrews came to appreciate the need of preserving a large variety of these newer and more miscellaneous books (even though they did not fall within the limits of either Law or Prophecy) satisfactorily explains the gradual and almost imperceptible formation of the Third Section of the Old Testament into a definite group called "Writings." It is in this newer set that the modern man finds the most interesting books of the Hebrew Bible—for here is a vast and interesting mixture of all sorts of things coming from many different ages. It is a grab-bag containing moral philosophy, hymns, dirges, romances, proverbs, psalms, idylls, love songs, apocalypses—all massed together!

Because things move slowly in the Orient it took a long time for these books of the Third section to win for themselves recognition as Scripture. It was only after a very long period of probation, full of curious windings in and out (the details will be given later) that they were finally admitted into the Bible. But they all had to run the gauntlet. When the race was finished the following books successfully emerged from a near-scriptural position to a fixed place within the Old Testament. Here they are:

Psalms
Proverbs
Job
Song of Songs
Ruth
Lamentations
Ecclesiastes
Esther
Daniel
Ezra
Nehemiah
I Chronicles
II Chronicles

2

Because of their high spiritual pedigree and intrinsic value in promoting the religious life of the nation the Psalms were placed first in the new collection. The idea that King David had a large share in their authorship was another strong reason why these devotional pieces were given such a high rank.

Nothing could be more certain than that no one man wrote all the psalms. That the tradition of the rabbis attributed them to King David was a part of that old oriental practice of circulating literary productions under the name of a national hero. To Moses they assigned all Law; to David they attributed the Psalms; and to Solomon was given the undeserved honor of being the author of Proverbs, Song of Songs, and Ecclesiastes. According to the Talmud, Moses even wrote the

Book of Job; and according to this same stream of extravagant tradition Abraham co-operated with David in writing the 89th psalm! Of course, the modern biblical scientist knows that many books were palmed off on the people under assumed or traditional names, perhaps without the slightest intention of fraud. It was just an old oriental habit which has curious survivals even to-day. (Did Colonel Chas. Lindbergh himself write the book "We" which now circulates with his name as author?)

As a matter of fact, the Psalms had a long literary history before people even thought of placing them in the Third section of the Bible. The very structure of the Book of Psalms reveals itself as a combination of smaller units, testifying to a process of successive development. Like all the other books we have thus far examined, the Psalms are composite in style, character, age, vocabulary and ideas. Over and over again they were revised and adapted in the long course of their development. Biblical scholars have written whole libraries on the subject of the Psalms in order to trace in minute detail the intricate story of those various stages of editing, compilation, and collection through which they passed. . . . Like wheels within wheels there are psalms within psalms.*

Three main divisions are revealed in this agglomerate mass of songs and poems (although these in turn are made up of so many smaller collections that it is almost impossible to bring out a clear-cut arrangement when none apparently exists).

---

*A few instances will illustrate this:
(a) Psalm 14 recurs as Psalm 53 (with variations).
(b) Psalm 31:1-3 is identical with Psalm 71:1-3.
(c) Psalm 108 is a combination of portions from 57 and 60.
(d) Psalm 40:13-17 recurs as 70, etc., etc.

The first forty psalms (2-41) are sometimes called the "Davidic" collection because most of them bear an ascription to the shepherd-king. The second collection (42-83) is known by biblical scholars as the "Elohistic" group and refers to those psalms in which the Hebrew name Elohim is used to designate the Divine Being, to the exclusion of the term Yahweh. The third collection (90-150) is made up mostly of anonymous pieces and is characterized by a complete absence of the familiar musical terms so frequent in the two preceding groups.

Originally, these three collections were independent of each other—this is clearly seen in the repetition of titles and the re-occurrences of actual pieces. Many pages could be written showing how this was done, but that would occupy too much time. One very characteristic example will suffice. If the reader will take the trouble to compare Psalm 14 with Psalm 53 he will not fail to observe that Psalm 53 which is in the Second collection is nothing more than an Elohistic revision of Psalm 14.

Is it possible to put our finger on any psalm that David himself wrote? No one can say with any amount of assurance. If David actually wrote poetry—and there is no reason to doubt that he could—then certain fragments may yet be preserved in this section of the Bible. Or, at least there may be a thin nucleus of his compositions. But where to find these fragments or how to put our finger on the nucleus is a problem that defies solution. It is just as impossible to locate the original psalms of David as it would be to find the original Ten Commandments of Moses. All ancient poetical compositions have been worked over by so many successive generations that the originals have not only been largely obliterated but what remains of them has been absorbed into adaptations and readaptations. . . .

When due allowance is made for a few psalms that bear marks of an early origin (and there is much evidence that psalms were written in the earliest days) still over nine-tenths of the total collection dates from the period after the Babylonian Exile. Many of the psalms, like the little collection known as the Psalms of Korah, were used by the choir-guilds in the Second Temple. This means that the Temple had a hymn book and the musical psalms were just those old hymns used over and over again so that our present collection grew up like Topsy. Viewed in this light, as an aggregation of several smaller groups, it is safe to say that the Psalms were compiled between the rebuilding of the Second Temple in 516 B. C. and the time of their inclusion in the Bible, presumably around 100 B. C.

While the Book of Psalms was meant to be a Jewish hymn book it has become—and this is the marvel—the book of devotion for all mankind. Although written in the language of an oriental people it is now as much the possession of the Occident as Dante, Shakespeare, or Ibsen. People know the psalms better than any other portion of the Hebrew Bible; and more non-Jews sing them week in and week out than ever chanted their sweetness in the most glorious days of ancient Jerusalem.

Although these Psalms were the cultic-hymns of the ancient Jews they embodied the finest type of poetical expression—and as pure poetry they have never ceased to interest and delight the world. Several years ago, when the author was a student at the University of

Chicago, he participated in the Florence James Adams Contest which annually confers prizes for the reading of poetry. While quite gratified to have won the first award, he was more elated over the choice of his winning selections. Each contestant had to read three poems, whereupon he chose the following: Psalm 139, Richard Le Gallienne's "May is Building Her House," and Vachel Lindsey's "Congo." Of the three pickings Psalm 139 received the most enthusiastic commendation. . . . As he carried off the gift of a seventy-five dollar check he wondered if the ghost of him who wrote the ancient hymn failed to smile.

Hundreds of men—it makes no differences if their exact names are unknown—wrote these Psalms. Consequently, the book is an anthology of devotion expressing every subtle shade of feeling from tender love to rank and cursing hatred. When at times we find in some of the Psalms elements of bitterness we must remember that they were written more than two thousand years before the civilized nations of the world (1914-1918) began to improve upon these old curses with their own up-to-date battle songs of lust and Hymns of Hate. . . .

3

Like the Book of Psalms the Book of Proverbs is a huge compilation from many sources. The old Jewish tradition naïvely ascribed the entire volume to Solomon notwithstanding the fact that the book itself expressly stipulates that certain sections came from different, and originally independent works.

In reality, Proverbs is a huge scrap-book containing those wise sayings of ancient Israel which over the centuries were minted into proverbial small coin. No one man could have written all the documents wrapped up in this book any more than one man could have penned the entire Psalm literature. Not in one age but in many were these tiny gems of inspiration gathered up and strung together. It is now a beautiful necklace, but it certainly has its separate beads.

A close investigation of this miscellaneous collection reveals at least eight pamphlets and a preface:

1. The Praise of Wisdom (chs. 1 to 9)
2. The Proverbs of Solomon (chs. 10 to 22:16)
3. The Words of the Wise (chs. 22:17 to 24:22)
4. Further Words of the Wise (chs. 24:23-34)
5. A Second Collection of the Proverbs of Solomon (chs. 25 to 29)
6. The Words of Agur (ch. 30)
7. The Words of King Lemuel (ch. 31:1-9)
8. The Praise of a Good Woman (ch. 31:10-31)

There is an old tradition about Solomon preserved in the Book of Kings that says he "was wiser than all men: and he spoke three thousand proverbs and his songs were a thousand and five." Maybe this item was originally just a royal publicity note, or it may be an exaggeration due to the idealization of a later age—(as the number of his wives was exaggerated to the staggering figure of one thousand)! No one knows exactly how many proverbs Solomon wrote. During his day the people of Jerusalem had large contacts with Egypt, Solomon himself having married a daughter of Pharaoh. The recently discovered Egyptian Book of Proverbs called the "Teaching of Amen-em-ope" seems beyond any doubt to have been used in compiling certain sections of this Hebrew document. The coincidences in thought, language, and style, as found, for example, in chapters 20:17 to 23:11, are so precisely like the Egyptian that it is impossible to believe the similarity to be purely accidental. . . . Yet no matter how much may be shown to have been borrowed, there undoubtedly is some measure of truth embodied in the Solomon tradition. He must have possessed shrewd native wit. But the bald reference in the Book of Kings could hardly be used to accurately detect the exact number of his original utterances.

Many isolated maxims in Proverbs go back to a high antiquity, but even these are so universal in character that it is impossible to assign a definite age to their composition. In all probability Solomon had a hobby of collecting proverbs just like certain people collect stamps. And it may be that his royal collection was the beginning of that larger collection that is now associated with his name—but nobody knows.

4

No one knows who wrote that daring drama called the Book of Job. Ancient Hebrew tradition sometimes ascribed it to Moses. In reality it is an anonymous document built up from an old folklore tale with Job as hero. Into this ancient framework the unknown author fitted the various discussions about life and its many dark problems thereby making out of Job a kind of Hebrew Prometheus bound hand and foot in the clutch of circumstances. And so, enmeshed in life itself— which may become at times the most horrible of all entanglements—it was no easy job for poor Job to get out. Perhaps Maeterlinck had the old fellow in mind when he wrote that fine thought on patience: "Man was only born but yesterday and has as yet scarcely begun to disentangle himself from chaos."

In its present form the Book of Job is a product of what historians call the "post-exilic" period of Hebrew literature. It is to be properly dated in the fifth or fourth century B. C.—that is, after the return of the Jews from Babylon. Coming from that far-off age (when Europe was in savagery and barbarism) it is nothing short of the wonderful to read Job's attempted portrait of himself, which may be taken to be a sketch of what the post-exilic age expected from its ideal Jew.

> I delivered the poor when he cried,
> The Orphan and him that had no helper.
> The blessing of him that was ready to perish came upon me,
> And I caused the widow's heart to sing for joy.
> I put on righteousness, and it clothed me;
> My justice was a robe and a diadem.
> I was eyes to the blind, and feet to the lame.
> I was a father to the needy,
> And the cause of him I knew not I searched out.
> And I broke the jaws of the unrighteous
> And plucked the prey out of his teeth.*

While Job is one of the most serious books of the Bible in its portrayal of the gloom and depression that overwhelmed an innocent man, still there is in the volume one gleam of humor. Job, as we know, was suffering not only physically but mentally, being tossed about by terrific storms of doubt. What he needed from his friends was sympathy and understanding, but instead they irritated him by their overweening conceit. Because he had been brought low they felt the need of

*Job 29:12-17.

lifting themselves high. Their glib tongues rolled off
a supercilious philosophy that nettled the old man. In-
. dignant at their vaunted superiority Job cut them with
satire:

> No doubt ye are the people
> And wisdom shall die with you.*

5

No one knows who wrote that choice piece of scep-
ticism called Ecclesiastes. Whatever may have been the
true name of the author there is no doubt that he hides
himself under a nom de plume when he calls himself
"Koheleth." He aimed to identify his personality with
Solomon as one who had amassed great wealth and
was "wiser than all who were before me in Jerusalem."

While it is the least biblical of all the books of the
Bible perhaps Ecclesiastes is the most human—surely
the most modern in tone and outlook. It employs a late
form of the Hebrew language so that it is certain that
Solomon could no more have been its author than
George Washington could have written Mr. H. L.
Mencken's *Prejudices*. Instead of the robust faith of
the Judæan highlands Ecclesiastes breathes a Greek atmosphere of melancholy and cold-blooded cynicism.
"It reminds me," wrote a great scholar, "of the remains
of a daring explorer, who has met with some terrible
accident, leaving his shattered form exposed to the en-
croachments of all sorts of foul vermin." Schopen-

---

*It is related that in Colonial New England a group of self-righteous in-
dividuals one day met in solemn assembly and passed three resolutions
whereupon the ghost of Job suddenly entered the room and pointing a
bony finger cried aloud: "No doubt ye are the people." These were the
resolutions:

First, Resolved that God made the world.
Second, Resolved that God made the world for His saints.
Third, Resolved that we are the saints!

hauer, who was a pessimist de luxe, once said that no one can fully appreciate Ecclesiastes until he is seventy!

Many striking similarities to the ideas and thoughts of Ecclesiastes may be found in non-Jewish writers, which all goes to prove that no one nation has a monopoly on pessimism. On the general theme of the emptiness of life, which Ecclesiastes pours out on almost every page of his book, Omar Khayyam matches that thought with the following lines:

> And this was all the Harvest that I reaped,
> I came like Water and like Wind I go.

. . . Perhaps more deeply pathetic (and at the same time more humorous) is the aching sigh of an old Greek:

> Here lie I, Dionysius of Tarsus, aged sixty years;
> I never wed; I wish my father had never.

6

Like the Book of Ecclesiastes no one knows anything about the individual authors who wrote that collection of voluptuous songs on Love entitled "The Song of Songs." Some scholars are inclined to believe that long before they were appropriated by the Hebrews and transformed for biblical purposes these songs were connected with the Babylonian religion, the Tammuz-Ishtar cult. Prof. T. J. Meek of Toronto has recently shown that "the structure of the songs is the same (two lovers representing god and goddess wooing each other and alternating in the praise of each other's charms); the general theme is the same (love); many of the phrases are quite identical. Both are liturgies of the fertility cult. . . ."

Nobody knows who wrote Lamentations or that novel called Esther. These books are all anonymous. The old traditions of the synagogue and the church that ascribed Lamentations to the pen of Jeremiah, and the composition of the Book of Esther to Mordecai, are nothing more than pious guess-work.

No one knows the name of that reverend gentleman who penned the Book of Daniel. For many centuries people have believed that Daniel himself was its author and that its story is a contemporary record of a captive Jew at Babylon in the beginning of the sixth century B. C. But this traditional view is no longer tenable. The Book of Daniel belongs to the Maccabean period, and reflects that age in its grotesque fancies and apocalyptic pictures. One should not think of Daniel as sober history but rather as a politico-religious romance. The year 167 B. C. may be taken as a fairly approximate date during which this story made its appearance. But even this should not be construed as precluding many elements in the book which are undoubtedly far older than the Maccabean uprising. . . .

And nobody knows who wrote the Book of Ruth, that most delightful of all ancient novels. Whoever the author was he has left a trail of pleasantness over the centuries haunting us like a vague and subtle perfume. The Book of Ruth has sweetened and gladdened the world. Millions of hearts have been touched by its simplicity and charm. It was this little love-idyll that made such a deep impression on Benjamin Franklin; and it may be that his fondness for it helped make him "the first civilized American."

7

If the reader will now open his Bible to the last verses of Second Chronicles and compare them with the opening verses of the Book of Ezra it will cause him less astonishment when scientific biblical scholarship declares that these books were originally one. The ending of Chronicles and the beginning of Ezra are the same; only it appears that the manuscript of Chronicles was torn in two at the wrong place: because the Book of Chronicles actually ends in the middle of a sentence!

II Chronicles 36:22 ff.	*Ezra 1:1 ff.*
Now in the first year of Cyrus, King of Persia, that the word of the Lord by the mouth of Jeremiah might be accomplished, the Lord stirred up the spirit of Cyrus, king of Persia, that he made a proclamation throughout all his kingdom, and put it also in writing saying: Thus saith Cyrus, king of Persia; All the kingdom of the earth hath the Lord, the God of heaven, given me and He hath charged me to build Him a house in Jerusalem, which is in Judah. Whosoever there is among you of all His people— the Lord his God be with him— let him go up. (The end)	Now in the first year of Cyrus, king of Persia, that the word of the Lord by the mouth of Jeremiah might be accomplished, the Lord stirred up the spirit of Cyrus, king of Persia, that he made a proclamation throughout all his kingdom, and put it also in writing, saying: Thus saith Cyrus, king of Persia: All the kingdoms of the earth hath the Lord, the God of heaven, given me; and he hath charged me to build Him a house in Jerusalem, which is in Judah. Whosoever there is among you of all His people— his God be with him—let him go up to Jerusalem, which is in Judah, and build the house of the Lord, the God of Israel, He is the God who is in Jerusalem.

Together with the books of Ezra and Chronicles must be placed the memoirs of Nehemiah. Originally, all these four volumes formed one large work entitled "Dibre Ha-jamin"—that is, "Annals," sketching the history of the Hebrew people from Adam down to the rebuilding of the Second Temple in 516 B. C.

Taken as a whole and re-arranged to tell a consecutive story these four books show themselves to be an historical compilation compacted partly out of auto-biographical materials written by Ezra and Nehemiah and partly out of older historical records. Like all the other books of the Old Testament these "Annals" were pieced together in such a way that the joints are easily recognizable once the reader's attention is called to them.

The question: Who wrote these Annals and why? involves an answer almost as intricate as the one we have just traced on the formation of the Pentateuch. And while the exact names of the men who worked them up are unknown there is no doubt that they were ecclesiastics of the Jerusalem Temple, for every page of their document drips with priestliness.

In order to fully grasp this let us cast a backward glance into the days following the return from Babylon.

After the Second Temple was rebuilt and the priests were in control of all things spiritual as well as temporal the need arose for a comprehensive history that would tell the whole story of the Hebrew People from a priestly standpoint. A new age always brings a new point of view (witness, for instance, the present day American histories which treat the Revolution of 1776 quite differently than the text-books of seventy-five years ago). Now the ancient Hebrews moved along with progress. It was only natural, having gone through the experience of the Babylonian Exile and the rebuilding of the Temple, that their priests felt that many things not so clearly understood by those who wrote before the Exile needed revamping. For example, the very existence of the Priest Code (unknown before the Exile) necessitated a new outlook and compelled a complete revaluation. All the former histories had been written before the Priest Code came into existence—consequently the older histories not only were full of unedifying stories but they contained much that was obsolete and superfluous. The newer age, so these priests felt, had brought with it a clearing of vision as to the nature of the nation's past, and many things originally not properly viewed or understood needed a corrective judgment in the light of the newer knowledge.

So, with these feelings uppermost in their minds, the priests set about writing a whole new history of the Hebrew people—it was to be a brand-new version. The ground already covered by such books as Joshua, Judges, Samuel and Kings was deliberately paralleled, only more attention was now given to the ministry of the Temple. To these priestly historians everything centred about the history of the ritual. Consequently, in order to include the story of the Babylonian Exile and the re-establishment of the Temple they went beyond the older documents and brought their account up to date by utilizing the memoirs of Ezra and Nehemiah. When they finished writing their history they had produced a new story (—or rather the old story in a new dress) which they called Dibre Ha-jamin—or the "Annals."

8

Now, when we compare the Books of Chronicles with the earlier national histories we are struck by several singular features which at once indicate this newer priestly point of view. The whole story of the Northern Kingdom (told at great length by the ancient histories) is almost entirely ignored by the newer priestly writers (the obvious reason being that the northern tribes had no allegiance to the Temple at Jerusalem: So why rehearse irrelevant things?). When it came to the sins of David and Solomon, which the older books portrayed in unvarnished language, the priests were scandalized by the odious blemishes; consequently, it was necessary to soften these discords. And so David's adultery and the rebellion of his sons are passed over in silence. Anyhow, why bring that up? Will the rehearsal of such unpleasant things tend to edify the people? And inasmuch as Solomon established the sacred Temple at Jerusalem why devote any space to the foreign women in his harem or dilate upon the looseness of his moral life? Isn't it much better to whitewash all these awkward and ugly facts?

No doubt the priests were right, after the fashion of their own thinking. And it is just because of such hyper-sensitive, moralizing ideas as these that they unhesitatingly blue-penciled everything that was undignified or odious. Consequently, the Books of Chronicles are nothing more than a priestly recast of Hebrew history in which the veil is carefully drawn over the faults and the mistakes of the old heroes and kings. By seeking to present the past in a puritanical dress they produced the story of their nation with a minimum of tarnish. We must remember that these priests were intense patriots; and patriotism as they saw it demanded a glorious past free from all manner of stain and blemish.

More than this. These priests were impressed with the idea: that whatever is had always been. Accordingly, they ascribed to previous ages the religious mo-

tives prevailing in their own. Having been trained
under the influence of the Priest Code, which distorts
Hebrew history by reading back into the past a ritual
development of a later period, it was only natural for
them to continue teaching and writing along this same
line. It is not sober history that we read in Chronicles
but an ecclesiastical romance. For that reason we ought
not be too hasty to blame the authors. They wrote as
children of the age in which they lived and such a conception of history was a part of their sacred creed. They
did not nonchalantly accept it—they passionately believed it! To them it was not distortion: it was the
Truth. And that is why, apparently with the purest
motives, these Chronicle-priests turned secular history
into Church history, habitually addressing the people
as a "congregation."

Just as Karl Marx in his Socialism sought the explanation of history in terms of a rigid "economic
interpretation"; and just as Sigmund Freud in his Psy-
cho-analysis sets up a strong emphasis upon "sex fac-
tors" as the master-key to unlock the tangled skein of
life's complexities; so these ancient Hebrew priests believed that the correct interpretation of their people's
history was to be found in the story of the establishment of the Temple with all its huge interests: priests,
levites, sacrifices, ceremonies, taxes, purification laws,
vessels, robes, furniture, musicians, gate keepers—and
a thousand and one details of ritual. It was one vast
scheme of holy things closely knitted together in all its
parts. When we read the two Books of Chronicles we
are really soaking up church history: it is as though a
group of London prelates had written the story of
Anglo-Saxon civilization in terms of the established
Church of England.

Because they present a distorted picture in the interests of their ceremonials and theology the records of Chronicles are filled with amplifications, idealizations and grand embellishments. Throughout the length and breadth of their pages there is a flourishing of high numbers and sweeping accounts. Their newer view of history demanded that the past be treated with grandeur and glamour: consequently, idealization of the old-time heroes went hand in hand with a high-powered exaggeration. In the older Books of Samuel, David is pictured as an outlaw who afterward succeeded in carving out an Empire with his sword—but in Chronicles he is transformed into a saint. In II Samuel 8:4, we are told that in David's victory over Hadadezer, king of Zobah, he took from the latter "a thousand and seven hundred horsemen." In I Chronicles 18:4 this figure is altered and David is now represented as having taken "a thousand chariots and seven thousand horsemen." In II Samuel 24:24, David is reported to have paid Araunah for his threshing-floor fifty shekels of silver. In I Chronicles 21:25 this old figure is exaggerated to "six hundred shekels of gold by weight." In II Samuel 6:1, David's warriors are numbered at "thirty thousand,"—but in I Chronicles 12:23-27 the figure is raised to more than three hundred thousand. . . . Such is the oriental imagination once it begins to frolic.

Like the Elohistic men, who toned down the crudities of the Yahwistic writings, so do these priests correct the ethical inadequacies of the old histories. Morality, like everything else in this world, has a history. And what passed muster in the days of rough warriors did not get by these educated priests.

One striking example—full of significance and in-

dicative of the tremendous moral progress made since
the early days—occurs in the story about King David
and the census. According to the old account in the
Book of Samuel, God is represented as having moved
David to number the people, for which, in a very capri-
cious mood (characteristic of old Yahweh), He afterward inflicted a plague on the innocent multitude.
This story was downright offensive to the higher ethical sense of these Chronicle-priests and so when they
wrote up a new account of the census they said that
Satan, not God, had incited David to do this thing.
And consequently it was Satan who inflicted the
plague!*

9

Satan—or God? Herein lies the whole difference between barbarism and civilization. Within the circum-
ference of that one little alteration in the Book of
Chronicles the story of the ethical evolution of the Hebrew religion is daringly told. For when a people can
regard the actions of their old and worn-out gods as
synonymous with the wiles of the Devil they have
taken the mightiest step forward. . . .

It is the tyranny of the dead that crushes a nation:
dead ideas, dead ancestors, dead laws, dead gods. And
the Hebrew priests were just strong enough not to be
crushed! They not only wrote a vigorous code of new
laws to surpass the old but they courageously undertook to write a new history with the idea of improving
upon the crude conceptions of primitive days. It is this
spirit of progression in ideas that they breathed into

*The references to the above passages are found in II Samuel 24:1 and
I Chronicles 21:1.

their people (despite the rigidity of the ritual they exalted) that has characterized the long course of Hebrew history. As "the thoughts of man are widened with the process of the suns," so each age clamored for its own particular expression. The new epoch had brought a maturer theology, and consequently the need for changing the old-time beliefs. So, in harmony with ethical progress—which is everywhere exhibited throughout the Old Testament—these priests frankly admitted that the Yahweh of their ancestors who could act so capriciously as to inflict a plague on innocent people was not their conception of what should be the conduct of the Divine Being. . . .

Like all the other religions of the Orient the religion of the Hebrews began as a cult devoted to sacred stones and trees. It tolerated the use and worship of images (teraphim). Its initial morality was the crude morality of the Stone Age. But as the thinking of primitive man improved his religion and his idea of God moved upward. When viewed in the light of scientific biblical study, the Old Testament is in reality a wondrous record of an upward climb filled with many backslidings but eventually reaching its destined peak. In it we see the workings of a slow and painful struggle from half-civilized ideas up to a high form of ethical monotheism. Out of the childlike fancies of the primitive oriental world the Hebrew mind shaped the loftiest and the most profound spiritual conceptions. And this constitutes its legacy to Civilization.

Once the modern reader of the Bible is made aware of this little known but fascinating story of moral and religious development contained within the Hebrew Scriptures he is apt to get that glow of satisfaction which passed over a little girl who having been shown for the first time the difference between the story in Chronicles and that of Samuel remarked quite naïvely: "My, how God has improved!"

CHAPTER IV

BY LIMITING THE OLD TESTAMENT TO BUT THREE SECTIONS THE ANCIENT RABBIS STOPPED THE GROWTH OF THE HEBREW BIBLE

"Of the making of books there is no end."

So said the wise man who wrote Ecclesiastes—the Omar Khayyam of the Old Testament.

He must have known what he was talking about because the little country of Palestine, toward the close of the second century B. C., was overrun with a murrain of growing volumes. Somebody had to call a halt, otherwise the sacred literature would know no bounds. For no sooner had the third section of the Bible been "sealed" and affiliated with the Pentateuch than a fourth division began growing into prominence This fourth collection of books is commonly known as the "Apocrypha," consisting of fourteen documents which at one time or another were regarded by the people as sacred scripture.*

Had the ancient rabbis permitted the expansion process to go on these books would have undoubtedly formed the next section of the Hebrew Bible, for even those people who did not venerate them as sacred scripture nevertheless esteemed them as "near-scrip-

*The following books make up the Apocrypha:

I Esdras	Baruch
II Esdras	Song of the Three Children
Tobit	History of Susanna
Judith	Bel and the Dragon
Remainder of Esther	Prayer of Manasses
Wisdom of Solomon	I Maccabees
Wisdom of Sirach	II Maccabees

tural." But history decreed against them. The continued growth of the Old Testatment was stopped short by an exclusion act; for the rabbis were determined that the Scriptures were to consist of only three sections: Pentateuch, Prophets and Writings. There was to be no fourth part. And so the Apocryphal books were deliberately kept out of the strict limits of the authoritative sacred literature.*

This drastic action on the part of the rabbis shows how greatly alarmed they were at the manner in which all kinds of books were flooding the market. Something had to be done. If not, where would it all end? So, in order to discuss the important matter of limiting the Bible—the rabbis were always fond of discussion—they determined to meet together from time to time in semi-national assemblies. Various councils occupied themselves with these grave questions until the famous Council of Jamnia (100 A. D.) gathered up all the loose ends of scriptural argument and once for all brought final and authoritative agreement. When the smoke of discussion died down the *completed Hebrew Bible as we now have it emerged*.

2

Besides the Apocrypha there was a large and growing number of books that were being circulated under false names—books that are now classed as Pseudepigrapha, which means "falsely ascribed." Although that is a long and cumbersome title it fittingly char-

---

*Several centuries after the rabbis had excluded the Apocryphal books from the Jewish Bible the question of their canonicity was taken up by Christianity which engaged in a bitter controversy over them. The Catholic Church stubbornly maintained that these books were true scripture whereas the Protestants just as stubbornly excluded them.

acterizes those writings which profess to be by authors from whom they are not in reality derived. Not only were they rejected from the synagogue by the Jews but the Christian leaders also energetically opposed them. They were literary trouble-breeders of the worst kind.

One of the most famous of this group was called the "Book of Enoch," professing to come from the pen of an ancient biblical character by that name. Another book called "The Assumption of Moses" makes an effort to be an authentic account of an address of Moses to Joshua in which the great Lawgiver foretells the course of history. In the "Testament of the Twelve Patriarchs" each of the twelve sons of Jacob appears and relates his life history. Without the least scruple the most curious and fantastic ideas were put into the mouths of ancient heroes. There were, in addition to these more important Pseudepigrapha, a pestiferous host of lesser ones claiming to have been written by Abraham, Job, Adam—in fact, the name of any hero who was long dead was deliberately used to express the thoughts of a living author.

In the light of this situation it is not difficult to understand why the rabbis were alarmed. What concerned them most was the irresponsible way in which people were mingling the latest editions of these newer authors with the ancient holy documents. In other words, the rabbis felt that it was high time to draw a definite line between the really old literature and the newer crop of books that were now clamoring for attention and confusing the people. Even way back in the second and first century B. C. (just as now in the twentieth century A. D.) the latest books were the noisiest! By their fictitious titles and fantastic claims they were fast placing the sacred classics in danger of serious neglect. There was only one way to handle this situation and that was to come to the immediate defense of the old-time Holy Books.

3

It was not an easy matter to settle the intricate problem of what should or should not constitute Scripture. In fact, it took many years of acrimonious debate to finally decide what books should be included in the Bible and what ones excluded. The wise men wavered in their opinions almost as much as they agreed. And many a battle royal was staged. Perhaps the fiercest bout of them all was fought over the "Song of Songs." Being a collection of erotic love-poems of the most sensual kind it is no wonder that many rabbis found it offensive. Only the supposition that the Songs had been written by King Solomon permitted the collection to have any standing whatsoever, for the "Song of Songs" never once mentions the name of God, it contains no word of prayer or praise and lacks all concern in theological problems. Then why have it in the Bible? asked the old-time Puritans.

Just about as it was ready to be hammered down, a gifted man with a mind strangely capable of all kinds of fantastic interpretations stepped to its rescue. His name was Rabbi Akiba, and he was an acknowledged leader and mystic. In deep and impressive tones he told the assembly a few things about the Song that no one before had ever known. He said that the Song, far from being a profane document, was the holiest and most sacred of all books in the third division of Scripture. Then he went on to indicate that one had to be a mystic to understand that in reality the Song has nothing to do with earthly love or passion but that it is an allegory symbolizing the relation between God and his chosen people. In other words, God is the lover full of fierce passion, and Israel is His holy bride! "Therefore," declared the venerable and long-bearded saint, "he who for entertainment sings the song as though it were a profane lyric will have no share in the future world." And that settled forever its scriptural status.

This peculiar method of reading into a book (or extracting out of it) ideas altogether foreign to its original intent is known as "Allegory." By means of its subtle powers all kinds of intellectual legerdemain was made possible so that the early rabbis found it a very convenient tool with which to twist the Scriptures: that which was openly objectionable and offensive was easily transformed or sublimated.

And what the rabbis used with rapturous delight, the Christian theologians appropriated with ecstasy!

For over a period of fifteen hundred years Allegory was the acceptable Christian mode of handling the Bible. Not until the days of Martin Luther, in the sixteenth century, were its wild pretensions and gross extravagances seriously checked. It is amusing that the early Catholic Fathers, following close upon Rabbi Akiba's allegorical juggling, pounced upon the "Song of Songs" with joyous glee. To them it represented nothing more nor less than Christ's love for his bride —the church! And any one who dared to believe that the "bride" was anything other than the Roman Hierarchy was solemnly persecuted.

But Allegory was not confined to Jews and Christians. The Greeks used it most profusely in order to explain away crude elements in Homer and the poets.

Persian believers in the Koran were not slow in applying it in the interpretation of the odes of their great national poet, Hafiz. Here is an exact parallel in Mohammedan literature to what happened in the Hebrew. Hafiz, as is well known, sang of wine, and of love, and of nightingales, and of roses—in fact, of beauty in every form. How can such sensual poetry be made orthodox?—that was the question that bothered the ecclesiastical authorities in Persia and their pious ministers of the Mohammedan religion. In order to make the odes of Hafiz acceptable they must be allegorized —that is, people must be led to believe that they are not at all sensuous but on the contrary they represent mystical revelations of things divine. And so the Persian commentators explain that "the wine" signifies the true faith, and that "the beloved lad" stands as a symbol of God, and that "the intoxication" means pious ecstasy brought forth by a deep contemplation of the divine works and words, etc. This has, indeed, been carried so far, that pilgrims from all parts of Persia now resort to the tomb of Hafiz, and almost regard that frivolous poet as a saint.

There were other books besides the Song of Songs that occupied the attention of the Rabbinical Schools which were in full swing at this time. The Talmud (the collective name for rabbinical lore) has preserved for us many interesting notes about these discussions which were long and weary and full of learned trifling. The Book of Ecclesiastes, for example, had almost as hard a time getting by as the Song of Songs. Its cold-blooded cynicism was regarded as a freak, and various rabbis keenly felt that it was out of harmony with the rest of the Bible. But there were others who frankly liked it, and so they did not hesitate to manipulate its original text and twist its original thoughts so as to make the book less objectionable to the conventional belief of the age. (That is why it is so necessary in an intelligent understanding of Ecclesiastes to draw a sharp line of demarcation between the original kernel and what was subsequently added in the interests of orthodoxy.) After these many changes and alterations had been made, the battle raged on with less opposition. Finally, when the unorthodoxy of the book had been brought into a fair conformity with the orthodox tradition of Solomon, it was pronounced "holy" and given a place of honor in the Scriptures.

The Book of Esther and the Book of Ezekiel also came in for plenty of punishment. They were lashed by the rabbinical tongues until it seemed that there was no hope for them. More than once they were about to be turned out. But somebody always came in with a "holy" argument and somehow they managed to stay: their presence in the Bible means that they finally got by—only, however, by the skin of their teeth.

4

But all this squabbling about Song of Songs and Ecclesiastes was mere child's play compared to the battle the rabbis had to wage against the rising tide of Christian literature that came near wrecking the Hebrew Scriptures.

With the sudden success of Christianity and the rapid spread of all kinds of Christian books a new element of red-hot danger was added—an alarm far more serious than anything that had ever crossed the path of Judaism. In order to defend the sanctity of the old-time writings the rabbis were forced not only to denounce the literature of the new sect as dangerously heretical and filled with insidious errors but they had to make definite pronouncements in order to repudiate the scriptural claims of these various new books. Something had to be done at once to stop the growing heresy. Pious Jews by the thousands were reading the Gilionim (Gospels); for they were doubly seductive, because on the one hand they were regarded as Jewish in origin, and on the other they professed to carry the message of a new dispensation.

Until recent years our knowledge of this particular period of Hebrew history was almost a total blank. Only after the most painstaking research have historians and biblical scholars been able to patch together some idea of what took place. It was an age of vast confusions—that we now know. And, of course, the explanation of the scantiness of our information is attributable to this factor. But it is now certain that the fight put up by the rabbis against the Gospels—particularly by Akiba and his contemporaries at Jamnia—was strong enough (and filled with enough alarm) to bring the Hebrew Bible to a rigid close so that no other writings of any type whatsoever would be given a chance to be called, or regarded, as "inspired" scripture. . . . The rabbis slammed the outer gate in the face of the Apocrypha and the Gospels—and once inside the synagogue they locked the door and bolted it.

THE NEW TESTAMENT

PART IV

WHAT HAPPENED TO THE NEW TESTAMENT WHEN THE SEARCHLIGHT OF SCIENTIFIC INVESTIGATION WAS TURNED ON IT

In exploring the Christian Scriptures many things were found which at first were considered very strange and disquieting— but everywhere there has come a triumphant sense that light has arisen in darkness.

CHAPTER I

THE STAGE IS SET: A SWIFT GLANCE AT THE
SALIENT POINTS

CENTURIES before the New Testament was written Alexander the Great hoped for a "marriage of Europe and Asia."

Had the warlord been born in the fourth century A. D. instead of the fourth century B. C. he would have seen his wish fulfilled, not in the field of politics but in religion. For Christianity proved to be just such a union of the East and the West.

Beginning in the near East as a small and insignificant Palestinian sect the new religion overleaped the boundaries of its parent faith, Judaism, and after a few brief centuries of rapid development and phenomenal growth, entrenched itself firmly in the Western world. The infant Faith began at once to centralize its power at Rome so that the bishop of the City of the Cæsars became the Pontifex Maximus—the Pope, meaning thereby the recognized and supreme authority over the most imposing institution the world has ever seen.

Hand in hand with this phenomenal rise in centralized power there went the absolute control of the Bible, particularly the New Testament upon which the church established her gigantic claims. As a vast and highly organized hierarchy overtowering in her pride of power it was not at all difficult for Rome to maintain a fixed and exclusive right to interpret the Scriptures. In fact, under the mental conditions of the Middle Ages she could hardly have done otherwise, for it must be remembered that the church stood alone as the potent, excluding, conserving, and unifying force in the lives of men. And "Church-power" was not simply a public favor—it was actually installed in human opinion to such an extent that her ecclesiastical representatives could declare to the world that she, and she alone, as God's custodian possessed the true and only keys of correct understanding and that consequently this conferred upon her an infallible divine right to give an infallible divine interpretation to the Bible.

Being an age of implicit faith men willingly accepted this kind of teaching, which was strong just because it had assumed a grand air of finality. Scarcely any one thought of appealing to the Scriptures against the power of the Pope. No one in those days had the remotest idea of creating any trouble by setting up the authority of the Bible overagainst the authority of the church, for it was the Age of Faith when almost everybody believed that the Bible and the church spoke the same language. And even if some individual here or there had an idea of defining the authority of one as distinguished from the other he was sure to be quickly suppressed.

By merely branding all unfavorable thinking as heretical or erroneous, the obstinate supporters of advanced thoughts would soon find themselves out in the cold, excommunicated by the strong arm of the Pope. For the church conceived it to be the supreme duty of man not to think for himself but to accept the official teachings of Rome without even concerning his head in an endeavor to know what it was: the church knew—and that was sufficient. As an illustration of how an intelligent man felt under these stultifying conditions there is the case of Peter Abelard, one of the most gifted thinkers Europe has ever produced, who had a series of life-long conflicts with the papal system.

It was in the year 1113 that Abelard betook himself from Paris to Laon, where he intended to spend some time listening to Anselm, a famous theologian who was drawing large crowds of students to his lectures. This was Abelard's impression:

"So I came to this old man, whose repute was a tradition, rather than merited by talent or learning. Any one who brought his uncertainties to him, went away more uncertain still: He was a marvel in the eyes of his hearers, but a nobody before a questioner. He had a wonderful wordflow but the sense was contemptible and the reasoning abject."

It is unfortunate for a man to be born before his generation. In the monasteries of mediæval learning Abelard was an incongruity, as much out of place as Mark Twain's Connecticut Yankee in King Arthur's Court. Being so far advanced beyond the stupidity of his age it was most certain that the great thinker was headed for trouble. His fellow churchmen accused him of thrusting his face into heaven and peering into the secrets of God. Worse still. It was alleged that he used too much reason: "what is more against reason than by reason to endeavor to transcend reason?" And so Abelard moved along to his Golgotha, his contemporaries being determined to scalp him. Finally, the crisis of his life came in the form of a prolonged intellectual duel with that ghostly and austere monk, Bernard of Clairvaux, who represented the church in all that was mystical, supernatural and unreasonable.

In denouncing Abelard, whose cause of offense was his too constant application of reason to theology, St. Bernard used the language of the cloister: "The faith of the righteous believer does not dispute. But that man . . . has no mind to believe what his reason has not previously argued."

This, of course, is just one dramatic incident out of scores of such encounters between the spirit of Reason and the dogmas of the church but it is a true cross-section of the whole organism of repression. . . .

The spirit of Rome commanded men to believe first—and then reason (if that be at all necessary). "Learn first what is to be believed," declared the saints of the church, meaning that one should be zealous to first accept the official teachings of the Papal hierarchy and then, if possible, try to find out reasons for upholding them. And suppose no sufficient reasons were to be found? Then, the believer must fall back on the spiritual principle: "I believe even though it be incredible" (*Credo quia incredible est.*)

Mediæval Catholicism taught that Truth was not to be arrived at by Reason. On the contrary, Reason must bend its knee before that solemn mass of teachings which Tradition had already declared final, and forever "settled." Beyond this settled limit, judged to be eternally fixed, no one dared to go except on pain of excommunication or death.

But the method of Abelard's mind was just the exact opposite of all this. It was his rule to use reason first and through the pure agency of intelligence arrive at what is to be believed. "How, then, is the faith of any people, however false, to be refuted, though it may have arrived at such a pitch of blindness as to confess some idol to be the creator both of heaven and earth? As according to your own admission you cannot reason upon matters of faith, you have no right to attack others upon a matter with regard to which you argue that you ought yourself to be unassailed. . . ." Here was a dilemma that could not be evaded. What was the church to do about it? Her answer was given at the Council of Soissons where Abelard's teachings were officially condemned and his famous book zealously consigned to the flames. . . .

Such a rigid control of the mind is not only intellectually preposterous but utterly repugnant to the modern man. Yet, in justice to the mediæval church, it must be said that the modern man did not then exist —except of course in an isolated case like Abelard who was a rare exception. Just as it is always easier to have hindsight than foresight so it costs us little or no effort to give our idea of *how* things should have happened in the past instead of trying to understand *why* things happened the way they did. The Catholic Church was not so much the cause as the result of the social stagnation and universal ignorance that swept down over the Middle Ages. She was the true product of her times, as much as science is the product of the modern world. Consequently, it is not only absurd to denounce her history, it is stupid as well. One might with as much sense, or lack of sense, denounce the French for having had a revolution, or the Bolsheviki for overthrowing the Czar. It is too often forgotten that within the portals of this same intolerant institution the learning of antiquity was feebly yet effectively preserved. Over the Middle Ages there hung dark and dismal clouds and, had it not been for the little light of knowledge which the Roman Catholic Church struggled to keep burning and jealously guarded, it is certain that on the whole, conditions would have been even worse than they actually were.

Furthermore: each epoch in history has its own mental atmosphere—a certain number of leading ideas which cement the social structure. Of the many ideas that characterized that period perhaps none was so important and all-embracing as the concept of Authority. If our views on this subject are vastly different, it is because our world is so modern. But in mediæval times Authority was conceived of as one and absolute: the very idea of two separate authorities would have been just as unthinkable and as confusing as two rival popes. And it was just because the mediæval mind conceived the Bible and the church as a mystical total that it took many hundreds of years to separate the two. In the Middle Ages the spirit of pure reason was simply too weak to tackle the job—just because the spirit of dogma was too strong. It was not until the dawn of the Renaissance and the rise of the Reformation that men began to sense a distinction between the human ideas *in* the Bible overagainst the supernatural dogmas of the church *about* the Bible.

2

Time is the essence of all things. By the middle of the fifteenth century new and progressive ideas were beginning to mass themselves on the frontiers of European thought. Slowly they began to openly challenge the old conceptions and assail them in their most sensitive spots. The spirit of reason which had been silenced in Abelard now became stronger so that under the fierce rays of intelligent thinking the huge glaciers of Tradition which had kept men's minds in cold storage for over a thousand years were showing a perceptible amount of thawing. Everywhere men began to sense a stir of life which always comes in the thrill of unknown things looming up above the horizon. It was a time pregnant with change, a period of discovery and the rapid acquisition of all kinds of knowledge. Printing was invented in 1452; and new facts became the order of the day as information began to pour in. Forty years later Christopher Columbus reached the unknown shores of America. Expansion now moved in all directions . . . commerce . . . travel . . . discovery . . . adventure. . . . It was no longer possible for people to live in a religious world limited by the old ideas. "O new age," cried Ulrich Van Hutten, "Study is flourishing, minds are awakening, it is a joy to live."

In that era of feverish expansion no invention came to be more closely linked with the progress and the development of human thought than the discovery of printing. It made the new age inevitable by setting loose upon Europe a whole new flock of ideas. From out of their hiding places the literature, the philosophy and the science of Antiquity were drawn into the open, cleansed from the dust and neglect of the ages and put through the press. Overnight typography became the Fountain of Youth perpetuating the world's thought.

And now information, which had been almost prohibitive to the average person, was made wondrously accessible. It no longer took an enormous amount of labor to produce a book. On the basis of the old system just one fair copy of the Gospels was a difficult job: a complete Bible in manuscript form being a prodigious undertaking. Even the very shape and bulk of the old parchments made them hard to handle. But now these documents which had been the luxury of the great lord or prelate were no longer needed. Printing outmoded the old methods, and while it threw an army of angry copyists out of their jobs, it brought books within the reach of the small man's purse.

As we look down the long and winding avenues of history it may be difficult, for us who wallow in a plethora of printer's ink, to picture a time when there were no books. Before the invention of the printing press people had to produce their manuscripts by the slow process of handwork and it took many months—even years —to finish making just one good copy. It took twenty-one months to produce a single code of *Les Canons de Gratien*, a famous mediæval law book. At that rate it would take 5,250 years to produce 3,000 copies.

. . . Encumbered on all sides and lacking the medium of the printed page, it is no wonder that mediæval men suffered from a painfully slow dissemination of ideas. That, in a large measure, explains the darkness of the mediæval world—and that is why it has been appropriately called the "Dark Ages."

As long as printing was unknown the church did not find it at all difficult to guard the Bible from inquisitive eyes. She looked upon the Scriptures as her own treasure whose secrets were to be withheld from too close an investigation. And so long had these holy documents been pedestaled in sacred veneration that their absolute sanctity was deemed to be eternal. This attitude, greatly assisted by the complete isolation of the Bible from the people, enabled the theologians to treat both the Old and the New Testament as a superhuman product.

But with the rise of the printer's art the Bible plumed its wings and abandoned the cloisters of the mediæval world. Movable type changed the spiritual map of Europe. . . . In 1456 Gutenberg issued the first printed edition of the Scriptures (in Latin). . . . With this initial effort Bible reading began to spread like wildfire. Just to get on the inside of the Scriptures and discover for oneself what it was all about grew into an insatiable Gargantuan literary appetite the like of which mankind has never seen. . . . And from that day to this the Bible has continued to be the world's best seller!

But this "pestiferous" business of wide-spread Bible reading did not meet with the approval of the leading churchmen of Rome who feared that too popular or too intimate an acquaintance with the Scriptures would tend to reduce the supernatural halo with which the sacred Book had been invested for so many centuries. Censorship of the press suddenly became a part of a vast machinery of Roman resistance. In his determination to keep the Gospels out of the hands of the people Pope Paul IV, in 1559, placed a ban on all Bibles in modern languages (enumerating forty-eight editions). His successor, Pope Pius IV, continued the same repressive policies. In addition he expressed the idea that indiscriminate reading of the versions did more harm than good, consequently he would not allow laymen to read the sacred book except by special permission of a bishop or an inquisitor on the ground that inasmuch as the Scriptures surpassed even the understanding of the wise and the learned it was dangerous for the average person to indulge himself.

It is an easy matter for the twentieth-century man to read a Bible. Perhaps that is the reason he does not appreciate what a long and bitter struggle had to be waged against mental intolerance before this simple right was conceded. When the great translator Wycliffe presented to the English people a version of the Bible in their own language he was immediately described by Archbishop Arundel as "that pestilent wretch, John Wycliffe, the son of the Old Serpent, the forerunner of Anti-Christ, who has completed his iniquity by inventing a new translation of the Scriptures." In this same spirit Charles V and Philip II passed a decree aimed at the Netherlands to inflict the death penalty upon that person caught reading the Bible in any language which he could understand.

But apparently, all the decrees, persecutions and loud denunciations did no good. People were reading the Bible and were determined to continue doing so. The more they were cautioned against investigating the holy Scriptures the more they studied. So finally realizing the utter futility of strangling the press the church gave in and even went so far as to authorize her own Catholic edition (now called the "Douai" Bible).

3

With the wide-spread diffusion of knowledge sweeping changes were brought about. They came so suddenly, and caused so rousing an appeal to intellectual freedom that the huge mediæval church was alarmed. For almost a thousand years Rome had jealously exercised the sole authority of declaring what was or what was not the truth, and she was determined not to yield to the demands of the new age which were impiously seeking to question that right.

But long before the church could set in motion any effective measure to fight the new spirit, the age of the Renaissance—for that is the name by which the new learning is called—was already in full blossom. So far had the demands of reason made their inroads upon the intellectual life of Europe that the most capable thinkers within the church had already been captured. Valla, Erasmus, Reuchlin, Colet, Grocyn were names to conjure with, and each one of them was an ardent supporter of the "new" learning with its emphasis upon the human instead of the supernatural side of life. "We by our diligence," wrote Erasmus, the most representative of them all, "have smoothed a road which previously was rugged and troublesome, but in which henceforth great theologians may ride more easily with steeds and chariots. We have levelled the soil of the arena in which, with fewer obstacles, they may now display those splendid processions of their wisdom. We have cleansed with harrows the fallow land which heretofore was impeded with briars and burs. We have swept away the impediments, and opened a field wherein they who may hereafter wish to explain the secrets of Scripture may either play together with greater freedom, or join battle with more convenience."

. . . So it came to pass that "the egg that Erasmus laid was hatched by Luther," which was the pointed way of saying that the men who created the Renaissance were responsible for the birth of the Reformation. Unrest and dissatisfaction in political, economic, intellectual and religious circles, hastened the day of open revolt against the restrictions of Rome. Europe had long been conscious of sitting on a huge mass of suppressed molten lava that was soon to blow up and hurl the mountain of papal authority from off the Bible. It was just a question of time when the eruption would take place.

4

In a German monastery far from the concerns of the new learning a monk was battling with his soul. Although he had been educated in a great university his mind was untouched by the intellectual currents of his day. He possessed a commanding personality and a singular genius for leadership but he was no theologian nor scholar nor scientist. His interest was in practical religion and it was at this point that he came into conflict with the church. Faster than he realized a great movement of revolt gathered about him and overnight Martin Luther became the storm centre of Europe.

Luther would have failed to establish Protestantism had not the idea of throwing off the yoke of Rome been widely entertained over a long period of time. Cleavage was in the air when Luther appeared on the stage of history. Already the essence of Protestantism had been determined. And no matter how grossly it may have at times deflected from its genius, it was at bottom the right to reason and to think.

Of course, it was not to be expected that the early Protestants could exercise reason in its fulness: they were still too close to the old system in which they had been nurtured to completely break away from its mediæval character. Yet this much must be said for its bold and daring accomplishment: it set up a new order of things. By refusing to accept any longer the official interpretation of the Bible from the halls of the Vatican, Luther broke through the one power that had kept the Bible from the people. It was this unobstructed access to the Scriptures that Luther had in mind when he wrote "Proinde liber esse volo"—Henceforth I mean to be free.

In fairness to the Roman position it must be stated here that the Scriptures had always been regarded by the Catholic Church as the final authority. But this was in theory only: for inasmuch as Scripture is obscure the church alone reserved the right to tell what it means. Consequently, the assumption of this right elevated the church's authority for all practical purposes over that of the Scripture. The authority of the Bible was given only lip-service, the real authority was the church. "In order to restrain petulant spirits it (the church) decrees that no one relying on his own skill shall, in matters of faith and morals . . . wresting the sacred Scriptures to his own sense, presume to interpret the said sacred Scriptures contrary to that sense which holy mother-church whose it is to judge the true sense of the Holy Scripture, hath held and doth hold . . ."

This official declaration of Catholicism (taken from the Council of Trent) is perhaps the clearest statement of the position of Rome: the authority of the church must forever be over the Bible.

But Luther and his followers insisted that the authority of the Bible must be supreme over the church.

And that was the *Deadlock*.

5

In place of the Pope the early Protestants exalted the Bible, giving it a monstrously fantastic supremacy. Thus having thrown overboard one kind of infallibility they now accepted another, that is, Bibliolatry—the exaggerated veneration of the Scriptures as an infallible rule of faith and practice. "Scripture," declared Pastor Quenstedt, one of the most representative of the Lutherans, "is a fountain of infallible truth, and exempt from all error; every word of it is absolutely true, whether of experience, of dogma, of morality, or of history." . . .

Happy to get rid of the Pope and in the first blush of their success, these "reformers" fondly imagined that what they now had was a divine code to guide them, a revelation consistent with itself in all parts, flawlessly accurate, and free from internal contradictions or imperfections. In order to hold their position against the sharp attacks of the Roman Catholics who were now maintaining the untrustworthiness of Scripture the Protestants were led to defend the Bible more zealously than before. "Not a word is contained in the Holy Scripture," thundered Voetius the renowned Protestant professor at Utrecht with an air of grand and imposing confidence, "which is not in the strictest sense inspired, the very punctuation not excepted."

And thus the Bible became to the Protestants the rigid "Word of God," literally inspired without the slightest defect for—so it came to be believed— "nothing exists in the Scriptures which was not divinely communicated." With unconditional veneration they placed the Scriptures on a supernatural pedestal as the supreme object of idolatrous worship so that to even speak of misspellings in the Bible was regarded as a blasphemy against the Holy Ghost. In one loud chorus the Protestant preachers led their people to believe what John Owen so characteristically declared to his own Puritan Congregation: "The Scriptures of the Old and New Testament were immediately and entirely given out by God himself, His mind being in them represented unto us without the least intervening of such mediums and ways as were capable of giving change or alteration to the least iota or syllable." Even as late as 1861 the famous Dean Burgon, in a sermon preached at Oxford University, pictured God as a superhuman ventriloquist. "The Bible," declared this churchman, "is none other than the voice of Him that sitteth upon the throne. Every book of it, every chapter of it, every verse of it, every syllable of it (where are we to stop?), every letter of it, is the direct utterance of the Most High. The Bible is none other than the Word of God,—not some part of it more, some part of it less, but all alike the utterance of Him who sitteth upon the throne, faultless, unerring, supreme."

And that is how the Protestants having discarded the Catholic type of mediævalism quickly created one of their own—equally as bad, if not worse.

While the vast majority (of the Protestants) were tenaciously holding to a literal acceptance of a perfect, flawless Bible, there was just a small handful of scholars who asked the uncomfortable question: "What are the facts?"

The next chapter contains their answer.

CHAPTER II

A SAGA OF RARE ACCOMPLISHMENT: WHAT HAP-
PENED WHEN SCHOLARS COMPARED THE NEW
TESTAMENT WITH THE OLD MANUSCRIPTS

IT seems to be the nature of every reaction that it carries the pendulum to the full length of the opposite direction. The belief in the infallibility of the Scriptures was an extremely sharp swing away from the ecclesiastical despotism of Rome which had taught for so many centuries the infallibility of the Pope. Like the French revolutionists who overthrew the tyranny of the Bourbons and set up a new tyranny of their own, so the Protestants in breaking away from the yoke of the Papacy devised a new yoke which in almost every respect was just as tyrannical as the one they had so bitterly fought.

It is sad but true that for every one hundred steps civilization takes forward it seems to take ninety-nine backward. Yet even that one step is an undeniable gain: it helps mankind to disentangle itself from the talons of chaos. All those who took up the sword against the "divine right" of Kings may have at times lapsed into forms of government equally as bad. But the significant result amid all the turmoil and backsliding is the *one* step gained. The moment men got it into their heads to fight "divine rights" the old tyrannies were headed for their doom.

Now with the doctrine of the infallibility of the Pope it was this way. Intelligent men, for many rea-

Religious Book Club, Inc.

80 LAFAYETTE STREET   NEW YORK, N. Y.

In Account with
Rev. D. F. Helms
726 Brice Ave
Lima, Ohio 11231 D

April, 1929

UNRAVELLING THE BOOK OF BOOKS	$2.75
POSTAGE	.12
TOTAL	$2.87

sons other than religious ones, gradually grew weary of Roman pretensions until finally, under the leadership of Martin Luther, they junked the whole idea. But it is not easy (mentally speaking) for people to violently break away from the things with which they have grown up. Actually panic-stricken at what they had done, the Protestants—those who protested against the Pope—had to quickly devise something to take the place of that which was now demolished. Having been nursed and suckled on the mediæval idea of an "infallible" authority it is not at all astonishing that they found it impossible to get along without some form of it. Like a man who divorces his wife and immediately feels the need of a new companion, the Protestants could not get along with Infallibility and yet they could not get along without it. Consequently, in the zeal of a fervent faith, they established in place of the supremacy of the Pope the greater supremacy of the Bible.

We have already seen how the awakened intelligence of Europe had overcome the old superstition as to the occupant of St. Peter's chair being the errorless, flawless representative of Christ on earth. That idea was now gone—utterly and forever. But how about this new-fangled Protestant belief of an errorless, flawless Book? Could it hold itself together? Or, was it too doomed to the rubbish heap?

2

The first serious blow to this fanciful theory of a perfect Bible resulted from a pulverizing investigation of the "text" of the Scriptures.

If the holy writings are to speak for themselves, so

argued the scholars, let us then go directly to the old manuscripts and compare them word for word. Only in this way can truth be sifted from error. That sounds to us of the twentieth century like a very reasonable and straightforward method—yet it took hundreds of years for men to arrive at it, just as it took centuries before navigators got courage enough to sail around the continents in order to disprove the idea of a "flat" earth. Investigation was the spirit of the new age with its "Back to the Manuscript" movement. And now began the study of Greek, because the New Testament was originally written in that language. Everywhere throughout Europe men rushed in with feverish heat to master the linguistic key to unlock the Christian Scriptures.

We can now see that it was the only sensible thing to do, although there were many who did not like the idea of subjecting the Bible to analysis. They would have preferred to let things alone in the spirit of a familiar mediæval caution: "Press not the breasts of Holy Writ too hard, lest they yield blood rather than milk." But truth has never discovered by caution. Only a fearless daring combined with hard work has overcome error, particularly against those subtle forms that have been time-honored and shielded by special privileges.

Once started, nothing could stop the progress of investigation. Despite opposition, excommunication, and anathemas it had to move forward. The minute and painstaking labor which the study of the text of the New Testament required was vigorously carried on by scores of scholars in various countries. The sum total of this most elaborate and careful investigation proved above all else one thing: *that of the many hundreds of New Testament manuscripts in existence no two were absolutely alike!*—a shattering conclusion that rocked the churches of Christendom.

Instead of a perfect biblical text that people had been led to fervently believe in, scholars found thousands of variations ranging all the way from simple mistakes and careless omissions of the copyists to very serious blunders of a major significance—yes, even to out and out fraudulent passages deliberately inserted into the Scriptures by pious bigots who wanted to prove their rival theological dogmas.

Perhaps the best example—and certainly the most egregious fraud in the whole New Testament—was cleverly put into the fifth chapter of the First Epistle of John, verse eight. The original text as contained in the oldest manuscripts read as follows:

For there are three that bear witness: the Spirit and the water and the blood and the three agree in one.

Somewhere in the fourth century this passage was altered in the interests of the dogma of the Trinity so that in its new dress it read:

For there are *three that bear witness in heaven: the Father, the Word, and the Holy Spirit; and these three are one. And* there are three that bear witness *on earth:* the Spirit and the water and the blood: and the three agree in one.

It is not known definitely who mutilated this text, although many of the world's leading scholars believe it was the work of Priscillian, a Spanish bishop who was finally excommunicated from the church in 300 A. D. At first Priscillian's words were inserted by

many copyists as a mere marginal note, and then slowly by imperceptible degrees they were incorporated
into the main text of the Epistle as an exceptionally
juicy argument to prove the doctrine of the Trinity.
In those days, before the printing press, it took a long
time for spurious readings (no matter how valuable
they were for bolstering up theological doctrines) to
get into the majority of the manuscripts. The corrupted
words usually floated around for many years, sometimes centuries, before they found a snug place in the
body of Scripture. And that, of course, explains why
it has been possible for scholars to check up on the
fraudulent passages. By comparing the latest manuscripts with the very oldest ones it was evident that this
particular passage in the First Epistle of John is an
invention utterly unknown to the earliest authorities.

However, more than a thousand years passed before
any one dared to openly question the genuineness of
this verse. Finally, in 1516, the great humanist and
scholar, Desiderius Erasmus, published for the first
time an edition of the New Testament in Greek which
was based on his efforts to purify the text from all
orthodox corruptions. In the course of his labors, carried on in Switzerland, Erasmus found what others before him had noticed: that the text of the Epistle of
John had been seriously tampered with. A careful
search through several Greek manuscripts at his disposal revealed an absence of the "three witnesses" interpolation. Being a man of intelligence, and not hesi-
tating to exercise the right of a mild critical judgment,
Erasmus saw nothing else to do but to reject this wording as spurious. So he published his first edition of the
New Testament without it.

But no sooner had this omission been noised about than a storm of protest rose against him. For many centuries the theologians had regarded this particular verse as one of their great "proof texts" in support of the doctrine of the Trinity (although that doctrine is not to be found in the New Testament). Erasmus' omission threw them into convulsions for they had no desire to see their favorite text invalidated. Blue with rage they widely denounced him and cruelly attacked his book both in England and on the Continent—the University of Paris being the noisiest and bitterest in her anathemas.*

All intelligent and honest vesions of the Bible now omit the verse. But in Erasmus' day only a few fearless thinkers dared to declare it spurious. Father Richard Simon, who already had gotten himself into ill-repute on account of his Old Testament research, did not hesitate to come out against it. Even Martin Luther consigned it to the waste-basket. . . . But progress is always slow in matters affecting religion. Despite all sound scholarship, accurate investigation and good judgment, the orthodox wings of the various churches insisted on keeping up the fictitious words. To most pious people Scripture simply was not "holy" scripture without the sacred error. And, as an illustration of the slowness of progress, the corrupted verse is still honored in several versions of the Bible which are read even to-day from thousands of pulpits in all parts of the world.

*In his early days Erasmus had been a student at the University of Paris. Many years later he wrote somewhat humorously: "I carried nothing away from it, but a body infected with disease and a plentiful supply of vermin." Rabelais recorded a similar experience with regard to the food and lodging at this great seat of mediæval learning.

3

Another familiar passage originally had no place in the New Testament.

Most any one who has heard of the Christian Scriptures knows the Lord's Prayer. It is undeniably a gem of spiritual beauty. But even here the text has been altered by a Doxology which occurs in the thirteenth verse of the sixth chapter of the Gospel of Matthew.

As the verse now stands in most Bibles it appears:

"And bring us not into temptation, but deliver us from evil; for thine is the kingdom, and the power, and the glory, forever, Amen."

Of course, that reads very beautifully and very innocently; but when this familiar portion of the Lord's Prayer was compared with the oldest manuscripts it was found to be entirely wanting! That was quite a severe jolt to those who were loudly proclaiming a perfect and infallible text. Eventually, honesty, at least among thoughtful people, had to prevail, and for that reason the words: "For thine is the kingdom, and the power, and the glory, forever. Amen." had to be stricken out of every corrected edition of the Bible, or relegated to the secondary importance of a mere footnote.*

Even after this demonstration there were those who, wedded to the idea of a perfect Bible, insisted upon the genuineness of these words believing them to have been the exact utterance of Jesus (—for no other reason

---

*Aside from this, the revisions of the Bible have shown that many passages and scores of expressions which have been implicitly accepted for generations, and quoted as the very word of God, were in fact the erroneous translations of imperfect readings.

than their presence in the New Testament). But if the testimony of the manuscripts is insufficient, one may turn to the Bible and give it a chance to speak for itself. What do we find? Here is the Gospel of Luke which has a version of the Lord's Prayer, and the Gospel of Luke knows nothing about this last sentence of kingdom, power, and glory! In fact, Luke's version is much older than Matthew's, clearly indicating how the famous words were no part of the orignial primitive form.

Matthew's Version

6:9-12:

After this manner therefore pray ye: Our Father who art in heaven, Hallowed be thy name. Thy kingdom come. Thy will be done, as in heaven, so on earth. Give us this day our daily bread. And forgive us our debts, as we also have forgiven our debtors. And bring us not into temptation, but deliver us from evil. *For thine is the kingdom, and the power, and the glory, forever. Amen.*

Luke's Version

11:2-4:

And he said unto them, when ye pray, say, Father, Hallowed be thy name. Thy kingdom come. Give us day by day our daily bread. And forgive us our sins; for we ourselves also forgive every one that is indebted to us. And bring us not into temptation.

It is now known that various doxologies were used in different places throughout early Christendom and that several ways of expressing it struggled for supremacy until finally one form prevailed over all others and was accepted. It is this accepted form that soon became fixed to Matthew's version. But in reality it was no part of the original.

4

Not only have the manuscripts shown us that short verses here and there have been interpolated into the Christian Scriptures but they have given us the concrete example of a whole story bodily incorporated into the Gospel of John. This particular story happens to be the prize of the New Testament. It deals with the subject of adultery—that persistent type of conduct as old as civilization which, like the poor, we have with us always. Jesus—so the story runs—refused to criticise the adulteress: he condemned the sin but forgave the sinner. . . . Whether the incident is historically true or not makes no difference as far as its value to humanity is concerned. It is sufficient that it is among the rarest pearls in the spiritual treasury of mankind, certainly it is the finest short story ever written.

Fortunately, this story has been preserved in the Bible where it is now incorporated in the eighth chapter of the Gospel of John. But—and here is the rub—the oldest manuscripts omit it altogether. Originally, it had no place in the New Testament writings. However, it was so supremely typical of the Nazarene, his compassion for the suffering and his understanding of human frailty, that it made its way into the Bible at a very early date. But before it found a resting place in the Scriptures it wandered about like a waif. Some of the later manuscripts have it at the very end of the Gospel of John as a kind of an appendix. In other manuscripts it appears as a marginal note often written in a small hand to distinguish it from the true text; and sometimes it is even found with asterisks about it in order to indicate doubt as to its authenticity. Still other authorities put it at the close of Luke, feeling, of course, that it was not a genuine part of John. Eusebius, an ancient church historian, declared it was in the Gospel according to the Hebrews. It really makes no particular difference what disposition is made of it. To be sure, it deserves a place in the Bible: it is so beautiful, so true, so wondrously good. It is as full of the radiant spirit of Jesus "as the diamond is full of the sun"—but nothing is more certain than that the story did not originally belong to the so-called "immaculate" text.*

There is just one more example that ought not be overlooked while we are on this subject of textual criticism for it is most interesting as an illustration of how the early scholars demolished the idea of a perfect text. This particular instance deals with the Gospel of Mark.

A careful investigation of the oldest manuscripts threw the entire ending of this Gospel into the realm of spurious or false reading. Beginning with the ninth verse of the last chapter there is a clear indication of how the ancient scriptures were tampered with. Like the Book of Chronicles, which ends abruptly in the middle of a sentence, so does the Gospel of Mark break off quite sharply as though the original manuscript had been torn. The oldest Greek codices entirely omit the present well-known ending of Mark (which is a false piece tacked on) while other authorities have preserved a different version not so familiar, except to scholars.

It is impossible to tell just what happened to the original close of this Gospel. In ancient days books suffered all kinds of curious fates. It may be that the last leaf of the volume was worn thin or lost and consequently a new ending had to be written. Or, perhaps, as seems more plausible, the original ending contained an account of the resurrection that was in conflict with the other gospels, consequently it was stricken out by

*Many other examples of interpolation and corruption could be easily given. And were this book a treatise in textual criticism the illustrations could be piled up sky-high. For those who desire to read into this subject more fully a helpful bibliography will be found at the end of the book.

some ecclesiastical authority. But no one knows exactly how or why the gospel was broken off, although there have been many ingenious conjectures to explain it. At any rate the "mutilated" Gospel of Mark is far from being a "perfect" text divinely accurate.

an un-happy way of stating it.

5

With the publication at Oxford in 1707 of John Mill's famous book on the variations and corruptions of the New Testament the theory of a perfect text vanished into the same thin air out of which it had been so ignorantly created. Not all the overwhelming power of dogma could stand up under the crushing blows administered by the testimony from the manuscripts. Mill very ably and very learnedly computed that the variations in the Christian Scriptures were in the neighborhood of thirty thousand. Yet, his estimate was small because it was based on comparatively few manuscripts.

I think the variations were 160,000 to 175000

No sooner had Mill finished his monumental work than he was followed by other investigators, such as Richard Bentley, William Mace, J. J. Wetstein, J. A. Bengel, Johann Semler, and J. J. Griesbach. From the already huge figure of thirty thousand the variations began to rise. What with the finding of fresh manuscripts and with each successive analysis, it soon reached the staggering figure of one hundred thousand. After more than two centuries of close study and research the latest computation—a staggering increase—places the number in the neighborhood of one hundred and seventy-five thousand! . . .

Enough water has now run under the mill for us to appreciate one significant fact in all this labyrinth of research, a fact too frequently ignored by those whose interest in the Bible is stupidly limited to a morbid gloating over the evidence of imperfection. Such people are usually blind to the positive value of textual criticism which has shown that notwithstanding hundreds—yes, thousands—of minor variations in the text that there is a substantial unity and agreement which is even more impressive than the errors. As well might one fasten his attention on the huge number of variations in Shakespearian literature to the utter neglect of its underlying unity. After all, no one is going to throw Shakespeare overboard because the early editions of his works need textual reconstruction in an attempt to get back to the wording of the autographs. In this respect the writings of both the Bible and Shakespeare may be compared to the Pyramids which have suffered from long centuries of abrasion, mutilation, and strain. Still their mass is solidly there in almost the same shape in which the old Egyptians finished them. When biblical scientists fearlessly removed from the text of the Scriptures the accretions of later ages and then proceeded to restore the purity of the correct reading they only did in a literary way what archæologists seek to do when they undertake the restoration of an ancient monument or a forgotten temple long buried in the sand and ashes of the centuries. . . .

The debt of gratitude the modern world owes to the scholars who have brought to light hundreds of facts concerning the text of the Bible must not diminish the equally great debt we owe to the old manuscripts themselves, these priceless memorials that have been preserved over the centuries. For without the manuscripts to fall back on it would have been im-

possible for scientists to discover the corruptions, interpolations, and fraudulent passages that mar the beauty
of the Testaments. The story of the manuscripts, how
they were written and then tucked away in the dark
recesses of half-forgotten monasteries, is in itself a
chapter in the romance of adventure that is full of
thrills.

To a great many people it must be quite a shock to
learn for the first time that there are, at present, no
original writings of the Bible in the sense of the modern world possessing the autographs. Whatever biblical
manuscripts there are to-day in the great libraries and
museums of the world are simply "copies" of copies.
In fact, distressing as it might seem at first, the very
oldest manuscript of the New Testament is as late as
the fourth century A. D.* All the originals, the autographs, perished at a very early date—even the first
copies of the originals are utterly gone. Excessive usage
combined with the fierce fires of persecution have
wiped them out—forever.

It is just this situation that makes the science of
Textual Criticism so difficult. If we only possessed the
autographs, then there would be no disputes—all questions could be easily and quickly settled. But that is not
the case. A heavy fog hangs over the pristine beauty of
the originals so that at its very best all that textual criticism can possibly hope to do is to arrive at an *approximately* pure wording. Yet approximate truth is far better than downright error.

Owing to the loss of the autographs we may never
be in a position to settle all the disputed points and

*All the old writings of antiquity like Homer, Herodotus, Plato, Virgil
and scores of others are known to us only by very late manuscripts. Like
the documents of the Bible the autographs of these classics are gone.

minor differences that naturally arise when scholars compare one manuscript with another. Still, we are deeply obligated to textual criticism for the great things it has accomplished, for no ancient document is free from blunders of some sort. By thoroughly investigating the oldest manuscripts it has succeeded in establishing (upon universally recognized principles) a far greater and more accurate knowledge of what the New Testament authors actually wrote than was known during the mediæval ages when people blindly accepted every corrupted reading as divine truth. And in all that is vital and essential the books of the New Testament (as we have them in their present form) may be honestly regarded as genuine reproductions of the original works.

6

Before building a bridge across a chasm one must understand something of bridge-building. And before a man can become a competent textual critic he must understand something about ancient book making. The study of manuscripts, intricate and complex as it is, demands a very special skill all of its own. Yet there are certain rudimentary things of splendid and absorbing interest that are open to the untrained or uninitiated. For instance, we may easily learn that the old manuscripts of the New Testament are divided into two classes, according to the form of the writing used. The very oldest manuscripts—that is, those written between the fourth and the tenth century—are called "Uncials," because they were written in Greek capital letters. The younger manuscripts from the tenth century and later use the smallest script, a kind of running hand: these are called "Minuscules," or "Cursives."

Of the Uncial manuscripts there are only about one hundred and fifty scattered in the various libraries and museums of the world. The Cursives on the other hand are far more plentiful, running up into the grand figure of about three thousand. All of them, uncials as well as cursives, are exceedingly valuable to book collectors. Many of them are very beautiful and exhibit great skill in penmanship.

Because the uncials are older they naturally represent the greatest authority in determining the correct text of the New Testament. It would carry us too far afield to examine individually and separately each one of these valuable documents. Many delightful books have been written about them describing in detail their age and composition together with such matters about their text as has enabled scholars to pursue their work of careful examination.* It will be enough for our purposes here to tell the story of just one of the oldest uncials, perhaps the most famous and priceless of all New Testament manuscripts. How it was found is a romance in adventure as absorbing as Carnarvon's discovery of King Tut's Tomb. And inasmuch as our present knowledge of this rare uncial is knit up with the indefatigable labors of one of the greatest biblical investigators and antiquarians who ever lived we will try to get acquainted with Constantin Tischendorf, the man to whom the world of scholarship bends its knee in gratitude.

Born in 1815 in Lengenfeld, Germany, Constantin Tischendorf received his education at the University of Leipzig where he became a teacher and where he

*Among the most distinguished manuscript scholars of all times are Karl Lachmann, Samuel P. Tregelles, B. F. Westcott, F. J. A. Hort, Von Soden, and Caspar Rene Gregory.

began his great career as a manuscript scholar. Possessed of a vivid imagination it soon occurred to young Tischendorf that hidden away in the dust and darkness of the old monasteries and tombs of Syria, Egypt, and Palestine there must be huge stores of documents coming down from the earliest Christian centuries. The vision of hunting for these treasures in the out-of-the-way places of civilization gripped his mind. Although miserably poor "so that he could not pay for the cloak that he wore" he managed by hard efforts to set out on his first expedition to the Orient in 1844.

After spending several weeks in Egypt with comparatively little to reward his efforts he followed a new course to Suez and the Sinaitic Peninsula, for he was determined to visit the Monastery of St. Catherine, located in the bleak desert regions on the sacred mountain supposed to have been the actual site where Moses had received the Ten Commandments. "I did not see the convent until we were come into its immediate proximity. It lies in a long and narrow vale between the mountain of Saint Epistemius or the Jebel ed Deir, and Horeb; but it comes into view most beautifully, with its fine garden of cypress, pomegranate, and orange trees giving a friendly greeting over the gray stone walls. The convent itself, with its walls towering to the height of forty feet, looks like a small fortress, and the want of any entrance, that can properly be called a door, strengthens the impression. The only entrance is thirty feet high, to which the visitor is pulled by a rope. A crowd of Bedouins were already gathered under this door, and they heralded my arrival by loud cries and the discharge of their fire-arms. But before I could enter upon my rope-journey upward, I was asked for my credentials. I presented the two letters from Suez, which were immediately drawn up into the convent."

Not wishing to lose any time Dr. Tischendorf at once began his hunt in the gloomy library which turned out to be exceptionally rich in manuscripts. That same evening, as he was nervously examining several volumes on the shelves, his eyes fell on a large fuel-basket of waste paper resting on the floor whose contents apparently were ready to be used for the fire. The basket was full of mouldered parchments of little value, and Dr. Tischendorf after looking them over was about to throw them all back when to his great surprise and bewilderment he chanced upon a number of miscellaneous leaves written in Greek uncials. . . . At that moment the world turned upside down in his head and he saw all the colors of the rainbow. . . .

But his excessive delight was a mistake; he should have cautiously concealed it. For his exuberance set the ignorant old monks to thinking. Suddenly the parchments became valuable in their eyes, and when Tischendorf tried to find the rest of the manuscript the next morning it was gone! No amount of urging on his part could get the monks to admit the presence of the remainder. . . . Realizing that he had unwittingly blundered, Tischendorf had to content himself with permission to take back to Germany a fragment of but forty-three sheets.

The idea that his plans had been seriously miscarried and stupidly botched haunted the great scholar. Again and again the desire came to go back and make an attempt to find the rest of the manuscript, for he considered himself cheated out of the fame he had so

Monastery of St. Catharine where Tischendorf discovered the famous Sinaiticus Manuscript.

unintentionally let slip through his fingers. Finally, in 1853, he set out on his second search to the Orient and paid St. Catherine another visit. But it was a dismal failure. Nobody in the monastery knew anything about the uncial manuscript he was after. It was a terrible disappointment to high expectation when Tischendorf returned to Europe empty-handed.

But still the idea haunted him! He must go back just once more to satisfy himself. Six long years now passed by before he could focus all the necessary arrangements for a successful last attempt. But this time he was determined to go with carefully laid plans. Being somewhat of a diplomat, and realizing the far-reaching influence of the Czar over the St. Catherine monastery, he shrewdly waited until he had received the full support of the House of Romanoff. He did not have to wait long. Within a few months imperial patronage was graciously extended. And so, backed by the powerful Czar, who as head of the Russian Greek Catholic Church granted the scholar special protection and extraordinary permission to thoroughly ransack the monastery, Tischendorf set out for his third visit to St. Catherine,— a modern crusader in a search of something more important than the Holy Grail.

This time Tischendorf had calculated wisely. The Czar's influence did the trick, securing for him a hearty welcome when he put in his appearance at the convent. The entire library was now thrown open to him, and immediately Tischendorf plunged into the sea of manuscripts in a last desperate attempt to find his treasure. Day after day from early morning to late at night he searched but still there was no sign of any part of the particular uncial he wanted. Having exhausted every possible nook and corner he was now convinced that the manuscript must have been stolen from the monastery or used for fuel by some ignorant monk. So, thoroughly disgusted and disappointed he was prepared to leave, and gave orders to his servants to engage his horses and camels for the return journey back to Cairo. . . .

But something providential happened. He had taken a leisurely walk that afternoon with the steward of the convent when the conversation turned on the subject of old manuscripts in which Tischendorf regretted his ill-success at being unable to find what he wanted. Coming back from their promenade the monk invited his German guest to his own dingy room where he naïvely informed Tischendorf that he, too, had been absorbed in a Greek Bible and would be very happy to have the scholar look it over. Too ignorant to realize what he had in his possession the old monk pulled out a huge piece of red cloth in which he had wrapped up the loose and disjointed fragments of his manuscript. On its being unrolled before him, Tischendorf, to his unspeakable surprise and delight, saw the very document he had given up all expectation of discovering! It proved to be the complete New Testament—the identical manuscript he had been in search of for fifteen years, belonging to the identically same codex from which he had taken forty-three leaves on his first visit.

Although mad with excitement and drunk with success Tischendorf feigned a beautiful nonchalance. He had learnt his lesson and was now careful not to excite his host. And so he managed to hold himself together until he reached his own room where he was allowed

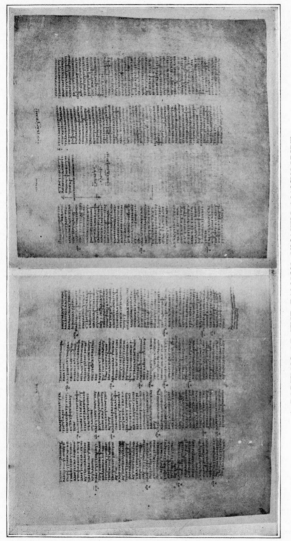

A PORTION OF THE FAMOUS SINAITIC MANUSCRIPT.

Reduced one-fifth from the fac-simile edited by Professor Lake and published by the Clarendon Press (Oxford and London).

to take the coveted manuscript over night conveying it like nuggets of gold. Once in his cell he let himself go, leaping and dancing for joy. "I knew that I held in my hand the most precious Biblical treasure in existence—a document whose age and importance exceeded that of all the manuscripts I had ever examined during twenty years, study of the subject. I cannot now, I confess, recall all the emotions which I felt in that exciting moment, with such a diamond in my possession. . . ."

It was a huge triumph. But all was not success as yet: there were additional troubles—how to get the manuscript out of the hands of the monks. After several tantalizing experiences filled with heart-breaking delays Tischendorf was finally able to have his prize transferred to Cairo where he received permission from the head of the monastery to present it "under the form of a loan" to the Czar.

His success was now complete. It overtopped all his labors. Thrilled to the depths of his soul in having attained his highest wishes the learned critic presented his great treasure-trove to Emperor Alexander II on the 19th of November, 1859, in the Winter Palace at Tsarkoe-Selo. . . . Ten years later, in recognition of his monumental labors the Czar issued an imperial ukase making him a hereditary noble of the Russian aristocracy.

And that's how the poor lad of Lengenfeld became "Count" Constantin Tischendorf.

CHAPTER III

THE COLLAPSE OF SUPERNATURALISM: THE STORY
OF HOW THE "HUMAN" SIDE OF THE BIBLE
BEGINS TO BE SEEN FOR THE FIRST TIME

FIFTY years after the death of Dante the Republic of
Florence endowed a lectureship in order to comment
upon the *Divina Commedia*. From that initial effort,
now after the passage of several centuries, it has been
estimated that there are over three thousand books
written for no other purpose than to explain the poet's
immortal vision.

What is true of Dante is true of other great classics.
Inasmuch as they stand in need of some explanation in
order to make them intelligible they have all become,
in the course of generations, the subject of endless
comment and interpretation. . . .

Immortalized by the accumulated reverence of many
ages it was not only natural but even necessary that
there should grow up around the Scriptures a vast
structure of explanation. No written document is ever
as simple as it seems—this is particularly true of all
ancient writings. One needs only to look over the huge
pile of literature that has gathered around the Constitution of the United States within the short period of
one hundred and fifty years to appreciate the colossal
edifice that has been reared upon its comparatively
simple and modern words. This is all the more astonishing when one realizes how close we are in point of
time to the founders of the Republic. In the case of the

Bible the distance that separated the mediæval church from the authors of the New Testament was a yawning chasm of many centuries; the need, therefore, of explaining the Scriptures whose thoughts, words, and phrases belonged to another age was an inescapable and imperious necessity. Just as the Supreme Court of the United States undertakes to give the last and final word as to the meaning of the Constitution so the ecclesiastical councils undertook to declare what was, and what was not, the truth in relation to the Bible.

It was inevitable, considering the mediæval temper of mind, that there would have to be a lot of juggling and twisting of Scripture in order to make these old writings fit the dogmas of the young church. As a result of this manipulation there grew up from the very earliest centuries an elaborate system of Biblical interpretation known as Allegory which at bottom was nothing more than a method of reading into the Bible (or extracting out of it) what was never there.

We have already noted that Allegory had been used by the Hebrews and the Greeks with varying degrees of success long before the rise of Christianity. But with this, as with so many other things, the new faith felt the need of appropriating a tried instrument that could be pressed into the service of handling the complex machinery of the church. So Allegory was given a prominent place in the tool-chest of Catholicism. With its ingenious use, as we shall soon learn, it performed brilliant feats of legerdemain mostly fantastic, absurd and vicious, but also at times very spiritual and very unselfish. The world has always had intellectual balloons but never so many as during the fancy-breeding influence of Allegory.

We will better understand the temper of this remote
age when we realize that each epoch in history has its
own set of characteristic thoughts and that Allegory
suited the mediæval mind to a nicety. It fitted into the
atmosphere of myth and marvel in which these people
moved and had their being. Knowing how few of us
can escape the thought-patterns of our immediate environment it is doubtless true that had we lived in
those days we too would have been under the domina-
tion of its method, for Allegory proved to be as appealing to the Dark Ages as Jazz is for America.

The more Allegory developed the more grotesque
and erratic it became, for it gave to the theologian
whatever he wanted for his purpose. With its subtle
jugglery he could prove anything (not even the sky
was the limit because, as a theologian, he had access to
Heaven). If, for example, he wanted to prove that it
was the duty of every man to make private confession
to a priest he merely cited the story of Jesus raising the
dead before a few witnesses which was taken to mean
that Christ intended that each Catholic priest possess
the mystical power to raise the dead soul or the dead
conscience to a new life. If he wished to demonstrate
the supremacy of the Roman hierarchy he had only to
refer to the story of Noah and the ark which, according to Allegory, shows that inasmuch as there was but
one ark so there is but one church, and, that Noah
merely symbolizes the Pope who guides the Ship of
Truth through the dark waters of this world's sin and
corruption. . . . Verses six and seven of Psalm VIII:
"Thou hast put all things under his feet: all sheep
and oxen, yea, and the beasts of the field" were made
to prove that God put all things under the feet of the

Pope: the sheep means the Christians; the oxen refers to the Jews and heretics; and the beasts of the field are the pagans.

The intense seriousness with which the church used the allegorical method made it possible for her to so befuddle the Bible that in a manner far removed from the intentions of its original authors the stupendous claims of Rome were made to receive their sanction. She abused scriptural texts to establish her own tyranny as when the hideous crimes of the Inquisition were justified on the basis of a passage in the sixth chapter of the Gospel of Mark: "He constrained his disciples to get in." She encouraged deceit to entrap and ruin heretics on the authority of St. Paul's ironic reference: "Being crafty I caught them with guile. . . ." And hand in hand with this use of Allegory and misrepresentation the church carried a very clever protective device in her solemn declaration that there could be no true interpretation of the Bible without the aid of the Holy Spirit, who is only found in a council approved by the Pope.

Occasionally we hear feeble protests against this kind of abuse but they made no more impression than a penny fife in a brass band. As far back as the ninth century Agobard, Bishop of Lyons, appreciated the necessity of correcting these extravagances. "If you once begin such a system who can measure the absurdity which will follow?" But Agobard himself could not resist using the very method against which he directed his caution. For as long as the social, economic, and mental conditions which supported mediævalism were in the saddle so long were men unwilling to think for themselves, and just so long was the church determined to keep up her profitable trade of paralyzing the Bible. But just as soon as the intelligence of Europe awoke from its stupor and lethargy people realized that the allegorical method was a huge incrustation that had to be removed if there was to be any mental freedom or any direct access to the Scriptures. . . .

It was in the sixteenth century, particularly in the initial stages of the great Reformation, that Allegory was dumped overboard. Luther himself contributed no mean effort to help his generation get rid of it. In one of his sermons he spoke contemptuously of those who would turn the Bible by means of this type of misrepresentation into "a nose of wax," and elsewhere he remarks that the church's use of the detestable method has broken up the Scripture into so many various senses making "mere rags and tatters, which serve for the teaching of neither faith nor hope nor morals." After declaring that each passage of Scripture has but one clear, definite and true sense of its own, the great Reformer goes on to say that it must be certain that all other meanings injected into it are but doubtful opinions, "empty speculations," "the scum of Holy Scripture," "so much dirt." In short, "Allegory is a sort of beautiful harlot who proves herself specially seductive to idle men." It may even degenerate into a mere "monkey-game" (Affenspiel).

Out of Luther's sound position (although it must be said that owing to his early training he never completely emancipated himself from the allegorical method) beneficial enfranchising influences have come. In place of the Allegory Luther pushed forward as one of his main principles the use of common sense in the interpretation of the Bible. "The Holy Ghost is the all-simplest writer that is in heaven or earth; therefore his words can have no more than one simplest sense, which we call the scriptural or literal meaning."

As simple and as straightforward as Luther's words now appear to us, it was at that time a very radical change in attitude, for the church had made a standing dogma of the "obscurity" of the Bible which served to keep it safely out of the hands of the people. But Luther declared that Scripture was plain enough to be understood without the aid of a priest and that consequently there was no need for any elaborate system of interpretation. "If the Scripture is obscure, which they (the Romanists) attempt to explain, who will certify that their explanation is certain? Another new explanation. But who will explain that? So it goes on forever; I will have no part of it called obscure."

With the Lutheran vindication of the right of private judgment the huge Allegorical pillar once so powerful crashed to the ground and with its tremendous support forever gone the Temple of Unreason began to weaken.

2

It may seem extraordinarily strange to us, now that we are accustomed to it, that there should have been a period in civilization when men knew practically nothing about the idea of history. Even little tots in our modern grammar schools soon become acquainted with the fact that all things have undergone development. But far back in the depths of the Middle Ages such thoughts were practically unknown even to the most learned. Ecclesiastical teaching in a very high handed manner overrode all the rational requirements of what the modern man calls "history."

To the mediæval person everything of great value had a supernatural origin. There was the divine right of Kings, the divine right of the Popes, the divine right of the Councils, and in the midst of all this "divine" thinking there stood the Bible which was regarded as the divinest of all divine things, the most supernatural in the whole realm of supernaturalism. Under the sway of such ideas it was a foregone conclusion that men would treat the Scriptures not as a human document written by men but as a collection of holy oracles spoken by God—a miraculous communication of facts not otherwise to be known. This attitude of mind accounts for the fact that from the sixth century until the rise of the Renaissance in the fifteenth—a vast stretch of a thousand years—there was practically no study of the Bible to be termed scientific. The few who investigated the Scriptures had no interest in finding out the truth of its origin, for the very simple reason that no one regarded it as a human product. As late as the thirteenth century the pious monk, Bonaventura, declared what most everybody solemnly believed, that "the progress of Holy Scripture is not bound to the laws of reasonings and definitions, like the other sciences; but, conformably to supernatural light proceeds to give to man the Wayfarer a knowledge of things sufficient for his salvation. . . ." The very idea that the sacred writings had a human side was as unfamiliar to the mediæval man as the notion of the sphericity of the earth.

It was not the Bible alone that was unknown to the people of the Middle Ages; the whole of Antiquity with all its classical authors (the so-called pagans) were equally isolated in the dense ignorance of those times. Each age has its dominant mood, and the Dark Ages rested upon a simple and naïve faith. Whatever scraps of information people possessed about the antique world were accepted by everybody with ready belief. No attempt was made to draw the line between myth and historical fact. With the same unreasoning and uncritical faith men accepted with equal satisfaction the campaigns of Cæsar and the legend of the Trojan settlement of Latium or the mythological doings of Romulus of whom it was actually and really believed that he was suckled by a she-wolf and fed by a woodpecker before becoming the founder of Rome. Mediæval men were just as childlike in dealing with the traditions regarding the Greek philosophers as in dealing with the legends of the Apostles—they swallowed it all in one blissful gulp. And they were happy as long as they were ignorant.

But, to quote a humorous placard recently seen on an old Ford automobile: "this can't go on forever." There is always a limit to ignorance and unreason. Sooner or later the awakened good sense of man was sure to break through the mechanics of a grotesque supernaturalism which had been closely geared into the machinery of Scripture. . . .

This brings us to the age of the Renaissance—that great period in European history which witnessed the Re-birth of the human intellect. Out of it were forged the tools of the new order that was eventually to displace the old. By asserting the right of Reason to investigate all things the Renaissance turned out to be the greatest single force in demolishing the ancient dogmas and the blind credulities of the church. By slow degrees it created a vast feeling of dissatisfaction and unrest so that long before actual rebellion broke out intelligent people were chafing against the trammels of mediæval ways of thinking.

Now it is significant in telling this story of how scholars slowly arrived at the true understanding of the origin of the New Testament in terms of human development (instead of the fanciful illusion of a supernatural revelation) that the term "Humanism" is the very name by which the spirit of the Renaissance is best known and most appropriately characterized.

Humanism not only asserted the independence of man's mind from all outside control but it dared to look upon the teachings of the church (both Catholic and Protestant) from a human standpoint, and not as an independent development outside of the ordinary processes of history. "It is not necessary," wrote the great humanist Erasmus, "that we should refer everything in the apostolic writings immediately to supernatural aid. Christ suffered his disciples to err. . . ." Such an admission coming from the most influential thinker of Europe made plain the new disposition on part of the leading scholars of Christianity to minimize supernatural activity. If the Good Book is a message written by God; if it is a letter which was mailed in heaven and handed down to earth by the postmasters Moses and the Prophets, or Jesus and the Apostles, then no one has a right to question it. But if this Book was written by men, then it contains a human element, and the only way to study a human document is not to close one's eyes and ask nothing but to use the ordinary methods of common-sense inquiry.

The enlightened minds of this period soon realized that the primary requisite in getting at the true, inner side of anything is to first get rid of superstition; for no intelligent study of the Bible could get under way as long as its writings were regarded as a divinely supernatural product.

And now began a long series of great intellectual battles that overhauled the thinking of Europe from one end to the other. The sixteenth, seventeenth, and eighteenth centuries may be all rolled together in telling the story of the warfare of reason against unreason, of naturalism against supernaturalism, of common sense against the dark forces of obscurantistic faith. It was, in short, a struggle of the awakening powers of modern science and the historical process against mediævalism and its extravagant pretensions. . . .

People frankly became sceptical and determined to stop believing in fairies.

3

It was particularly in England by the opening of the seventeenth century that Humanism found its acknowledged leadership.* Already there had been a growing belief in the uniformity of natural law with the habit of steadily seeking natural causes to explain things instead of resorting to supernatural agencies. Strange and uncommon events like earthquakes, electrical storms, or cyclones were no longer looked upon as the cunning devices of evil demons or the perpetrations of ghosts and witches. Men began to explain the world and its complex happenings in terms of Na-

*Humanism went under different names in different countries. In England it was called "Deism"; in France "Enlightenment"; and in Germany "Illumination."

ture's laws. An eclipse of the sun which would have frightened mediæval people as an omen of strange meanings was now understood as an astronomical fact devoid of any religious significance.

It was this new and growing scientific attitude applied to the book of Nature that was to be carried over and applied to the book of Scripture.

As early as 1624 a young English cavalier, Sir Edward Herbert, better known by his later title, Lord Herbert of Cherbury, wrote a deistic book entitled *De Veritate*. Sir Herbert was a man of wide travel and observation. He had acted for many years as the English ambassador at the French Court, where he came under the sway of certain "advanced" thoughts that made a profound impression on his mind and were later reflected in his writings.

The significance of Lord Herbert's *De Vertitate* is in the argument it sets up: that the great and vital truths of Christianity have sprung most naturally from the innate reason of man and were not in any sense the gift of a supernatural communication from God. In fact, argues Lord Herbert, the most sensible beliefs of Christianity have been shared by the wise and good men of all ages and races many centuries before the birth of Christ. Consequently, intelligent men can no longer conceive the Bible as a special, or a peculiarly supernatural, revelation bestowed by divine favor upon Christians (particularly when all peoples the world over who never heard of Christ have an understanding of the fundamental truths of morality and religion).

Pursuing this same line of thought, but in another book, *On the Religion of a Layman,* Lord Herbert dwelt on the difficulties that surround the average person in his quest for fundamental truth. Because of their constant appeals to the supernatural the clergy are chiefly responsible for blinding the people; they denounce reason as a "human" faculty entirely too depraved to be of genuine service. But Herbert warns his readers to be cautious of those who make a habit of minimizing man's most glorious possession. Far from being a depraved faculty, Reason alone is the resplendent crown of every human being. And it is in the light of Reason, not in its absence, that Lord Herbert asks men to read the Bible. If they do that they will soon find in the Scriptures many things not of equal moral value. By the simple and unobstructed exercise of his reason man will naturally let go of the rubbish therein heaped up—and by the same reason he will also prize its worth-while teachings. . . .

Lord Herbert's volumes were the mere beginnings of the fireworks. Already England was on the tip-toe of excitement with all kinds of controversial essays and tracts being shot off the press. Soon a brilliant galaxy of authors—John Milton, Thomas Hobbes, John Locke —lit up the overcast sky with a colorful intellectual display. . . . Men were beginning to think deeply in staid old England.

In the midst of all this excitement there appeared an anonymous little book that had wrapped up within its pages a big message. It was entitled *Christianity Not Mysterious*—a very bold title which its author flung into the wide open spaces where it caused a considerable explosion of indignation. It was soon discovered to be the work of John Toland, a young Irishman who proved to be as influential in the latter part of the seventeenth century as Thomas Paine in the latter part of the eighteenth. "I demand to what end should God require us to believe what we cannot understand"—that was the spirit of this youthful thinker from Dublin.

It was in 1629 that Toland's literary bomb first struck those vestigal remains of mediæval ideas rotting in a dead theology. He wrote his book, as he himself says, in order to show that "there is nothing in the Gospels contrary to reason, nor above it; and that no Christian doctrine can properly be called a mystery." Such a purpose was a direct attack upon those among the clergy who were teaching just the very opposite doctrine to the people, namely, that Christianity and its Bible are full of knowledge "too deep and too wonderful" to be understood by mortal man. The British people having so long regarded the Christian Scriptures as a volume of mysteries to be unfolded by interpretations still more mysterious it is no wonder that Toland's book was regarded as a punch into the sacred midriff of theology. As harsh as it was there is no denying that it carried the vigorous spirit of the newer age that frankly regarded supernaturalism as a hiding-place for all sorts of beliefs contrary to common sense. "If the writers of the Bible never seek to confound or mislead, but to convince the mind, it follows that the best way to get to their meaning is honestly to use our intellects following the same rules of interpretation which we should apply to any other book. Reason being in this way the channel through which we receive revelation, it is impossible that we can receive as Divine what is contrary to reason."

Toland was but a young man of twenty-five when he wrote, and his book suffers from much haste and immaturity. It has an air of arrogance with not a few rash speculations. But beyond these limitations its main point was acknowledged by thinking people to be sound. Theology had long used the phrase "above reason" as a clever device to invest the Scriptures with an authority they did not possess. By the use of these words the most absurd ideas were given a lofty finality. In Toland the demands of common sense found a champion. Instead of following the old method of first accepting the Authority of the Scriptures as divine and then proceeding to consider its contents, the young Irishman insisted on the very opposite procedure—that is, first examine its contents and then see how much of it commends itself to one's intelligence. . . . This, of course, was the fundamental principle of that other famous young man, Benedict Spinoza, from whose writings Toland learnt many valuable lessons. As a matter of fact, one of the charges levelled against Toland and his tribe was that "they read Hobbes and Spinoza, and learned to laugh at Balaam's ass and Samson's locks, then to ridicule all supernaturalism."

Young as he was our daring author was no fool. He realized that the rigid orthodoxy of his time would fight him to the last ditch. "Some will not thank me, it's possible, for so useful an undertaking; and others will make me a heretic in grain for what I have performed already. But as it is Duty, and nobody's applause, which is the rule of my actions; so God knows, I no more value this cheap and ridiculous nickname of a heretic than Paul did before me: for I acknowledge no *Orthodoxy* but the *Truth*." So iniquitous was his book considered, and so ubiquitous was the denunciation that the clergy rang from their pulpits against him, that a certain man on being asked why he ceased to attend church answered that he was accustomed in his youth to hear something about his Savior Jesus Christ but that now all the talking was about John Toland. . . . The highest tribute paid to *Christianity Not Mysterious* must be credited to the Irish Parliament upon whose orders the book was burned before the gate of the House "in the august presence of the sheriffs and the constables of the City of Dublin."

Scarcely had the storm raised by Toland subsided when the attention of the thinking world was engaged —this time even more acrimoniously—by Thomas Woolston who had been a fellow of Sidney-Sussex College in Cambridge. . . . During a brief period of but two years, 1727-1729, Woolston dashed off a series of half a dozen pamphlets entitled "Discourses on Miracles" wherein the very serious question of the historical character of the Gospels was raised for the first time. Had Woolston's writings been less eccentric he would perhaps have escaped being so severely raked over the hot coals of indignation. Not only was he deprived of his Fellowship and prosecuted for libel but he was sentenced to a fine which he was unable to pay and so died in prison. Surely he knew in advance the odium that was awaiting just around the corner. But maybe that very realization made him all the more determined, in order to arouse the public intelligence, to use as spiked and rough-shod a manner of presentation as the English language could command.

There was no vagabond doubt in Woolston's mind on the subject of miracles. For that reason the influence of his pamphlets cannot be discounted; they served their purpose since in the boldest and most trenchant manner he examined the miracles of Christ as recorded in the Gospels and showed with much ability and shrewd common sense that because of their gross inconsistencies they contained many unhistorical and untrustworthy elements. With unmistakable directness he assailed the genuineness of supernatural occurrences by showing them up as "incredible" history. *So?*

Woolston's discourses had tremendous circulation, exerting a very wide and far-reaching influence. Scores of replies were hurled at him, it being estimated that upward of sixty pamphlets were written in vindication of Christ's miracles. . . . Voltaire who was at that time in England was greatly impressed by them and when he came to write his own article on "Miracles" in his famous *Philosophical Dictionary* he did not fail to discuss Woolston's importance. "It seems to me that among the moderns, Thomas Woolston, doctor of Cambridge, was the first who dared . . . and who brazenly maintained that none of the miracles of Jesus Christ had really been worked. He wrote without method, without literary charm, and in a rough and jumbled style, but not without vigor."

An English visitor who came to see Voltaire in his old age chanced to discuss with the Frenchman the great changes that had taken place since the days of Woolston. "When critics are silent," caustically observed the venerable philosopher, "it does not so much prove the age to be correct, as dull."

Progress at best is curiously fitful, now in one country now in another, with long intervals of marking time between its various stages. Shortly after Woolston's death English leadership in critical thought—which had been of brief duration—died down. . . . The torch of progress passed over to Germany.

Was it not the Wesleyan revival that changed the situation in England?

4

By the opening of the eighteenth century the spirit of Rationalism had made such a wide appeal to biblical scholars that there was no longer any hesitancy about going directly to the Scriptures in order to consider its documents at first hand in much the same way in which men were handling the histories of Greece and Rome, divesting them of their legendary accretions and sifting myth from fact in an honest endeavor to trace out the correct historical process. The new spirit began to proceed on the principle that no document however sacred or beautiful can claim exemption from investigation.

The English pioneers—Lord Herbert, Toland, Woolston—opened the eyes of intelligent men. But it was left to the Germans to give the world a vigorous arousing, for now, on the soil of the Fatherland, the sharpest kind of investigation began to get under way. This would have been utterly impossible had not the breadth and universality of Humanism already found a group of men possessing a thoroughgoing dislike and antagonism to ecclesiastical authority and supernatural ideas.

Of course, on all sides there was a shuddering repugnance at the aggressiveness of those who were demanding the right to treat the New Testament in this way. Having been accustomed to look upon the Gospels with solemn veneration and holy awe it was not to be expected that devout and pious Christians would calmly sit by and watch their sacred book analyzed without a strong protest. Anything that is cherished always stands on a high and guarded pedestal: in the case of the Scriptures this pedestal exalted the Bible to an overtowering height far beyond any other possession in Christendom. For what book is a true manifestation of God's omnipotence but this? What book was ever supernaturally guarded against all error but this? And for what book besides this can it be claimed that its authors were especially prepared in their task by divine selection and supernatural endowment? Through this book God actually spoke to the world. . . . With such a belief it is no wonder that each word of the supposed revelation was passionately guarded. It assumed for the Bible an immunity from error. And just because it was considered different from other books it was not to be read like other books. Consequently, there were many earnest pleas not to subject the Bible to an investigation, for after all —so it was claimed—the very fact that the Scriptures had been under the shelter of the church for eighteen centuries thereby exempted it from methods one would ordinarily use in treating any other book.

Now, when there is added to this deep reverence for the Scriptures the greater reverence for the central figure of the Gospels—the personality of Jesus— it can be readily appreciated what a large amount of courage was needed to undertake the task of investigation. Only the undaunted desire to know the truth—a tremendous tribute to the human mind—kept the biblical scholars close to their task in face of terrific opposition; for it must not be forgotten that every advance in thought was regarded by the masses of the people as a veiled attempt to degrade the Bible.

For that reason the new learning made its way very gradually, not, however, without severe conflicts with the old. Yet, it was everywhere evident that the time was ripe for an understanding of Christianity without miracle, a simple account of things that anybody could fathom without being constantly befuddled by the intrusion of ecclesiastical ideas masquerading themselves as being "above reason." Men felt that the mediæval church's interpretation had not been a true interpretation—it sorely obscured and almost completely destroyed the historical character of the New Testament. The Bible had been hugged so closely and so affectionately that its humanity was almost squeezed out of it. . . . This way of handling the Scriptures, sincere as it was, had torn the Bible limb by limb from its historical setting. Therefore, the present need was to heal the fractures and dislocations.

Just exactly how this was done will be told in detail in the next chapter on the Higher Criticism of the New Testament. But before men could practise the Higher Criticism it was necessary first of all to get rid of the intolerable dogmatism that the Bible is a divinely supernatural book.

5

Toward the end of the century—to be exact, in 1781—there appeared in Germany an essay whose very title sums up the intellectual revolution which had taken place in intelligent minds. In that year Gotthold Lessing published a paper on "A New Hypothesis Concerning the Evangelists Considered Simply as Human Historians." By and large this treatise was an open attempt to take the Gospels away from narrow theological grounds and make them an affair of history. With this in mind, Lessing began sketching the story of early

Christianity and arrived at the idea that there must have sprung up on Palestinian soil various collections of the sayings and deeds of Jesus which were composed in the native Hebrew dialect, the Aramaic language which Jesus and the apostles spoke. Now, the Gospels are written in Greek. What does this signify? Clearly one thing: that behind their present Greek form there must be a vast unknown ocean of original Aramaic sources out of which the Gospels were compiled. (When we come to the chapter on the Higher Criticism of the Gospels we shall see what an important part this "Aramaic" idea plays in reconstructing the true story of how the Gospels were written.)

At the age of 59, after he had become a member of the Berlin Academy and had the pleasure of seeing his finest dramatic works published, Lessing was appointed head of the ducal library at Wolfenbuttel. The appointment removed him from the hustling world outside to a quiet world within shifting his interests from the field of dramatics to the realms of theology. But whether inside or outside a library Lessing was a man of action with a shrewd eye for undiscovered treasures. Packed away on the old shelves in half forgotten corners the erstwhile dramatist uncovered several important tracts and treatises which he published with considerable success. This led him on to a new discovery which concerns us in telling how the structure of supernaturalism went down in collapse. . . .

Now there lived in Hamburg a quiet and scholarly man who until his death in 1768 had been a teacher of oriental languages in his native city for forty years. During his lifetime he had published several books and as a man of wide culture he had read deeply into the

work of the English rationalists and the French ency-
clopedists. For his own intellectual satisfaction, and for
the benefit of a few select friends, Prof. Herman Samuel Reimarus wrote several short little papers (fragments) setting forth some very unconventional and advanced ideas about the Bible. But he refused to have
them published, feeling that the time was not ripe.

Lessing's acquaintance with the learned Reimarus
was acquired during the last year of the professor's
life which fortunately gave the dramatist time enough
in which to appreciate the splendid things this savant
had written. No doubt Lessing realized then, what the
educated world now knows, that Reimarus had made
a splendid attempt to form a corrected historical conception of the life of Jesus. Here for the first time in
the whole history of Christianity an ably equipped
mind turned its searching powers into an honest investigation of the most sacred character of western civilization.

Shortly after Reimarus's death, Lessing went to see
the professor's son and daughter in an effort to get possession of the deceased's manuscript. After many delays and much hesitation on the part of the heirs, Lessing finally secured permission to publish the fragments on condition that they would be sent out into the
world anonymously. With this pledge Lessing saw
them through the press under the title of the "Wolfenbuttel Fragments." In trying to avoid as much censure
as possible Lessing allowed himself certain liberties,
which, perhaps, were quite necessary considering the
importance of gaining a hearing in face of the orthodoxy of the German people and the hatred of the theologians. "They are, as I say, fragments of a work but

I cannot decide whether of a work actually finished and destroyed, or of one never completed. For they have no universal title; their author is nowhere given; and I have by no means been able to discover how and when they came into our library. Nay, I am not certain that they are fragments of one work, but I conclude as much from this, that they have all one object, and all bear upon revealed religion, and more especially the criticism of Bible history."

The publication of the "Fragments" produced a sensation throughout Germany, creating such a wild conflagration of controversy that the government was finally obliged to step in and stop the series. . . . But freedom of thought and discussion could not be so easily checked. Reimarus, with well-aimed and powerful blows, had dealt supernaturalism an ingnominious death. Furthermore, he dropped the sharpest acids of criticism on contemporary superstition in at least two of his fragments, one on "The Decrying of Reason in the Pulpit," and the other on "The Impossibility of the Revelation which all men should have good Grounds for Believing." But even still more revolutionary than these was Reimarus's famous document on "The Aims of Jesus and his Disciples" which became the world's starting point in a historical understanding of the central figure of Christianity.*

Perhaps because he was timid, or perhaps because he thought the time was not ripe to give his advanced ideas to the world, Reimarus preferred to go to his grave with his fragments unpublished. Yet he realized that in order to understand the Bible it was first necessary for

---

*The whole subject of the critical investigation of Christ is admirably well treated in Schweitzer's book *In Quest of the Historical Jesus*. This is an English translation from the German *Von Reimarus zu Wrede*.

men to get rid of the pestiferous notion of its divine origin. He claimed, what almost every sensible theologian to-day concurs in, that the Bible is to be read like any other book: as one would read the Dialogues of Plato, the dramas of Sophocles, or the Cantos of the Iliad. He imputed to the Old and New Testaments no inspiration beyond the loftiness of the intelligence that created it—such loftiness as may be found and recognized in all high literature. He recognized that the Gospel writers like other biographers depended upon the ordinary sources of information and hence did not receive the facts of the life of Jesus by supernatural communication. Taken all in all the writings of Reimarus, their intellectual honesty and historical spirit, may be summed up in one of his most pungent sentences which from his day to this has marked the long course of investigation. "That which is absurd and impossible, that which in any other history would be called falsehood, deception, outrage, and cruelty, cannot be made reasonable, righteous, and true by the added words: Thus saith the Lord."

6

As harsh and as brutally honest as the spirit of Rationalism undoubtedly was, it exerted by no means a wholly negative influence in undermining traditional beliefs. Men like Toland and Woolston in England, and Lessing and Reimarus in Germany, contributed something very positive. It is true that their rationalism served to shift the emphasis of European thinking. Thought is the greatest force in all the world; and the secret of progress is not in holding ideas forcibly but in holding forcible ideas. By projecting vigorous methods of scientific historical research they prepared the way for the creation of new moral and intellectual values.

One needs to take but a single illustration in witness of their beneficial influence. Here, for example, was the great question of Negro Slavery that agitated the United States from the founding of the Republic. Those pious Christians who defended this barbaric institution did so, in large part, on the authority of the Bible which they sincerely believed had declared for all time that the black man was destined to be the bond-servant of the white. If the Bible is not to be taken at its face value where then are Christians to go for their ultimate sanctions?—that was the great dilemma. The way out of this chaos, that went so far as to embroil the United States in a long and bitter Civil War, was indicated by that great preacher of Boston, a man who understood rationalism at its highest and best. In immortal and never-to-be-forgotten words Theodore Parker declared: "The Bible sanctions slavery. The conscience of mankind does not; the conscience of mankind must judge the Bible."

Although at first extremely feeble, the spirit of Rationalism with its truer comprehension of things was bound to win. The ancient theology, deeply entrenched and hoary with age, eventually had to be thrown on the scrapheap of time. And after the storms had settled down even the theologians themselves came around to a wholesome appreciation of the need of straining supernatural elements out of the Bible. . . .

With the collapse of Supernaturalism—for that is what the whole thing meant—common sense came into complete control. And when men saw the ancient

[handwritten margin note:] does not the Bible contain the Principle that destroy slavery?

[handwritten note at bottom:] may not the Bible be a human book recording supernatural as well as natural events?

Temple of Unreason lying in ruins they immediately realized that its débris had to be cleared off the stage in order to make ready for the scientific performance of the next act.

PART V

THE "NEW" NEW TESTAMENT

Not by chance or arbitrariness has so large a group of biblical experts reached so strong an agreement. Like explorers set down in the Valley of Diamonds they have discovered a new world bestrewn with gems, each one a flashing crystal of delight. . . .

CHAPTER I

THE HIGHER CRITICISM OF THE GOSPELS, OR THE TRUE STORY OF HOW THESE DOCUMENTS WERE WRITTEN

IT is sometimes thought—mostly however in half-educated circles—that the men who undermined the old theology and exploded antiquated beliefs were relentless enemies of the church and the synagogue, a sort of mixed and rowdy group of infidels, atheists, anarchists, and libertines. Such has long been the popular and misleading impression which glances at all biblical investigation as a dark and sinister menace.

Nothing could be farther from the truth. The founders of the science of Biblical Criticism were not only men of superb courage, with wide awake and unbefuddled power, but they were devotees of a very high type of religion, frequently far in advance of their respective denominations. These scholars were no ordinary group of thinkers. It is true that they were often harsh and blunt—they had to be in order to speak their minds against contemporary dislike for reason and investigation. It is often a thankless and ungracious office to tell the world what it least wishes to hear, and a man must be prepared to carry his cross to a Calvary for his pursuit of honest knowledge. With but few exceptions the scholars who undertook biblical science suffered the manifold hardships of excommunication, persecution, heresy trials, social ostracism, degradation, and loss of livelihood.

And yet, practically all of them received their training at the hands of the old-time orthodoxy. It was not that they disliked Tradition but they loved Truth more. And it was out of a sincere desire to purify the teachings of religion that they waged their battles upon ignorance and superstition. All this they did very reluctantly, and not as some foolish people think to batter down religion, but on the contrary to lay the spiritual foundations of civilization with greater security and in line with the advancement of knowledge and progress.

The adoption of an unpopular attitude always demands courage, as Ibsen has so well shown in his play *The Enemy of the People*. On the great questions of Life—and particularly as regards the modern outlook of the average man—there have been many vast changes within recent years. No longer are people satisfied with milk-bottle answers. Intelligent men and women show a justifiable resentment against being treated like infants. Years ago, for example, whenever an inquiry was made concerning the origin of the Bible some such innocuous reply as this was given: "Men spake with God, being moved by the Holy Ghost, and the result was the book which we call the Bible." That was considered an all-sufficient response. To-day it answers nothing!

An evasive answer always has behind it a desire to withhold something, fearing the fierce light of intelligence because there are skeletons in the closet. It was Matthew Arnold who severely criticised Colenso, not because the learned Bishop had written the truth about the Bible, but because his book made its appearance in English which everybody could read. Arnold said

that Colenso should have written in Latin primarily
for the scholars (since they alone would have read it
and the damage could not have been so great)! . . .

The science of Biblical Criticism rests foursquare
upon the position that the Scriptures have nothing to
fear, any more than the mountains must fear the science
of geology, or the stars the science of astronomy. The
Bible is just what it is, and all that men can do is to
find the truth about it. Honest scholarship therefore
seeks to destroy but one thing: misconception.

It was in this spirit of truth that the great Textual
Critics—all of whom were connected with some
branch of organized Christianity—cleared the way
through the deep underbrush of ecclesiastical teaching
by discrediting the theory of an "immaculate" and perfect text. It was essentially in this same spirit, despite
certain hasty conclusions and half-baked ideas, that the
rationalists in France, England, and Germany demolished the time-honored supernaturalism and set Christianity free from its huge growth of myth and miracles.
When all this valuable and preliminary work had been
accomplished, the road was made ready for a new turn
in its further development and extension. For it now remained for the Higher Critics to push forward the investigation of the New Testament along historical
lines. And it is this story of their accomplishment that
we will now pass in review.

2

Already intelligent men had realized that most of
the Old Testament books are not only anonymous but
highly composite productions. Certain writings traditionally ascribed to Moses, David, Solomon, Daniel

and others turned out to be utterly lacking in the
necessary evidences in support of such authorships. On
the contrary, these old documents bore unmistakable
earmarks of having gone through a long compilatory
process. That being the case with the Old Testament:
how about the New Testament? Are all its books in
reality the products of those Apostles whom church
tradition has so piously honored? Or, do these writings present the same kind of inescapable proof as to
plurality of writers?

Who were the true authors of the Christian Bible?

Were these men actually eye-witnesses of the dramatic incidents in the life of Jesus—or do their records
rest largely upon hearsay?

When were these books written: early or late?

Why were they produced?

To begin with there are the Gospels—four biographies of Jesus attributed to four different authors:
Matthew, Mark, Luke and John. Now the first thing
that strikes the alert reader of these four documents is
their wide resemblances and yet their very sharp and
stubborn differences. This presents at the very outset an
inescapable literary phenomenon that demands immediate explanation: inasmuch as these Gospels have their
similarities and differences, what is their inter-relation?

It was soon found out that of these biographies the
first three—Matthew, Mark, and Luke—are so definitely geared into each other that they belong in a class
by themselves, totally distinct from the Fourth Gospel.
Consequently, these three have been called the "Synoptic Gospels" because they contain substantially the
same material and are capable of being "viewed together" in parallel columns. On the other hand, the

Fourth Gospel has a very different arrangement, its construction does not follow the common plan of the other three. For example, this Fourth Gospel (traditionally called the "Gospel according to John") narrates no baptism and reports no temptation; it contains many new places and persons not mentioned elsewhere; and in addition it presents a portrait of Jesus altogether unique. In Matthew, Mark, and Luke the ministry of Jesus is preceded by an account of his baptism; and the temptation is given prominence. These three Gospels narrate, sometimes in almost verbal harmony, the same stories, the same journeys, the same colloquies, the same warnings—they even repeat the same misquotations. From first to last, amid minor differences, they present the teaching and work of Jesus from the same general point of view.

It will be recalled that in telling the inside story of how the documents of the Pentateuch were unravelled, scholars discovered four main sources: Yahwistic, Elohistic, Deuteronomic, and Priestly. Now, the narratives of the life of Jesus—somewhat similar to the narratives of Moses—are given in a fourfold tradition. What we have here is such a remarkable correspondence that for purposes of illustration we might compare Mark with the Yahwistic, Luke with the Elohistic, Matthew with the Deuteronomic, and John with the Priestly. However, there is a difference between the Pentateuch and the Gospels inasmuch as the four narratives of the Pentateuch were braided together into one piece while the Gospels remained independent.*

*In the middle of the second century A. D. a Syrian scholar by the name of Tatian took the four Gospels and wove them together into one story. His book was called *Diatessaron* (literally, the Book of the Four) and was the official gospel of the Syrian Church for about two centuries. It was finally suppressed.

Again: it will be recalled that the "inside view" of the Pentateuch shows that each document is a skein of many colors woven of many strands. In a similar manner each gospel, despite its seeming unity, is a composite literary product. While the very oldest Pentateuchal record—the Yahwistic—possesses an amazing unity, yet it contains within itself stories and laws of diverse origin and from many widely separated generations. One must always be willing to draw a distinction between the earlier age when a law or an idea was born and the much later period when it was reduced to writing. Particularly in the slow-moving Orient things passed from tongue to ear long before they were put on parchment. For this very reason all ancient writings are full of irregularities. The Gospels have their share of broken joints, mutilations, misfits and deformities—very far from being faultless historical records or exquisite specimens of infallibility. The large number of variations between them is indicative of a complex result of a complex process presenting many insoluble problems. One needs only a very brief acquaintance with these writings to appreciate how evident is their lack of correspondence. Huge boulders of discord and imperfection lie strewn along the rough and stony highway of their composition. . . .

3

We know that the Yahwistic document was the first written narrative of the Pentateuch. Do we know as much about the Gospels? That is to say: can we answer the question who wrote the first account of the ministry of Jesus?

A hundred and fifty years of the most assiduous effort pushed with unremitting zeal and tireless labor has not failed to arrive at some real results. Scientific scholarship has definitely established the priority of Mark as the first and earliest of the records setting forth the doings of the man of Galilee. It was out of Mark that both Matthew and Luke took the framework for their own writings, cleverly fitting into its arrangement their own distinctive material and coloring the whole by their own individual treatment.

We will look at the New Testament just as we looked at the Old—as a geologist sees the strata of the earth and tells us in what order the deposits were laid down. And in the light of what has already been told about the Hebrew sacred writings it is going to be very easy to understand the Christian. For the Orient did not change much in those days and the processes of literary production current among the Christian writers were about the same as they had always been among the Hebrews.

Going back for a moment to the Yahwistic document and the story of its composition we saw how it was built up from very old sources—literary fossils embedded in literary rock. The same is true of the Gospels: they all rest upon materials much older than themselves, each gospel representing a gradual accretion of records.

Mark—the earliest of the evangelists—is a document that may be conjecturally dated shortly before the Romans destroyed Jerusalem in 70 A. D. This means that a chasm of thirty or forty years separates Mark's written document from the ministry of Jesus—a long enough time to create a plastic body of oral teachings and a highly colored tradition embellished with fanciful stories. Even here in the United States in less than fifteen years after the death of Abraham Lincoln much was attributed to the great emancipator which, while bearing his spirit, is not in reality authentic. A forceful personality always sets in motion a stream of incessant assimilation and this is nowhere more clearly seen than in the Gospels which have reached their present form through successive stages of elaboration. . . .

Unfortunately, there are no historical references telling us how the Gospel of Mark was written. Consequently, all investigation is thrown back on the document itself and such meagre bits of tradition as come floating down the centuries. Only however by getting in on the inside of the narrative has it been possible for the biblical scholars to extract a reasonable story of its composition and growth. All this, of course, had to be done by that weary, laborious and round-about process known as the Higher Criticism.

An old tradition has been passed down the centuries which comes from the writings of Papias (about 125 A. D.) who was bishop of Hierapolis. Living close to the times of the early Christian leaders, much significance is attached to his famous report that "Mark, having become the interpreter of Peter, wrote accurately whatever he remembered, not, however, recording in order the things that were said or done by Christ." This reference is considered of great importance in establishing the fact that the Gospel of Mark has its basis in that oral gospel which he had heard directly from the lips of Peter. It does seem undeniably true that the Gospel of Mark bears traits of an eye-witness; and it can well be that its vividness and color are due to the personal reminiscenses which Peter communicated to Mark.*

We would like to know so much about those far-off interesting days. Unfortunately the outlines are obscured in dense fog. No one knows how the loose material of Peter's reminiscences was shaped into our present Gospel of Mark. No one knows for sure whether it was written in Rome (as many believe) or in some other city of the ancient world. We are simply left in the air with the uncomfortable feeling that the true details will perhaps never be really discovered.

<h1 style="text-align:center">4</h1>

Next to Mark comes Luke. Both men were of that younger Christian generation which had no personal acquaintance with the great Master and so had to get their information largely from what others said, or from what the friends of eye-witnesses had seen. Luke in particular makes no claim of having watched Jesus in action. His object in writing was merely to present a clearer and more complete account of the Galilean rabbi. That is all that he professes to do. And he is careful to tell us just that in his own very fine introduction:

"Forasmuch as many have taken in hand to draw up a narrative concerning those matters which have been fulfilled among us, even as they delivered them unto us, who from the beginning were eye-witnesses and ministers of the word, it seemed good to me also, having traced the course of all things accurately from the first, to write unto thee in order, most excellent The-

*There are some scholars who regard the present Gospel of Mark as a very much revised and expanded edition of the original Mark. The German scholars have called this hypothetical original "Ur-Marcus."

ophilus, that thou mightest know the certainty concerning the thing wherein thou wast instructed."

Luke was a Greek physician living somewhere on the shores of the Ægean Sea. He had been a friend of Paul, just as Mark had been with Peter.* In his part of the country all kinds of new-fangled stories and sayings about Jesus' work were being circulated, stories that were contradictory and very confusing. Greek Christians were fast getting muddled, they hardly knew what to believe. Among this large number of perplexed people there was a man of high position and intelligence named Theophilus who was a friend of Luke. Perhaps it was he that suggested to his physician to write a fresh account which would bring order out of chaos. Whatever the immediate impulse, Luke wrote. He undertook to bring together into one comprehensive account the best elements of the Jesus story according to his own lights.

One thing is certain: when Luke came to writing his own account of the ministry of Jesus he had a much easier task than his predecessors. He not only had an abundance of material from which to make selections but he had a good model in Mark's gospel, which he deliberately incorporated into his own. Of the total number of words in Mark nearly thirty-five per cent appear in Luke.

In many of the passages which Luke appropriated from Mark the verbal agreement is so very close that notwithstanding the little touches here and there added to enlarge, or modify, or explain the original there is absolutely no difficulty in recognizing the equivalent material, as the following illustration shows.

---

*Perhaps this is why the Book of Acts, now generally admitted by scholars to have been written by Luke, is so full of Paul.

From Mark 1:23-28	From Luke 4:33-37
23 And straightway there was in their synagogue a man with an unclean spirit; and he cried out, 24 saying, What have we to do with thee, thou Jesus of Nazareth? Art thou come to destroy us? I know thee who thou art, the Holy One of God. 25 And Jesus rebuked him, saying, Hold thy peace, and come out of him. 26 And the unclean spirit, tearing him and crying with a loud voice, came out of him. 27 And they were all amazed, insomuch that they questioned among themselves, saying, What is this? a new teaching! with authority he commandeth even the unclean spirits, and they obey him. 28 And the report of him went out straightway everywhere, into all the region of Galilee round about.	33 And in the synagogue there was a man which had a spirit of an unclean devil; and he cried out with a loud voice, 34 Ah, what have we to do with thee, thou Jesus of Nazareth? Art thou come to destroy us? I know thee who thou art, the Holy One of God. 35 And Jesus rebuked him saying, Hold thy peace, and come out of him. And when the devil had thrown him down in the midst, he came out of him, having done him no hurt. 36 And amazement came upon all, and they spake together, one with another, saying, What is this word? for with authority and power he commandeth the unclean spirits, and they come out. 37 And there went forth a rumor concerning him into every place of the region round about.

But the Gospel of Mark was not the only source that Luke employed in his writing. He used large extracts from one very important document which scholars designate by the symbol "Q" (which stands for the German word Quelle, meaning "source"). Knowing what we do about the compilation of various Old Testament books, Luke's borrowing from other writers without acknowledgment should give us no trouble. As has been pointed out in connection with the Hebrew Scriptures: the literary etiquette of the day did not think this manner of doing things at all wrong. There is an interesting parallel in an old English document called the *Saxon Chronicle* which uses somewhat the same method. This mediæval record is a huge compilation relating the history of Britain from Julius Cæsar's invasion to the accession of Henry II in 1154. But nowhere does the *Chronicle* give any information as to who were the authors of its several sources. Our knowledge is limited to the fact that it is a product of the slow growth of many centuries incorporating the works of a multiplicity of unknown writers.

Perhaps the *Saxon Chronicle* is not the best illustration because it covers several centuries of development and expansion. The Gospels, on the other hand, were written within a very short space of time. Still, they all exhibit the same type of compilatory growth. In its present form the Gospel of Luke (it is better to say "according to" Luke) is a braiding together of at least two main primary works: Mark's account and the Q-source; plus other material drawn from a wide variety of written as well as from oral traditions.

5

When the Higher Critics came to the unravelling of Matthew's Gospel they found that it too, like Luke, incorporated large sections from Mark,—nearly fifty per cent,—and in addition used that famous source (also used by Luke) called "Q."

Just to take one brief illustration of how the editor of Matthew copied the Gospel of Mark let us look at the following instance which produces a striking similarity down to the very words which Jesus was reported to have said.

From Mark 1:16-18	*From Matthew 4:18-20*
And passing along by the sea of Galilee, he saw Simon and Andrew the brother of Simon casting a net in the sea; for they were fishers. And Jesus said unto them, Come ye after me, and I will make you to become fishers of men. And straightway they left the net and followed him.	And walking by the sea of Galilee, he saw two brethren, Simon who is called Peter, and Andrew his brother, casting a net into the sea; for they were fishers. And he saith unto them, Come ye after me, and I will make you fishers of men. And they straightway left the nets and followed him.

Just as in the case of the Gospel of Mark there was preserved a bit of traditional testimony from Papias as to where Mark got his ideas about Jesus, so here too, in the case of Matthew, it is reported that Papias made the statement that "Matthew composed the oracles (of Jesus) in the Hebrew dialect and each one interpreted them as he could." Unfortunately the word "Oracles" (logia) is very vague, and it is uncertain just what is meant by it, although it is commonly supposed to denote a collection of the "Sayings" of Jesus. Whatever Matthew jotted down, one thing is certain: he compiled it in the Hebrew dialect, that is the vernacular Aramaic which Jesus spoke. In all probability it was this little document that created the basis of the present Greek-form of the Gospel of Matthew. If that be true it sufficiently explains why the early Christians held on to Matthew's name long after his "Logia" were translated into Greek and then expanded and joined to other material before it was finally revised and worked up into the present composition.

It is this Logia—a collection of the Sayings of Jesus found in both Matthew and Luke—that many scholars designate by the somewhat colorless symbol "Q." Just what "Q" is, may be gathered from the fact that the first preaching and instruction of the Apostles was carried on in Aramaic (Hebrew), the vernacular of Palestine. Naturally there would arise in this language a mass of brief forms containing the important "Sayings" of Jesus. Perhaps the most popular and significant of these records was the one compiled and used by Matthew. Now, due to the spread of Christianity among the Gentiles—to whom Aramaic was unknown —it soon became necessary to instruct the new converts in Greek. Consequently, it was of the utmost practical importance that the original Aramaic collections be done into that language which the majority could understand. Had Christianity remained a purely Jewish movement its literature would have been preserved in the dialect Jesus himself used. But because the new faith overleaped its boundaries it had to make its appeal to Greek-speaking peoples.

A comparison of the "Q" material as it is now preserved in the Gospel of Matthew does not always agree with the "Q" material in Luke. For this reason scholars believe that there must have been in circulation many Greek versions of this Q-source long before the editors of Matthew and Luke began their work.

While Matthew and Luke have much in common, since both used Mark as a source and also "Q," still there are wide differences that are very significant. For example, the genealogy of Jesus as given in Matthew does not correspond with Luke's.* All sorts of preposterous explanations were once concocted in order to harmonize this discrepancy; for it seemed unthinkable to devout Christians that the evangelists did not agree on so important a matter as the ancestry of Christ. At first, the Higher Critics were condemned for declaring that this error was not dictated by the omniscient God. Orthodox theologians actually looked upon the biblical investigators as though this discrepancy in the pedigree of the Master had never existed until their devilish Criticism came along and uncovered it. As a matter of fact, no biblical scholar creates any problems— the discrepancies and errors together with the fractures, leaps, and dislocations are already embedded in the text. All that any intelligent man can do is to offer a rational explanation of how these things have come about.

*The birth roll of Jesus fixed by Matthew 1:1-17 states that there were 42 generations between Abraham and Jesus (but actually mentions only 40). For the same period Luke 3:23-28 gives 55.

"SAYINGS OF JESUS."

This is a papyrus fragment found in Egypt. Undoubtedly scores of different versions of these "Sayings" circulated about the orient. The originals, of course, were in Aramaic, the language Jesus spoke.

Two hundred years of close study of the Gospels have brought many great changes—even among the least progressive wings of Christianity. No longer does any sensible person try to harmonize the two pedigrees in an effort to prove them to be supernaturally in agreement with each other. It is now realized that these divergent accounts are perfectly natural—just as natural as the two stories of Creation, of the two records of the Flood: they arise out of different sources employed by their editors.

Another illustration: Both Matthew and Luke give the Sermon on the Mount. But how different! Matthew knows only the Blessings; but Luke includes the Woes.

From Matthew 5:3-12

3 Blessed are the poor in spirit: for theirs is the kingdom of heaven.

4 Blessed are they that mourn: for they shall be comforted.

5 Blessed are the meek: for they shall inherit the earth.

6 Blessed are they that hunger and thirst after righteousness: for they shall be filled.

7 Blessed are the merciful: for they shall obtain mercy.

8 Blessed are the pure in heart: for they shall see God.

9 Blessed are the peace-makers; for they shall be called sons of God.

10 Blessed are they that have been persecuted for righteousness sake: for theirs is the kingdom of heaven.

11 Blessed are ye when men shall reproach you, and persecute you, and say all manner of evil against you falsely, for my sake.

12 Rejoice and be exceedingly glad: for great is your reward in heaven: for so persecuted they the prophets which were before you.

From Luke 6:20-26

20 Blessed are ye poor; for yours is the kingdom of God.

21 Blessed are ye that hunger now: for ye shall be filled. Blessed are ye that weep now: for ye shall laugh.

22 Blessed are ye when men shall hate you, and when they shall separate you (from their company), and reproach you, and cast out your name as evil for the Son of man's sake.

23 Rejoice in that day, and leap (for joy): for behold your reward is great in heaven: for in the same manner did their fathers unto the prophets.

24 But woe unto you that are rich! for ye have received your consolation.

25 Woe unto you that are full now! for ye shall hunger. Woe (unto you), ye that laugh now! for ye shall mourn and weep.

26 Woe (unto you), when all men shall speak well of you, for in the same manner did their fathers unto the false prophets.

Although the Gospel according to Matthew is an anonymous composition (the name Matthew having been attached to it by tradition) there is evidence that it was used largely by Jewish Christians in much the same way that the Gospel of Luke was used by Gentile Christians. Antioch, the rich and flourishing capital of Syria, contained a good size population of these Hebrews who had acknowledged Jesus as the Messiah. As one of the great centres of early Christianity it is now believed by many scholars that in all probability Antioch is the place, where between the years 75–80 A. D., the Gospel according to Matthew was pieced together and edited—not, of course, by the Apostle Matthew but by some unknown editor who did not even take the trouble to give out any names as to authorship.

6

The Fourth Gospel stands by itself. In style, arrangement, treatment, personalities, and material it is so vastly different from the other gospels that it has created its own special category.

The Jesus of the synoptics differs widely from the Jesus in John's Gospel not only in his actions and general spiritual character but also in his very words. Whereas the synoptics may be said to give a photographic view of Jesus this Fourth evangelist works like an impressionistic painter in his free handling of the colors of history. It is not so much a biography of Jesus that he is after but an *interpretation* of the life and teaching of the Master in terms of idealism, mysticism, and symbolism. While the synoptic Christ is portrayed humble of mind and heart, living in lowly submission to God's will the Christ of the Fourth Gospel is an idealized Figure, majestic in its unearthly glory and moving like a strange light upon the landscape of Judæa. Here is to be found nothing of that meek and forgiving Teacher that we knew elsewhere. This difference in the treatment of the Nazarene reminds one of the equally profound difference between Socrates as portrayed by Plato and the picture given by Xenophon.

Positive information as to who wrote this Fourth Gospel, where and when it made its first appearance, is very difficult to find. Many scholars believe that it was written in the city of Ephesus, somewhere around the year 100 A. D.

But by whom?

Church tradition ascribed it to the Apostle John, the son of Zebedee, one of the fishermen whom Jesus called to be a disciple. Years ago this view was easily entertained, but there now exists too much refractory evidence against assigning this Greek gospel to an Aramaic-speaking Galilean. That an untutored fisherman could have written so elaborate and so highly philosophical an account of Jesus has always presented a thorny problem. And so to most scholars John's authorship of the Fourth Gospel is unthinkable.*

Perhaps some other person by the name of John was its author? Or, perhaps John the Apostle merely wrote a fragment in Aramaic which served as the basis of an accretive compilation that has been cleverly worked up into its present Greek form? Unfortunately nobody knows the answers to these questions.

*Equally complex is the literary history of that strange and fantastic book called the "Revelations of St. John" which is also frequently referred to by its Greek name "Apocalypse." Church tradition naïvely assigned the authorship of this document to the writer of the Fourth Gospel although nothing is more certain than that one and the same man could not have been the author of both.

But this does not prevent us from enjoying the many fine and noble teachings embedded in this Gospel. For example, there is related the story of that delightful miracle that Jesus performed at a wedding feast in the village of Cana in Galilee. With no wine for the ceremony it looked as though the nuptials would have to be a rather dismal affair. So, on being informed of the situation Jesus changed the water, standing in the forlorn jars, into a delicious and sparkling liqueur.

Perhaps the author of this gospel never intended that people should accept his story literally. It is better understood as a charming piece of symbolism. What John wants to say is that without the influence of Jesus human life is like a lot of ordinary water growing stagnant in the jars. Yet this need not be always so; for once his magnetic presence is felt it possesses the magical power of transforming humdrum routine into sparkling experiences of abundant joy.

One of the least known, but yet one of the most delicately beautiful poems ever written deals with the subject of this particular miracle. Many years ago it was submitted by an English student to a university that had announced a very handsome award for the best verse dealing with Jesus' experience at the wedding feast in Cana. Many poems poured in—some scholars having attempted quite elaborate compositions. But the poem that won the coveted prize consisted of only one short line:

The modest water saw its Lord, and blushed.

CHAPTER II

HOW THE NEW TESTAMENT CAME TO BE LIMITED TO TWENTY–SEVEN BOOKS

SEVERAL years ago a professor of biblical literature at one of the large American universities asked his class this question: "What are the Epistles?" Among the many startling answers a certain young man wrote: "The Epistles are the wives of the Apostles."

In a sense he was right. As Christianity grew into an organized religion it soon became wedded to the Epistles of Paul, which are now known to have been the earliest of all the documents of the New Testament. At least twenty years before any of the Gospels were written, this restless and impetuous man was sending letters to his friends. He must have carried on a very large correspondence, although only a handful of his writings have been preserved.*

Paul was a busy man, earning his living as a tent-maker when he was not establishing new branches of his church. What then prompted him to write? Was it because he had a strong penchant for literature? Or, did he feel that Christianity was destined to become a huge success and that here was an opportunity, inas-

---

*The following Epistles are usually considered by scholars to be the "genuine" letters of Paul.

Epistles	Probable date of composition
I and II Thessalonians	51 A. D.
I Corinthians	55 A. D.
II Corinthians	56 A. D.
Galatians	56 A. D.
Romans	57 A. D.
Colossians, Philemon	61 A. D.
Philippians	62 A. D.

much as he was on the ground floor, to make himself
famous by writing the "first" documents of the great
religion that was to be?

It was not until the nineteenth century that these
questions were scientifically answered, for it was not
until that time that biblical scholars undertook a penetrating investigation of the Epistles. The first man to
pave the way to a correct understanding of Paul's correspondence was Ferdinand C. Baur, professor at the
University of Tubingen in Germany and founder of
the famous school of "Tubingen Criticism." In 1831
Baur published an essay on the "Christ-party in the
Christian Church" which presented the historical evidence that there was a strong faction in the Christian
community of Corinth which disputed Paul's claims
and openly disagreed with his theology. In order to
vindicate himself and uphold his views the tent-maker
wrote to the Corinthians. Consequently, it was not the
peaceful interests of literature that urged Paul to write
but bitter controversy in which he was forced to use
his pen in self-defense.

Paul had his enemies not only in Corinth but everywhere—in Rome, in Galatia, in Ephesus, at Colossæ.
He wrote out of sheer necessity. Opposition had raised
its ugly head and he was determined to meet it boldly.
As each new crisis presented itself he rushed with new
intensity to meet it, and therewith a fresh literary
output.

Written as they were in the heat of the moment,
nothing was farther from Paul's mind than the concerns of literature. He dictated his letters utterly unconscious of any rhetorical effort—in fact his paragraphs, vigorous as they are, frequently strike us as

clumsy and twisted. Least of all did he ever think that these notes, dashed off at white-heat, would some day become a part of a sacred collection of holy books!

True

Had Paul written to individuals no doubt all his letters would have quickly perished. But he addressed his communications to churches, and so they were preserved with fanatical zeal. In less than a hundred years after his death people were venerating his epistles next to the reported words of Jesus. So great was the name of Paul that many writings were attributed to him of which he knew nothing. It is certain that the "Epistle to the Hebrews" was never written by this great apostle; it is also certain that Paul never wrote that circular letter called "Ephesians." Yet the very fact that these writings have been assigned to him is just another evidence that stamps this tent-maker as one of the most forceful personalities of history.

Doubt it,

2

Alongside of the collection of Paul's letters, one finds in the New Testament a number of similar epistles of very doubtful authorship. These writings come from a much later period but they too breathe the atmosphere of opposition and warfare. Early Christianity which had long been pictured as a peaceful and loving communion living in paradisiacal harmony was actually nothing of the kind. Split and torn into all kinds of sects it was more like Joseph's coat-of-many-colors instead of Christ's seamless robe. The air was full of jealousy, bitter antagonism and innuendo. Those who believed one way spared no denunciation upon their brethren who could not see eye to eye with them. Even before he died, Paul witnessed his own churches, which he had worked so hard to establish, broken up into warring parties. It looked as though Jesus' disciples had come to bring not Peace but a Sword.

One of the great gains of scientific scholarship since the days of Baur has been to re-create this early atmosphere in which Christianity was struggling not so much from its foes without as from its hot dissensions within. The libraries of the world are now filled with a huge and growing literature which sets forth these absorbing historical facts. We come across strange words like "Gnosticism"—a form of belief which for a long time threatened to displace the teachings of Paul. Then we read about the "Alogi," the "Ebionites," the "Montanists," the "Marcionites"—various divisions which were far more antagonistic to each other than some of the modern denominations which still draw lines of demarcation within Christianity. In fact, it might be said that all the writings of the New Testament are controversial and each document when scientifically studied in the light of history betrays an important bias.

Of course, this does not mean that controversial literature has no value even after the heated issue has long died down. In a very true sense the Declaration of Independence is controversial in that it sets up republican ideas in opposition to eighteenth century England. Dante wrote his poem on a political situation which has long since been dead. Milton's *Paradise Lost* and Dean Swift's *Gulliver's Travels* have behind them the passion of a great controversy. While the average man may care little for what former ages fought about, still it is undeniably true that an intelligent understanding of the New Testament depends on a full knowledge of these antagonistic forces that brought it into existence.

Before the rise of Higher Criticism men looked upon the New Testament as a unity in the sense that the ideas, teachings, and the "outlook" of all the twenty-seven writings were uniform. Since Baur's day all this has been changed. Each New Testament document is frankly understood in terms of its own views without any attempt to conceal differences and inconsistencies. Even on so great a subject as the personality of Jesus, the New Testament contains the most opposite pictures. It is all so bewildering; and that is why a consistent biography of the Master is utterly impossible to achieve.

And that is why each denomination within Christianity sees its "own" Jesus! If you want a meek and lowly Jesus you will have no more difficulty in finding him than your friend who wants an exalted, majestic Figure. If you want a human Jesus who became divine— or, if you prefer a divine Jesus who became human, you will find both well represented in the New Testament. If you are looking for Jesus the revolutionist, or Jesus the conservative; Jesus of Paul, or Jesus of Peter; Jesus of Peace, or Jesus of the Sword; Jesus the Jew, or Jesus the Logos; Jesus the son of Joseph and Mary, or Jesus the son of Mary alone,—all these fragments of him are in the New Testament like scattered parts of a puzzle that is beyond any one's ability to fit together.* For all its matchless lucidity the teaching of Jesus as well as his personality is extremely complex.

There are certain characters of history that hang

*In the judgment of the writer the best account of Jesus is to be found in Prof. Shirely Jackson Case's recently published book entitled *Jesus a new Biography*, University of Chicago Press (1927).

with a kind of moonlike clearness and roundness of outline in a summer's sky. But not the character of Jesus. As far back as the days when Luke began to write his gospel there were already in existence the most varied attempts at a biography of the Great Teacher. Luke himself says so in the introduction to his gospel when he writes that "many have taken in hand to draw up a narrative." Luke wrote because he wanted to give (what he thought to be) a correct account. And from his day to this attempts have not been lacking. The modern book market is flooded with biographies of Jesus all the way from Frederick David Strauss and Ernest Renan to Papini and Emil Ludwig. These men have written because they think they have something new to say, or perhaps they believe they can give the baffling subject a different twist. (That's just why Luke wrote—he thought he had a better approach.)

But it is a hopeless task. The sources are too meagre and too divergent. Just as there is more than a single tradition of Moses in the Old Testament so there is more than a single view of Jesus in the New Testament. As wide and as different as is the picture of Moses painted in the Priestly Document from that of the Yahwistic, so wide is the outlook of the Gospel of John from the Gospel of Mark, or the Epistles of Paul from the moralism of James. Primitive Christianity was full of endless differences. Far from reflecting an original agreement the New Testament is a record of the most varied diversities.

3

At the very outset of its career Christianity was divided into a large number of separate communities with their separate beliefs. Unlike the disciples of Jesus, who wrote practically little or nothing, this younger generation of Christians (mostly gentiles) were writing with great heat and enormous output. Christian literature toward the close of the first century was exceedingly voluminous and followed along four main lines: Gospels, Acts, Epistles, and Apocalypses.

Slowly, gradually, half unconsciously there now began to spread among the Christians a general feeling that certain writings of the early teachers and leaders were just as holy as the books of the Old Testament. By the middle of the second century Christian communities were already reading the Gospels as sacred literature. In his "Apology" written to the Emperor about the year 140 A. D. Justin Martyr, who was a prominent figure in the Roman Church, pictures early church life: "On the day of the Sun (Sunday) all those of us who live in the same town or district assemble together, and there is read to us some part of the Memoirs of the Apostles, which" (he says elsewhere) "are called Gospels, and the writings of the Prophets as much as time permits." Here is an explicit statement of the high regard in which the Gospels were valued. This first step in the development of the new bible may be compared to the ancient Hebrew recognition of the Pentateuch as the first and most holy section of the entire Old Testament. And just as the Pentateuch came to be regarded as the direct inspiration of God through Moses, so the Christians cherishing the words of the Master began to feel that the Gospels contained even a still higher form of divine communication.

We get another glimpse of this period from an old document found in the Ambrosian Library of Milan, Italy. It is a mutilated manuscript badly torn and disarranged but it is very important, for it contains the earliest list of those books which the early Christian regarded as "Sacred Scripture." This Muratorian Fragment—for that is the name that scholars have given the document—comes from around the year 190 A. D. It makes mention of the Gospels, after which it places the Book of Acts next in importance. Then it gives thirteen Epistles of Paul, pointing out that "although four of them, Philemon, Titus, I and II Timothy, were written from personal feeling and affection, yet they are hallowed in the respect of the Catholic Church."

Being an age of many divisions with their many documents it is not surprising that the Muratorian Fragment should go out of its way to draw a line of distinction between books that are "Recognized" and books that are "Spurious." "Moreover," declares this interesting manuscript, "there is in circulation an Epistle to the Laodiceans and one to the Alexandrians forged in Paul's name and several others which cannot be received in the Catholic Church. The Epistle of Jude, however, and two with the name of John are held in the Catholic Church. We receive also that Revelation of John, and the Revelation of Peter, which later some of our body will not allow to be read in church."

The middle of the second century saw many Gospels in existence such as the Gospel according to the Hebrews, the Gospel of the Nazarenes, the Gospel according to Peter, the Gospel according to the Egyptians and many more that have perished and will never be known by name. But the majority of the books that are now in the New Testament were already being tentatively recognized. However, there were a few that were still seriously questioned: James, II Peter, II and III John, Jude, Hebrews and Revelations. Just as the books of Ecclesiastes, Esther, Ezekiel, and the Song of Songs were subjected to long discussion before they were allowed into the Old Testament so these seven minor books were very slow in getting admitted into the New. . . .

4

But this is not all! Here in the middle of the second century we see the religion of Jesus engaged in a serious conflict with a movement called "Gnosticism" which although much older than Christianity had much in common with the newer faith. The Gnostics ("the knowing ones") were people who looked for "knowledge" or revelation and "redemption" through visions of God and angels. By many weird and ascetic practices their followers would induce upon themselves fantastic experiences supposed to be the highest form of communication with the spiritual world. Now, Christianity had proved itself exceedingly attractive to these people and they poured into the churches in great number threatening to overwhelm it. For these Gnostic-Christians were not only prolific with their "visions" but they were equally prolific with their pens. They produced a large body of literature, mostly Gospels and Acts, which set forth their own peculiar views. Particularly they stressed the fact that Jesus secretly taught Gnosticism to the Apostles and it was this "secret" knowledge that they claimed to be the true Christianity. People in all ages—no less in the twentieth century than in the second—are always impressed by "secrets." Anything that loves mystery will not be content with desk-wisdom. And so Gnosticism flourished.

But the time soon arrived when it became necessary for the leaders of the church to drive out these heretics and destroy their literature. Just as the rabbis were forced to assemble the true Hebrew Scriptures in opposition to the Jewish heretics who were reading all kinds of false literature, so the Christian leaders found it necessary to define just what constituted the "true" New Testament in order to draw the line between the accepted and authorized books and those spurious gospels that were flooding the market. Hence the need of an authorized list of genuine books, those which might be appealed to by the church as a "canon" or rule and standard of belief. In this need the ascension of the New Testament literature began.

Out of this conflict certain books emerged as "sacred" scripture while others still continued under discussion. Even as late as the fourth century the question was not altogether settled. There is, for example, the evidence of Eusebius, a great church historian who gives us a summary of the situation about 324 A. D. He tells us of some books which he himself accepts although they are not usually acknowledged. "Since we are dealing with this subject," writes Eusebius, "it is proper to sum up the writings of the New Testament which have been already mentioned. First then must be put the holy quaternion of the Gospels; following them the Acts of the Apostles. After this must be reckoned the Epistles of Paul; next in order the extant former epistle of John, and likewise the epistle of Peter, must be maintained. After them is to be placed, if it really seems proper, the Apocalypse of John, concerning which we shall give the different opinions at the proper time. These then belong among the accepted writings. Among the disputed writings, which are nevertheless recognized by many, are extant the so-called epistle of James and that of Jude, also the second epistle of Peter, and those that are called the second and third of John, whether they belong to the evangelist or to another person of the same name. Among the rejected writings must be reckoned also the Acts of Paul, and the so-called Shepherd, and the Apocalypse of Peter, and in addition to these the extant epistle of Barnabas, and the so-called Teachings of the Apostles; and besides, as I said the Apocalypse of John, if it seem proper, which some, as I said, reject, but which others class with the accepted books. And among these some have placed also the Gospel according to the Hebrews, with which those of the Hebrews that have accepted Christ are especially delighted. And all these may be reckoned among the disputed books."

5

The New Testament was born in shock and conflict. It emerged as a "sacred" literature through internal struggle with heresy, and through the external fires of persecution. But at first no one thought of making a bible out of its separate documents. They were merely considered as books. However, familiarity and devotion, coupled with the need for written authority, soon changed these artless writings into a sacred collection. As they now lie beside each other they represent only a small selection of a very large body of literature produced by the primitive Christians. While the formation of the Old Testament covers a long period of many hundreds of years it is quite remarkable that the creation of the New Testament books was the work of little more than half a century.

Just as there were three stages in the formation of the Old Testament (Pentateuch, Prophets, and Writings) so the New Testament presents a somewhat similar triple division. First, the Epistles of Paul were recognized as authoritative; then came the Gospels; and last in the completed process was the acceptance of those books which had long been subjected to discussion. By and large, it must be said that the twenty-seven writings that make up the New Testament won out over a vast number of similar books through sheer intrinsic merit and by the authority ascribed to their reputed authors. For fully three centuries these writings ran the gauntlet of a severe selective process before the judgment of the Christian world pronounced them the sure oracles of God. No wonder men came to regard them as a divine revelation. . . .

It was the Catholic Church—that huge anchor of Faith—that eventually made it her business to rigidly define what documents were to be bound up in the New Testament. In spite of a lowly origin, and in the face of persecution, the young church grew rapidly. One of her main tasks was to guard against inside enemies—particularly those heretics called "Gnostics." They were far more dangerous to her progress than her pagan persecutors, for these Gnostics were busy fabricating new Gospels and Epistles to justify their novel doctrines. The need for a correct list of books was now made imperative in order to hold the church in a straight line. Whatever document could authenticate its claim to apostolic authorship or apostolic sanction was soon on its way upward to become "Holy Scripture." Eventually, only the "recognized" books were drawn together, and then slowly they were aggregated into a larger whole.

Three famous church Fathers living near the end of the second century,—Irenæus in France, Tertullian in Carthage, Clement in Alexandria of Egypt,—had much to do with settling the contents of the New Testament. And even of still greater importance was the work of Athanasius, the renowned archbishop of Alexandria, who sent a circular letter to all the churches under his control carefully listing by name those books which he considered authoritative. Athanasius' famous encyclical was dated Easter Day, 367 A. D.

It was not however until thirty years later that the whole matter reached a fixed settlement. In 397 A. D. an important church meeting (Synod) was held at Carthage in North Africa where a list was drawn up of those books which should be considered by all the faithful as "Holy Scriptures." Like Rabbi Akiba, who dominated the Council of Jamnia when the Old Testament was authoritatively closed, the great Christian theologian Augustine dominated this particular Synod. And it was here that the list drawn up by Athanasius was approved and the Christian Scriptures solemnly declared "fixed." . . . That year marked the coronation of the New Testament.

6

And now we are at the end of our long journey of exploration. There is, perhaps, only one question that needs to be answered. And it is this: How did it happen that the Old Testament was taken over by the Christians and joined together with the New Testament as an integral part of their sacred literature? At first blush it would seem that the Christians would only be too glad to get rid of the Hebrew Bible. Surely, it belonged to the people of another religion. Then why did they adopt it?

As a matter of fact there was a long and bitter controversy among the Christians of the second century on this subject. It was precipitated by a wealthy shipbuilder whose name was Marcion. In the year 144 A. D. this man founded his own independent church in Rome which soon developed many branches that were vigorous enough to last for several centuries. In order that his churches might be guided by a sacred literature Marcion drew up a list of books which he claimed represented the true Christian tradition. In this "heretic" bible Marcion placed a mutilated Gospel of Luke and ten Epistles of Paul. (All of the rest of the Old and New Testament writings he madly slashed out on the ground that the Jewish God, which he believed to be immoral, was not the real Father of Jesus Christ.) He even went so far as to mutilate every one of Paul's ten letters in a desperate effort to eliminate from them any favorable reference to the Jews.

Try as hard as he could to get rid of the Old Testament it was futile. No movement can escape history. Jesus was born a Jew, all his disciples were Jews, the man Paul, who gave Christianity to the Gentiles, styled himself a "Hebrew of Hebrews." Furthermore, the new religion began as a sect of Judaism, and even after it established its own independent life it kept drawing into its fold Jewish supporters. Long before any of the New Testament writings were born or even a shred of the Gospels was produced the early Christians had but one Bible, and that was the Hebrew Bible. Jesus never heard of the New Testament; he died before it was born. He was familiar with only one Bible—the bible of his own people. Likewise none of the disciples ever held a New Testament in their hands!

In view of these facts, which were deep-rooted traditions in the church, it was impossible to accept Marcion's ideas. Such a violent break with Christianity's historic past was regarded by the responsible leaders as freakish and fraught with serious danger. Far from being a millstone about the neck of those who were professing to follow the teachings of Jesus, the Hebrew Scriptures were regarded as the very foundation-stone upon which the new religion had reared her superstructure. With such a solid and sane recognition of her Jewish origin the Church was prepared to whip the rival Marcionites. . . .

After a long battle the shipbuilder's heretics and his mutilated bible finally went down into a dark sea of defeat; and from that day to this the New Testament has affectionately embraced the Old. 5-10-29.

My chief criticism of this writer is his cock-sureness about how & by what persons the O.T. was written & compiled. He pictures those early times & events as if he had been there & saw the whole affair, much like Wells writes his History of prehistoric times. He also too readily scraps all the supernatural.

While the Bible is
a human book, written
as other books are, ex-
cepting that it deals
with spiritual things,
yet it may be a true
record of some super-
natural events, as when
Jesus fed the 5000, or
opened the eyes of the
blind.

D. F. Helms.

BIBLIOGRAPHY

BIBLIOGRAPHY

OLD TESTAMENT

Part I

Chapter I. *Spinoza.*

Tractatus Theologico-Politicus. Benedict De Spinoza. Hamburg, 1670.
A Study of Spinoza. James Martineau. London, 1882.
History of Old Testament Criticism. Archibald Duff. New York, 1910.
Essays and Criticism. Matthew Arnold. London, 1883.

Chapter II. *Simon.*

Histoire Critique du Vieux Testament. Richard Simon. 1682.
The Massoreth ha-massoreth of Elias Levita in Hebrew with an English translation. C. D. Ginsburg. London, 1867.
Elements of the Higher Criticism. A. C. Zenos. New York, 1895.
Study of Holy Scripture. C. A. Briggs. New York, 1899.
Old Testament Criticism. E. McQueen Gray. New York, 1923.

Chapter III. *Astruc and Eichhorn.*

Conjectures sur . . . Genese. Jean Astruc. Brussels, 1753.
Einleitung in Alte Testament. J. G. Eichhorn. 1787.
Genesis of Genesis. B. W. Bacon. Hartford, 1892.
Documents of the Hexateuch. Vol. I. W. E Addis. New York, 1893.
An Introduction to the Pentateuch. A. T. Chapman. Cambridge, 1911.

Chapter IV. *Ilgen, Hupfeld, etc.*

Die Urkunden des Jerusalemer Templearchives. Karl David Ilgen. Jena, 1798.
Quellen der Genesis. Herman Hupfeld. Berlin, 1853.
The Pentateuch . . . Critically Examined. (Part I.) John W. Colenso. London, 1862.
Founders of Old Testament Criticism. T. K. Cheyne. New York, 1893.

Chapter V. *De Wette, Geddes, etc.*

Deuteronomium. W. M. L. De Wette. 1805.

Critical Remarks on the Holy Scriptures. A. Geddes. London, 1800.

Modern Criticism and the Preaching of the Old Testament. Geo. Adam Smith. New York, 1901.

The Composition of the Pentateuch. J. Estlin Carpenter and G. Hartford. London, 1902.

Decline and Fall of the Kingdom of Judah. T. K. Cheyne. London, 1908.

Deuteronomy, a Prophetic Lawbook. L. B. Longacre. New York, 1924.

PART II

Chapter I. *The Yahwistic Document.*

Introduction to the Literature of the Old Testament. S. R. Driver. New York, 1893.

The Legends of Genesis. Hermann Gunkel. Chicago, 1907.

The Bible and Modern Thought. J. R. Cohu. New York, 1920.

The Origin of Biblical Traditions. Albert T. Clay. New Haven, 1923.

The Literature of the Old Testament. Julius A. Bewer. New York, 1924.

The People and the Book. Edited by A. S. Peake. Oxford, 1925.

Chapter II. *The Elohistic Document.*

The Books of the Pentateuch. F. G. Eiselen. New York, 1916.

An Introduction to the Old Testament. Harlan Creelman. New York, 1917.

Sources of the Hexateuch. E. S. Brightman. New York, 1918.

The Authentic Literature of Israel. Vol. I. E. Czarnomska. New York, 1924.

Chapter III. *The Deuteronomic Document.*

Deuteronomy. S. R. Driver. New York, 1909.

The Book of Deuteronomy. George Adam Smith. Cambridge, 1918.

The Old Testament in the Light of To-day. W. F. Bade.
Boston, 1915.

Chapter IV. *The Priestly Document.*
The Documents of the Hexateuch. Vol. II. W. E. Addis.
New York, 1898.
*Constructive Studies in the Priestly Element in the Old
Testament.* W. R. Harper. Chicago, 1902.
The Messages of Israel Lawgivers. Charles F. Kent. New
York, 1908.
The Growth and Contents of the Old Testament. Charles
F. Kent. New York, 1925.

PART III

Chapter I. *Hebrew History.*
Judges. G. F. Moore. New York, 1895.
The Books of Samuel. H. P. Smith. New York, 1899.
*Historical Methods in the Old Testament (a paper in "Cam-
bridge Biblical Essays").* A. A. Bevan. London, 1909.
Israel's Historical and Biographical Narratives. C. F. Kent.
New York, 1925.

Chapter II. *Hebrew Prophecy.*
The Hebrew Prophet. L. W. Batten. New York, 1905.
The Kings and Prophets of Israel and Judah. C. F. Kent.
New York, 1909.
The Prophet and His Problems. J. M. P. Smith. New
York, 1916.
The Book of Isaiah. Geo. Adam Smith. London, 1927.
The Prophetic Books of the Old Testament. F. C. Eiselen.
New York, 1923.
The Second Isaiah. C. C. Torrey. New York, 1928.

Chapter III. *Hebrew Writings.*
The Psalter. A. C. Welch. Oxford, 1926.
The Psalmists. Edited by D. C. Simpson. Oxford, 1926.
The Book of Ecclesiastes. A. H. McNeile. Cambridge,
1904.
A Gentle Cynic. Morris Jastrow. Philadelphia, 1919.
The Book of Job. Morris Jastrow. Philadelphia, 1920.
The Book of Proverbs. Crawford H. Toy. New York,
1899.

The Wisdom of Egypt and the Old Testament. W. O. E. Oesterly. London, 1927.

The Song of Songs. Morris Jastrow. Philadelphia, 1921.

The Book of Daniel. James A. Montgomery. New York, 1927.

The Books of Ezra and Nehemiah. Loring W. Batten. New York, 1913.

The Books of Chronicles. E. L. Curtis and A. A. Madsen. New York, 1910.

Chapter IV. *The Formation of the Old Testament.*

The Hebrew Scriptures in the Making. Max L. Margolis. Philadelphia, 1922.

Canon of the Old Testament. H. E. Ryle. London, 1892.

The Origin of the Canon of the Old Testament. G. Wildeboer. London, 1895.

The Definition of the Jewish Canon (an essay in "Modern Theology and Related Subjects"). G. F. Moore. New York, 1911.

The Old Testament in the Jewish Church. (Lecture VI.) W. Robertson Smith. Edinburgh, 1892.

The Origin and Permanent Value of the Old Testament. C. F. Kent. New York, 1906.

NEW TESTAMENT

Part IV

Chapter I. *Church History.*

Christian Thought to the Reformation. H. B. Workman. New York, 1911.

Protestant Thought Before Kant. A. C. McGiffert. New York, 1911.

History of the Higher Criticism. Henry S. Nash. New York, 1906.

Biblical Scholarship and Inspiration. L. J. Evans and H. P. Smith. Cincinnati, 1891.

Chapter II. *Textual Criticism.*

Textual Criticism of the New Testament. B. B. Warfield. New York, 1886.

Our Bible and the Ancient Manuscripts. F. G. Kenyon. London, 1903.

History of the Textual Criticism of the New Testament.
Marvin R. Vincent.   New York, 1899.

The Reign of the Manuscript.   P. W. Sinks.   Toronto,
1917.

Textual Criticism of the New Testament.   F. G. Kenyon.
London, 1912.

Introduction to the Textual Criticism of the New Testament.
A. T. Robinson.   New York, 1925.

Chapter III.   *Rationalism.*

A History of the Warfare of Science with Theology.
Andrew D. White.   New York, 1908.

History of Interpretation.   F. W. Farrar.   New York, 1886.

Essays in Biblical Interpretation.   Henry Preserved Smith.
Boston, 1921.

The English Church in the Eighteenth Century.   G. J.
Abbey and J. H. Overton.   London, 1878.

History of English Rationalism in the Nineteenth Century.
A. W. Benn.   London, 1906.

Unbelief in the Eighteenth Century.   John Cairns.   Edinburgh, 1881.

The Philosophy of Religion.   Otto Pfleiderer.   London,
1886.

Critical History of Free Thought.   A. S. Farrar.   New
York, 1863.

PART V

Chapter I.   *Higher Criticism of the New Testament.*

The Bible in the Nineteenth Century.   J. Estlin Carpenter.
London, 1903.

Oxford Studies in the Synoptic Problem.   W. Sanday.   Oxford, 1911.

Sources of the Synoptic Gospels.   Carl S. Patton.   New
York, 1915.

The Four Gospels.   B. H. Streeter.   New York, 1925.

A Critical Introduction to the New Testament.   A. S. Peake.
New York, 1924.

Gospel Origins.   Wm. W. Holdsworth.   New York, 1913.

The Story of the New Testament.   E. J. Goodspeed.   Chicago, 1916.

Introduction to the Literature of the New Testament.   James
Moffatt.   New York, 1917.

Introduction to the Study of the New Testament.   A. H. Mc-
Neile.   Oxford, 1927.

Chapter II.   *Selection of the New Testament.*

Canon and Text of the New Testament.   Caspar Rene Gregory.   New York, 1907.

Canon of the Bible.   Samuel Davidson.   New York, 1917.

Text and Canon of the New Testament.   Alexander Souter.
New York, 1920.

The God of the Early Christians.   A. C. McGiffert.   New
York, 1924.

The Formation of the New Testament.   E. J. Goodspeed.
Chicago, 1926.

INDEX

INDEX

Abelard 219 f.
Abraham 10 f., 13, 67, 78, 89, 92, 95 f., 133, 153, 207
Acts, Book of 288, 304
Ainu 77
Agobard 255
Akiba, Rabbi 208 f., 212, 309
Alexander II of Russia. 251
Allegory 209, 253–258
Alogi 300
Alphabet (Hebrew) 142
Ambrosian Library. 304
Amos, Book of 174 f.
Anselm 219
Antioch 294
Apocalypse 295
Apocrypha 205 f., 212
Aramaic 271, 291 f., 295
Arnold, Mathew 280 f.
Astruc, Jean 35 f., 45, 48 f., 50, 63, 66, 92
Athanasius 309
Athens 139
Augustine 126, 309

Babylonia 122 f.
Baur, F. C. 298 f., 300, 301
Beersheba 10, 78, 114
Bengel, J. A. 242
Bentley, Richard 242
Bernard of Clairvaux 219 f.
Beth-El 50 f., 52, 53, 78
Bibliolatry 230 f.
Book of the Covenant 98 f.
Book of the Covenant (Little) 83 f.
Browning, Robert 8, 172
Burgon, Dean 231

Canaanites 11 f.
Cappel, Louis 22, 25
Censorship 225
Chronicles, Books of 196 f., 241
Colenso, Bishop J. W. 57 f., 153, 280
Colet 227
Corinthians 298
Creation Story 26 f., 34, 36 f., 41, 84, 132, 152, 293

Criticism (Higher) 42 f., 61, 270, 279 f., 286, 298, 301
Criticism (Lower-Textual) 21 f., 25, 42, 233 f., 242, 246, 279 f.
Cursives (see Manuscripts) 245 f.
Cyrus 134, 177

Dan 13, 78, 114
Daniel 195, 281
Dante 252, 300
David 9 f., 73, 79 f., 91, 171 f., 185 f., 199, 281
Deborah 169
De Mille, C. B. 165
Deuteronomy 9, 13, 20, 65, 68, 73, 106 f., 123, 127 f., 137, 150 f., 172
De Wette, W. M. L. 65 f.
Diatessaron (see Tatian)
Doxology 238
Duhm 153

Ebionites 300
Ecclesiastes 193 f., 210 f., 305
Eichhorn, J. G. 39 f., 48 f., 61, 63, 66
Elohim 28, 36 f., 40, 49 f., 92, 153, 187
Elohistic Documents 49 f., 52, 92 f., 123, 146 f.
Elzevir Press 19
Ephesians 299
Epistles 297 f., 304, 306
Erasmus 227 f., 236 f., 260
Esther, Book of 195, 211, 305
Eusebius 240, 306
Ezekiel 54 f., 56, 81, 122–131, 164, 180, 211, 305
Ezra 25, 138 f., 152, 163, 196

Flood Story 31 f., 34, 36 f., 86, 149, 132, 293
Fourth Gospel (see Gospel of John)
Fragmentary Theory 64 f.
Franklin, Benjamin 195

Geddes, Alexander 62 f., 66
Gnosticism 300, 305 f., 308

323